ANN WALKER

HEAVEN CAN COME LATER

HEAVEN CAN COME LATER

BY

ANN WALKER

EXCALIBUR PRESS of LONDON
13 Knightsbridge Green, London SW1X 7QL

PRINTED & BOUND IN U.K.

PUBLISHED BY EXCALIBUR PRESS of LONDON

ISBN 1 872080 65 0

INTRODUCTION

This is the true story of my life and the reason I have written it is to show people that no matter how life is to them, whether it be good or bad, we each have a friend in the spirit world whom we call a spirit guide. He or she is with us for a lifetime and even during our darkest hours they are right by our sides and despite the frailty of the human heart, they are there to help. It is also to show that not only do we have guides, or as some people call them, Guardian Angels, we also have with us our families and loved ones, that have gone to "spirit", with us always.

I believe everybody has a guide to help and guide them through life and this book is simply about my life before and after I met my spirit guide, White Arrow.

I dedicate this book, in reverence, to the cherished support and unselfish patience of my family, without which this book could not have been written. This book also could not have been possible without the help of my friend Valerie Smith, who gave me the inspiration and desire to start it, the help with writing it and the courage to finish it.

CHAPTER ONE

It was September 11th, 1942. Germany was at war with England and as they were dropping their bombs over England, so were many new babies being born. One of these newborn infants came into the world in Clacton-on-Sea in the early hours of the morning. Was this little child going to be set apart from the others, who could tell? What was in store for him or her? There were so many new babies being born at this time and it was everyone's dream that this new generation would be filled with hope and with the ability to bring peace into our troubled world.

A young girl of twenty-two was being wheeled into a maternity hospital. She was quite an attractive woman with fair hair and with the onset of labour was anxious about the safe arrival of her baby which, hopefully, wouldn't be too long to go. She sat patiently in the wheelchair as she waited for the nursing staff to wheel her into the small, stark but sterile delivery room. Everything was white and gleaming. The nurse said to the fair-haired young woman, "Don't worry, love, everything will be just fine. Sit there for a moment whilst I prepare the delivery table for you." She smiled at the young mother-to-be only to be stopped in her tracks.

"I'm sorry, nurse," said the young woman, "But I don't think I can wait any longer. I'm sure the baby's nearly there because I want to push!" She was trying not to make a fuss but it was obvious there was very little time to waste. The nurse immediately stopped what she was doing in order to examine the young woman.

"Yes, you're quite right, love. The baby's head's nearly there!" Don't worry, I won't leave you but I'll ring for the doctor to come at once."

She pressed the button for assistance and within seconds the doctor appeared. With his expert eye he knew exactly what was happening and said to the nurse, "This lady is well into the second stage. We'll have to act fast. Quickly, then, nurse. Let's get her onto the delivery table. I'm afraid we'll have to forget about the other deliveries for the time being. There's no time to lose."

Sure enough, they just managed to lift the young woman onto the delivery table when the head entered the world. The nurse reassured the mother-to-be and said softly, "Breathe deeply, my dear, and as soon as the doctor says you can push, push with all your might."

1

It seemed no sooner had the nurse uttered these words when the doctor commanded, "Push." and the baby entered the world. A smack was soon followed which instigated the first cry. A baby girl was born. And that baby girl was me!

As I lay in my mother's arms, little did my mother and I know that another war was about to break out. It was to last thirty-seven years, one which I had apparently chosen to experience. The explanation for that was to come to light many years later.

At this precious moment, however, there was only one thing my mother was interested in and that was her new daughter. She already had a young son, but, as she held me tightly to her bosom, she realized she had always wanted a fair-haired, blue-eyed girl.

My father was in the army and stationed at Clacton-on-Sea, hence my birth-place. My mother had no visitors the day I was born because Dad was in the army prison which they called the Guard House. He had been caught trying to desert and was punished accordingly. He was only twenty-three or twenty-four years old and at least six feet tall with dark hair and a very good-looking man. My mother suffered two miscarriages altogether, one before my brother was born and then another before I came along. On each occasion the loss of the unborn babies was due to my father's violence towards my mother which was mainly due to his being an alcoholic. Thankfully, he had not managed to hurt my brother nor me. My mother must have had a tremendous sense of relief to have succeeded in giving birth to both a son and a daughter.

Dad had come from a very poor Welsh family and was brought up during the Depression. Things during the 30's had been very bad so his family decided to move south, thinking it would be better for them all regarding employment and living conditions. Dad was only about sixteen or seventeen when they moved, along with his two brothers, Delwyn, who died during his twenties from tuberculosis, and Ivor, who died later on in life from cancer. He also had a sister who remains an enigma to me since I know so little about her, apart from the fact that she emigrated to Australia at an early age. Nobody in the family can remember my Dad's father who presumably died when he was a relatively young man, as indeed did many in those days, and Dad's mother died when I was only about one or two years old, so I don't have many recollections of her either. According to those who knew her, she went out one evening and dropped dead in the street from a heart attack. Apparently my father didn't attend her funeral for I'm afraid his drink was far more important to him and it was my mother's side of the family who went instead.

2

Dad met Mum when he was in his twenties and Mum was nineteen. Mum came from a big family. In fact there were eight children in all. When Mum was born my grandmother was not married and when she met her future husband, my maternal grandfather, he married my grandmother and decided to adopt my mother, who was by then about nine months old, and bring her up and accept and love her as if she were his very own child. This fact was kept a secret from her for many years so, while she grew up, my mother did not realise that she was really only half-sister to her four younger brothers and three sisters. Under the circumstances, my mother was incredibly lucky to be such an accepted and well-loved member of a supportive, large family and the truth made not a scrap of difference to their feelings towards her.

As I said, Mum was only nineteen when she met and fell in love with my Dad. After all, he was always immaculately dressed and never left the house without combing his hair first or polishing his shoes. Very soon after they met, Mum became pregnant. In those days it was regarded as unforgivable and shameful to be both young and pregnant outside of marriage, so the only thing they could do in their situation was to marry as soon as possible. Having said that, Mum was well aware of Dad's drinking problem which had started since he left his native Wales, and actually went to consult a member of her family as to whether she should go ahead and marry him. She did love him, and wanted to give her baby a name and do the right thing, but was very worried and concerned about his excessive drinking. She was told in good faith to go ahead with the marriage, if not for him, for the sake of the child she was carrying. Personally, I believe no-one can advise and that it was fated for Mum to marry him. However, she took the advice and married my father, but his drinking got steadily worse and there was nothing anyone could do to change the fact.

Mum hoped their first child would be able to bring change and fresh hope into his life, but my mother had a miscarriage. She very soon became pregnant again and this time successfully gave birth to Raymond, my brother, in June, 1940. My father became more and more drunk all the time and showed violence not only to my mother but to his young child, too. By the time Raymond reached his second year he was totally deaf and dumb. There were many stories going round at the time when doctors diagnosed Raymond as suffering from tuberculosis of the hip, not forgetting his sudden speech and hearing loss. Some said it was due to my brother having fallen from his high chair, getting his leg caught in it in the process, and so you can see why there were conflicting views held in the family as to why and how he was struck deaf and dumb, and now also had T.B. The doctors all claimed it was due to the shock of his fall, and yet my relatives had seen my father hit my brother around the ears and head many a time. It is hardly surprising, therefore, that they suspected this had contributed to his problems. I only hope to God the doctors were right - but I doubt if anyone will ever know the truth.

****

During my early years I hardly saw anything of my brother, mainly because he was in and out of hospital all the time, so my memory of him at a young age is very limited. I do remember, however, that we never seemed to stay for long in one place and were always on the move. By the time I was about five I vaguely recollect there being gaps when I didn't see my mother, nor my father, and I believe this was because I was put into care from time to time when my mother couldn't find adequate shelter for the two of us. Being of such a tender age my memory of this soon faded and this went on until I reached the age of eight when I was more capable of understanding what was going on and taking notice of the events as they occurred. It was around this time that I can clearly remember getting ready for school one morning. I was eating a slice of toast and having a cup of tea for my breakfast when Mum called to me. I loved her so much and she always gave me a kiss and a cuddle before I left for school in the mornings. This particular day, however, she seemed upset and it looked to me as if she had been crying because her eyes were very red. She squeezed me so tightly I could hardly breathe and she said, "I love you, Ann."

"I love you, too," I replied, wondering what all the extra attention I was receiving was about, not that I didn't enjoy it! The trouble was, I was running a bit behind schedule and was due to meet my friend on the corner before we set off for school so I quickly gave her a hug back and, after kissing her on the cheek, I rushed out saying my goodbyes, in the typical fashion of any average eight-year-old. Half of me would have longed to have stayed at home with Mum and for that lovely cuddle not to finish and to stay in her arms. I was too young to sense anything was wrong, not even when Mum came rushing out behind me, repeating loudly that she loved me and to be careful. I assured her I loved her too and that I'd be careful and, after making my promises to her, I gave Mum a wave and walked towards my friend who was already at the street corner waiting for me. We were in the same class at school and arrived nice and early at school that morning. When we went into our classroom we both mucked about, throwing books at each other and chasing each other around the desks. I was always happy at school and enjoyed my lessons but I was now beginning to realise the unhappiness my father was causing the family so in a way I felt safe at school. My friend and I sat next to each other in class and we still had mischief on our minds as our first lesson commenced. We were giggling and passing little bits of paper with

4

silly notes scribbled on them to each other.

Suddenly the classroom door opened and in walked the Headmistress. It was amazing what a sobering effect she had on us all and we all sat in silence as she spoke in private to the class teacher. After the teacher had received her instructions from her peer she called out, directing her voice at me, "Ann Pinkham, will you go with Miss Edwards to her office, please."

I pushed my chair back saying, "Yes, miss," and walked out of the classroom behind the Headmistress. Miss Edwards was a very strict woman in her forties and usually wore grey or tweed suits and brogue shoes. She wore her greying hair in a bun, which made her look even more severe, and when she wore her spectacles she had an air of authority about her which even her staff recognised. She told me there were two ladies waiting to meet me and she showed me into her office. I had never set eyes on the women before so it didn't mean much to me at the time. I was told to sit down on the chair and Miss Edwards had a brief conversation with the two women which was all going over my head. I wasn't really interested in what they were saying but more anxious in getting back to my classroom and my friend. After a couple of minutes I was starting to feel bored and began to kick my legs from front to back, knocking the back of the chair with my shoes.

One of the strangers turned and smiled at me but I didn't like her and glanced the other way, tossing my head up in a disapproving manner.

"Stop that, Ann," said Miss Edwards.

That made me stop in my tracks. I looked up and apologised, after which the three women carried on talking. Eventually, my headmistress got up from her desk and called to me, "Ann," as she walked over towards me. "You will have to leave with these ladies as they will be taking you to a new home."

I immediately thought to myself, Oh, Mum, where are you? I said and did nothing for a moment, but looked towards the door and started to run for it. It would only take me five minutes to run home to Mum and she would stop them taking me anywhere, I thought. I didn't get very far from the door when one of the strangers grabbed me by the arm.

"No, Ann, you have to come with us, I'm afraid," and promptly sat me back on the chair. She went on, "It's no use trying to run away, you have to come with us and that's all there is to it."

I could feel the tears slowly building up but I was adamant they wouldn't see me cry so I took it out on the chair legs again by banging my shoes against the chair, but this time I got away with it as no one said anything to stop me. They whispered something between themselves and then one of the ladies walked towards me and said, "Come on, Ann. Let's go."

I was afraid of them and of what they were suggesting so I leant back in my chair, frightened to move or speak. I wanted my Mum. This was the first time I can remember anything bad happening to me and I was terrified. The woman grabbed hold of my hand and pulled me up, then started walking to the door with me dragging my feet behind. I knew I had no choice but to go, but where we were going I had no idea and that really frightened me. We got outside the school gates where a parked car was waiting for us. The other lady had caught up with us and unlocked the car door whilst the other one, still holding my hand, pushed me gently into the back of the car.

The women both got in and spoke quietly to each other as I looked at my school. I could see my classroom from where I was sitting and wondered if I would ever see my friend again and if she would miss me. My main worry though was, naturally, what would my Mum say? As I looked out of the car window I said to myself, please, Mum, come and get me. You wouldn't let these strangers take me away, would you? Please, Mum, do something. I could not contain my despair any more. The great big lump in my throat just seemed to explode and I cried uncontrollably.

The car was started up and we set off and as we passed the houses and buildings we went past my own house. As we approached it I got up on my knees to look out of the back window, hoping I would see Mum. The tears were streaming down my cheeks as I looked at our front door. There was no sign of Mum, nothing at all and, as the car gathered speed, the house began to fade out of focus until I could see it no more. I sat back down on the back seat and cried out, "I want my Mum. I don't want to go with you," and I leant against the car door. With that, the car came to a grinding holt making me fall to the floor. The woman in the passenger seat got out of the car and got into the back next to me. By this time I was really sobbing, thinking the end of the world had come, for they were taking me away from my Mum and I didn't know if I would ever see her again. I didn't even know where they were taking me.

The woman sitting next to me changed her attitude and for the first time showed some compassion. She held me closely and said softly, "Come on, love, you'll see your Mum soon. It won't be long, I promise."

6

Very soon after that I cried myself to sleep, propped up against the lady. I woke up some time later with a start when the car had stopped. I rubbed my eyes and sat up straight to look out of the car window. All I could see was a large building in front of us. From an eight-year-old child's viewpoint it looked just like a castle but it was in fact a convent called St. Anns. We had driven all the way to Orpington in Kent, miles away from my home and my Mum.

CHAPTER TWO

We got out of the car and the two women took me inside the convent. It was all so bewildering to me. I just couldn't understand why my Mum wasn't there waiting for me or why I had been taken there at all. The three of us sat in a room until a nun came in to greet us. Once again I was terrified because they all spoke to each other so quietly, completely ignoring me. After a little while the two women left and I was now alone with the nun. I was more scared of her than I was of the two women, and that was bad enough. "Come along with me, Ann," she said to me and off we went along some corridors until we came to a large room. I later learned it was called a dormitory and there were eight beds in the room. When the two women had arrived at my school to take me away with them they had with them a small suitcase for me with some essentials I would be needing. The Sister showed me which of the beds would be mine and told me to unpack the suitcase. She told me she would return in ten minutes when she would take me to the dining room and introduce me to the other children.

I was soon to learn that the convent was a place where children from similar backgrounds to mine were sent and many of the children there were as unhappy as I was because we had been taken from our mothers or fathers.

I tried very hard to resign myself to the fact that I may as well make the most of my situation and after a couple of weeks had settled down. Although I got on well with the children and the nuns, I was never truly happy being away from Mum. I didn't think I would ever be able to adjust to that side of things.

In all I was at the convent for about eighteen months and was now over ten years old. One day I was sitting in my classroom, having a lesson with all the other children, when once again I was summoned to go to the office. This time the "Headmistress" was called Mother Superior. I sat outside her office, wondering

7

what I had done wrong to warrant being sent for. I could her voices coming from inside the room and I could tell the Mother Superior was speaking to another woman but, because I didn't recognise the voice, I didn't take that much interest in it.

Suddenly, the door opened and Mother Superior came out into the corridor. "Ann," she said, "Please come inside, will you?"

Mother Superior had such a lovely kind voice and she went on to say, "There is somebody here who would very much like to see you," and she smiled sweetly.

I got up from the chair and stood still for a moment, remembering the last time I had found myself in a similar situation. What was to happen to me this time? I wondered. Mother Superior looked at me almost as if she could read my mind because she said, "Go in and don't be afraid, Little One. You'll be so happy when you know what this is all about".

Years later I was to be referred to as "Little One", but by a different source.

I opened the door tentatively and as it swung back I saw Mum sitting on a chair right in front of me. I was so overawed I couldn't move for a moment. After all this time I was with my mother once more and this time I didn't, or more to the point, couldn't hold back the tears. They flowed freely as I stood there, hardly bearing to blink in case I was dreaming. Mum was crying also and got up with her arms outstretched to me.

"Ann, darling," she cried, and I rushed into them, longing for them to hug me. No words were uttered, no words were necessary. Instead we just held each other tightly, never wanting to ever let go again. After what seem like an entirety Mum wiped away her tears and said, "Come on, love. I'm taking you home now."

I looked up at her to make sure she really meant it and that I didn't make a mistake. I loved her so much and here she was at long last to be with me again. I had to ask that burning, nagging question which had been eating away at me, "You won't leave me again, will you, Mum?"

Mum hugged me so tightly, saying reassuringly, "No, darling, I promise, I promise."

One of the nuns came into the office with my belongings and Mum and I walked out of the office clinging on to each other. I couldn't bear to think we would ever be parted again and, I dare say, I think Mum may have been of the same opinion.

The Mother Superior was still outside in the corridor and, as we came out to thank her for all they had done for me, she shook Mum's hand and smiled at me, wishing us both all the very best. I said my goodbyes and we walked out of the convent and into the sunlight which was one of the most wonderful moments of my life.

It was a gloriously sunny day and I felt so happy. From a very early age I had learnt not to ask Mum many questions about her and Dad and I wasn't going to start now. I was just relieved and delighted to be with her. We walked to the bus-stop, and all the way home on the bus Mum asked me to tell her all about the convent and what the people there were like. She showed much concern about my well-being and if I was worried about anything, and if there was anything at all I was to discuss it with her. For ten years old I was a deep-thinking child, and maybe was growing up too fast, but I knew I had to somehow convince Mum I was fine.

We got off the bus at the top of our road and no sooner had we gone a few yards when Mum suddenly grabbed hold of my hand. I looked around me to find out what had startled Mum to do such a thing and in the distance I could see my father walking towards us. Mum continued to hold my hand tightly and we walked towards him. I had been away for so long that in a way I suppose I had missed my Dad in a strange way and was pleased to see him. As he approached us all he said, however, was "Hello," and started talking to Mum, completely ignoring me, which I found very hurtful. We all went home together and as the day went by it was as if nothing had really changed since I was at last at home with them both. They were still doing the same things as before I went away, that is, arguing and shouting at each other. When I went to bed that night I could hear them arguing as they had always done, but somehow it didn't matter. I was with my Mum now and, hopefully, nothing was going to change that.

Life continued very much as before I went away but I was older now and I was more aware of the beatings and abuse my father was giving my mother and now I was hating him for it. I found that whenever Dad entered the room I would go out of the room and go into my bedroom, for I knew if I had stayed he would start picking on me also and I couldn't face that. It was bad enough bearing the bad language he used on Mum. On numerous occasions when Dad would be getting ready to go out he would polish his shoes and, if he started a row with me and the answers I came up with didn't suit him, he wouldn't think twice to hit me with the shoe across my head or face, causing me great pain. He would only do this if Mum was out of the room, for instance, if she was washing up in the kitchen, so it was better for me to stay away from him altogether.

9

After a year or so we moved to West Harrow to a lovely big flat and it was at this stage that my brother came home to live with us, after living so long in a hospital and then special schools for the deaf and dumb. Raymond and I had our very own bedrooms and I was so pleased to have my brother living at home with us. I knew he couldn't hear the beatings and foul language my father used and in a way I was relieved that he couldn't, for I remember even at that age thinking he had suffered enough. I was twelve years old when my brother came home and the next couple of years were extremely difficult to get through for me. Whether it was because I was becoming an adolescent and the changes in my body were affecting me as they do others of my age, or if I was becoming more aware of what was happening I don't really know, but it was probably a combination of the two. One thing I was certain about was that I couldn't bear to see Mum suffering the continuous beatings and verbal abuse she was receiving from Dad. Time and time again I ran away from home during these years but the police always managed to find me and take me back home. I was in such a dilemma and was creating a two-fold situation as I was making Mum unhappy when I kept running away, but then again I couldn't stand seeing her distressed and frightened all the time. The trouble was, there didn't appear to be a solution to it all as we were both too scared of Dad to do anything about it.

Those awful couple of years left a scar on me which lasted many years. There was one particular night during that period which I can remember so clearly even to this day. It was a typical night which summed up what it was like at home and which led me to hate my father so much. I had been watching television that evening with Mum when suddenly Mum said to me, "You'd better go to bed now, Ann, your Dad'll be in soon."

I sensed urgency in her voice and knew my father was due to come in any time. I was used to this as it was an everyday event so I kissed Mum goodnight, hoping she would be alright. I went to bed that night, forgetting to put the wardrobe behind my bedroom door, and Mum called out to remind me to do so. I acknowledged her request and after I had move it into position, I sat on my bed and stated at it, thinking, good, no-one would be able to push the door open with that large piece of furniture in the way, and I got into bed.

I took a book from the dressing table and started to read it. I very soon became deeply engrossed in the story when suddenly I heard Dad coming up the stairs. I put the book down and slid down between the bedclothes, hoping that everyone would have a quiet, good night. By the way, a quiet, good night to me meant all the shouting and bawling would be over and done with in ten minutes, even if you included Mum receiving a clout. However, that night nobody was that lucky. I heard Mum ask Dad if he wanted anything to eat and by this time I felt sick - I always did, night after night - never knowing if it was to be a good night or not. I heard Dad moving about in the front room and call out to Mum, "Yes, Letty, I wouldn't mind a sandwich." He sounded fairly amicable and in a good mood. Great, I thought, and grabbed one of my pillows and put it over my head. I had been reading a love story and as I was trying to get off to sleep I was in a sort of day-dream, remembering the lovely story.

All of a sudden, I heard an almighty scream. The fear in me brought tears to my eyes. I had shed so many tears in the past, but there they were, back again. Every night, when I went to bed, I always thought that I wouldn't be able to cry any more or experience the pain of fear within me any more, but once again it was happening. Like I had always done in the past years, I tried to press the pillow against my ears so I couldn't hear the shouting and crying, but it made no difference. I could still hear the slaps and the punches and Mum's screams. I took the pillow away from my head when I realised there was no point in it being there. I desperately wanted to help Mum and push the wardrobe away from the door. I hated him so much but I had to live by Mum's words of warning.

"You'll only make it worse for me, Ann, for if you get hurt I just couldn't stand it."

I hated everything and everyone, except for Mum of course. Why her and why me? What had we done to deserve such treatment?

I got out of bed and went towards the wall which was next to the front room. I put my ear as close to it as possible for I wanted to know Mum was safe. Suddenly, all went quiet for a few seconds, apart from Mum sobbing very softly. There was no more screaming from her and no more shouting from Dad, which pleased me as I thought it must all be over. I could then hear Dad going into the kitchen, not that I cared what he did as long as he left Mum alone, and then I could hear a scraping, dragging noise. For a moment I wouldn't make out what the noise was but when I heard my father coming back I heard him trying to open the door between the kitchen and the front room. There was obviously something obstructing his way, something which was preventing him from opening the door, but I didn't know what. All went quiet again and the deathly silence scared me but I daren't move from the position I was in in case I made a noise.

Just then, Dad called out to Mum, "Letty , open the door."

"No!" I heard Mum say.

"Please, I won't hurt you, I promise," said Dad.

I was still standing there, not daring to move in case he heard me. I was praying for Mum not open the door to him but to stick to her guns, when I heard her call out to him, "Tom, I'm sitting on the window sill. If you push open the door, I'll jump!"

I thought to myself, My God, am I hearing things? Mum had never in her life said such words before to him, not that I was aware of, anyway.

Dad tried different tactics and this time tried to soften the tone in his voice. He said, "Open the door, Letty. I love you. I promise if you just let me in I won't hurt you. Please, Letty, love."

By this time I was crying softly, hoping Dad wouldn't hear in case it made matters worse. I went over to my bed and lay down, putting the pillow partly over my head, hoping that no-one could hear my sobbing, and also trying to hear Mum's reply at the same time.

She said to Dad, "If you come in, Tom, I'll jump."

"Oh, please don't do that, Mum. I love you," I said to myself quietly.

Then I heard my Dad speak again, still in his wickedly enticing way.

"Letty, I love you more than anything. You know I didn't mean to hurt you." With this, I thought, as I had done so many times before in my young life, I've heard it all before, Dad, you can be so devious when you want to be, and I prayed Mum wouldn't open that door.

Dad continued to call out to Mum, pleading with her to let him in. I could never, and definitely would never, trust him nor his sweet talking, so I pulled my pillow closer over my ears, terrified for Mum's safety.

After a couple of minutes I could hear the scraping, dragging sound again. I thought to myself, No, no Mum, please don't. I knew that whatever it was she had put behind the door, she was now removing it because she had believed Dad's pie-crust promises. Even at my young age I knew my father better than she did, but she allowed him to enter the front room where she stood all on her own.

"Tom...." I Heard her cry, but it was too late, within a split second there was an

12

almighty scream and then more screams. It went on for a good ten minutes, but it seemed a lifetime to me, so God knows how long it seemed to my poor mother.

After the screaming came the long silence. All I could hear was my father walking to the bathroom and then towards the bedroom. I couldn't hear my Mum at all and I didn't know whether she was dead or alive. She had always told me never to come out of my room, whatever happened, until she told me to, so I cried myself to sleep instead. I couldn't get the screaming out of my mind it was truly the worst experience I had been through and the hate for my father was so deeply rooted and embedded in me, I never, forgave him, from that day on.

The following morning I woke up, still not knowing if Mum was alright or not. I got myself ready for school and after a while thought I could hear her out in the kitchen. Yes, I was right, thank God she was alive. I rushed out of my bedroom towards the kitchen to Mum who had her back to me. Dad must have already left for work and she was cooking my breakfast.

I said, with a cry in my voice, "Oh Mum, thank God you are alright. I was so frightened after what happened last night."

Mum slowly turned round to face me and I saw for the first time the injuries she had sustained from the previous evening's attack on her. Her face was black and blue and one eye was so swollen it had doubled in size. My feeling of hate for my father immediately increased ten-fold from the night before and there was a look on her face as if she wanted to cry but she couldn't because it hurt so much. How could a man get away with it? Why should it be allowed? I asked myself as I looked at her, but what could I do. It was so unfair, so terrible, and was the worst hiding my mother had ever had. It was the first time I had seen my mother's face so badly beaten up it was to leave an emotional scar on me for the rest of my life. At only thirty-six years old, my mother had suffered more brutal kicks, punches and both physical and mental cruelty than most people ever witness in a whole lifetime, and I wouldn't wish it on any other living soul.

After that dreadful night, things went from bad to worse. I kept running away and the authorities eventually found they could not allow this so they made me a Ward of Court. However, they allowed me to stay with Mum and Dad, but only because they were aware of the closeness and bond between my mother and me. By the time I reached fourteen and a half I left school. I had made good friends with a girl called Sheila and spent most of my time round her house until in the end it was suggested by her family that I leave home and move in with them. Mum agreed to this, and she and Dad also moved on. They didn't tell me what their new address was and I felt very guilty for leaving her alone with Dad but, knowing Dad only too well, I wasn't surprised she didn't tell me where they had moved to because she probably thought it would keep the peace if I wasn't informed. Raymond had also left home and went to live with some friends of his, so he was out the family scene, too.

CHAPTER THREE

As Sheila and I had left school and neither of us had a job, we had plenty of time on our hands and we used to hang around in cafés in Harrow to combat our boredom. One day I was feeling down in the dumps as I wished I knew how Mum was and where they were living. Sheila tried to cheer me up but to no avail.

"I'll tell you what will cheer you up and get you to stop thinking about your parents," said Sheila, jumping up from her chair with excitement. She was always full of fun and her wonderful sense of adventure appealed to me. However, I really didn't want to know what her wild scheme might be and told her so.

Sheila wouldn't take no for an answer and produced a tube of pills from her handbag.

She drew my attention to them and, after I questioned her as to what they were for, she told me they were supposed to cheer people up when they were depressed or worried about something. She went on to say, "I've never tried them myself, but I bought some because I've been told they are really good. Anyway, what harm will it do just to try a couple?" Why not, I thought to myself and so we shared the pills between us. There were twenty pills in the tube so we had ten each.

The following morning we both felt terribly ill from the effects of the pills because they had kept us awake all night. Apart from that, they certainly made me feel carefree and safe for the first time in my life. I enjoyed that feeling but didn't want to take any more and neither did Sheila, so after the effects wore off we decided not to do it again.

Although Sheila was a good friend and her parents were kind to me, I was beginning to miss my own home and family, strange as it may seem. Blood is

14

thicker than water and nobody, but nobody can ever take the place of your mother. Despite the fact that Sheila's parents were very supportive and protective towards me, I felt I could never call it *my* home. I couldn't have wished to have had a nicer family to look after me and I didn't want to offend them, but my mind was made up.

One day I decided it would make an enjoyable day out to go and visit my mother's youngest sister, Shirley. Her real name was Ruth, but my mother started to call her Shirley at a young age because she had such lovely, fair curly hair, reminiscent of Shirley Temple's, and the nickname stuck with her for the rest of her life. I confided my feelings of wanting to leave Sheila's house to my aunt and she suggested that I should come and live with her, my uncle George and my cousin David. I felt this would be a step in the right direction and so i said my thank-yous and farewells to Sheila and her family and went to live with my relatives. It was the next best thing, as far as I was concerned, to live with Mum's sister as I couldn't live with mum herself. They treated me well and I soon found myself a job in a paint factory and tried my best to live a normal life. In spite of all my hard efforts to find peace, however, I was still not entirely happy, simply because Mum wasn't there, and I missed her very much.

My aunt and uncle spent hours talking to me and were indeed a tower of strength. They filled me in by telling me some of the goings-on that had occurred in the past, which I was unaware of at the time because some of it was history before I was born, and the rest was when I was a youngster. They stressed time and time again that Mum was completely terrified of Dad and they told me about Dad's appalling behaviour towards my mother. They kept nothing from me and painted the dismal picture in true colours. I asked them why on earth had Mum never left Dad and they said she had, on numerous occasions, but somehow or another Dad always managed to find out where she had gone and won her back with his devilish ways. Mum's family cared about Mum and how Dad was destroying her, but admitted there was nothing they could do. They were only too well aware Mum was being badly treated but, whenever one of them confronted my father about it, he apparently used to put on an act about how much he loved us all and never admitted to anything to the contrary. It was revealed that nobody liked my father and they always felt sorry for my mother, Raymond and me. There was a lot I knew about my father and the way he mistreated Mum but during my stay at my aunt and uncle's house they certainly opened my eyes to it all. Dad even went as far as breaking my mother's shoulder during one of his fits of temper, and, as he was such a huge man, it is no wonder nobody wanted to interfere between man and wife in case he set on them also. During those days there were no such things as shelter for battered wives or social services so I was now able to see the

15

difficulty Mum had when trying to escape from Dad. It seems she really didn't have much choice but to stay and put up with it, especially when I was around, and it was a case of putting up with it and suffering the consequences.

I was still a Ward of Court as I lived with my aunt and uncle and now I had a Probation Officer who had to be kept informed of my whereabouts. She was aware, therefore, that I had been living at Sheila's house and then with my aunt and uncle. I also had to let my Probation Officer know if I ever wanted to change my job but, being the kind lady that she was, she invariably helped me as much as she could. When work at the factory became too monotonous for me, I asked my cousin Joyce if there was any chance of her getting me a job at her company. She worked for a baby clothing firm and luckily she was able to get me one. I enjoyed my work there a great deal. Joyce and I were of the same age and, because the two of us were the eldest cousins in the family, we had been friends ever since I can remember. Nevertheless, although I loved my job, being with Joyce and living with Aunty Sheila, I gradually found myself missing my mother more and more, but I had no idea where she was living or what she was doing, nor indeed, what had been going on in general since I had left home. I tried desperately hard not to hurt my Uncle George's feelings, but one day I summoned up the courage to tell him how I was longing to get in touch with Mum and he said to me,

"Ann, it is entirely up to you, love. We understand how you must feel. Both your aunt and I want what's best for you, just as long as you are happy. You must do what you think best."

You can't imagine how much that meant to me and I was so glad they understood why I had to find the lady who meant everything to me, my Mum.

By now I was fifteen and a half years old and still working at Snowman's, the baby clothing factory. I decided to wait a couple of weeks until I thought it right time to start my search for mum. I had a good home with my aunt and uncle and a good job, but I was desperately missing Mum now. No-one knew where she was and, however hard I tried, I kept coming up against blind alleys. I was now becoming obsessed about seeing her again but it seemed an impossible task to track her down. I was beginning to withdraw into myself and into a deep depression.

One day, during my lunch-break, I went to the local parade of shops near to where I worked. I needed to find a chemist as I had a terrible headache that day and popped in to buy some tablets to take the pain away. As I waited to be served my

16

eyes moved along the shelves. There in front of me were the same pills I had tried that day with Sheila. As I stared at them I remembered the wonderful feeling of upliftment they had given me and the sense of security and freedom they gave me.

The assistant asked me what I wanted and when she returned with the headache pills asked me if there was anything else I wanted.

I said, "No thank you, that's all," and walked back to work.

All that afternoon I couldn't stop thinking about the "magic" pills. So far in my life nothing had made me truly happy and I kept going over and over in my mind to the day Sheila and I took those pills. It wouldn't do me any harm, surely, to try them once more. I just needed to feel everything was right with the world again, and this was the only way I could think of which would create that illusion.

By the end of the afternoon I had talked myself into going straight back to the chemist after work, praying that they would still be open. To my relief, the chemist was still open, so I walked in and bought a tube. Funnily enough, I declined to take any of the pills straight away because I could vividly remember how awful Sheila and I both felt the morning after, because we were so tired as the pills kept us awake all night long. So when I got up the following morning I looked at the tube sitting on my lap, and somehow or another I knew I'd be foolish to take them and that it was wrong. I felt so disenchanted with my life, however, that as I opened the tube I thought to myself, Yes, I'll just take a couple for now and see how it goes.

I felt sure that a couple of them would be sufficient, that I wouldn't get used to them, but how wrong I was. Within a month I was well and truly hooked on them. I wouldn't say I was happy taking them, but they helped me to cope with life a lot easier and i felt with their help I could take each day as it came along. The lift they gave me to overcome the hurt I had been feeling for such a long time was incredible, and I was determined I wasn't going to hurt any more. To me, the pills were my safeguard against life in general. They didn't appear to affect me in a way that other people would notice, and somehow or another life carried on as if nothing was wrong. That is, until one day when my uncle and aunt asked to have a word with me. I had been careless at work and someone had seen me taking some pills and had informed them. By this time I had no intention of giving the pills up as it was the only means of support I knew for carrying on. My aunt and uncle were not angry with me, surprisingly enough, but intensely worried. I told them a few lies and managed to convince them it wasn't as bad as they thought, but from that time on they kept a very careful watch over me.

Not long after that I made up my mind it would be best for me to leave. They all understood and I told them I would be living back with Sheila and her family for a while. I was coming up to sixteen now, and soon I would be too old to be a Ward of Court, but until then I had to tell my Probation Officer of my whereabouts.

I didn't stay for long at Sheila's and moved in with some other friends who were the same age as me. They were all aware of my taking pills but all vowed to try and help me stop taking them and see sense. They, too, were wonderful to me for they never ran me down,but tried to persuade me that this kind of lifestyle was not in my best interests. Perhaps some of them guessed the reason I was taking drugs but, then again, we were all so young, reckless and, particularly in my case,very mixed up, so escapism was a common answer to problems.

As the time went by, the drugs began to make me feel very, very ill, although of course I would not admit that it was the pills which were the cause of why I felt so bad. I suspect I wasn't aware of the fact that they were the reason for my weakening physical state. I thought my health was A1 and that there was nothing to worry about.

One Friday, however, one of my friends I was living with came with me to town to go shopping. We had a good day out and, tired and weary, caught a bus back home, but during the trip on the bus I suddenly developed stomach pains which were so severe that they made me double up. They became so acute that the bus driver had to stop the bus and an ambulance was sent for. I was subsequently taken straight to Harrow-on-the-Hill hospital, where two doctors examined me. I can still remember them arguing as to whether it would be better to keep me in overnight for observation or not. They were unaware that I had been taking drugs, but did decide that acid had formed in my stomach and was the cause of the pain. They sent me home on the Saturday morning, after I had spent one night in hospital, and said that there was nothing they could do for me. Despite all this, that evening I still felt terribly ill. I tried to distract myself by meeting my group of friends at the "Drop In" Café in Harrow, but eventually I gave up pretending everything was fine and asked one of my friends if I could possibly sleep in the back of his car until I felt a bit better, to which he agreed.

When I woke up I found that he had driven me back to the hospital, because everyone was so worried about me and frightened to see me in such a bad way. The lady doctor whom I had seen when I first collapsed arranged for me to be admitted for observation and told me that my friends were all waiting outside the room, apprehensive and scared in case I was annoyed with them for having taken me back to hospital. Of course I didn't blame them, how could I? They, in turn, were pleased to see I was now safe and relieved to see I was in good hands.

The doctor decided to keep me in that Saturday night. I still don't know how the doctors managed to do it, but miraculously they were able to find my mother and contacted her to inform her of her daughter's plight. I didn't even know where she was living, so how on earth they did I don't know. One day during my stay in hospital the sister told me I had a visitor. I had been resting for a couple of days now and feeling a little better. I thanked her and sat up in bed, preening myself ready to receive my mystery visitor. I looked up and there she was; Mum was standing next to my bed. Words cannot express how thrilled I was to see her again, and we fell into each other's arms, cuddled each other and cried. I felt like pinching myself to make sure it was really happening. Mum asked me if I was feeling any better and we found we had so much to catch up on. I must have changed a lot in the twelve months we had been apart and had grown up rapidly in that time. As a result, my mother must have found it difficult to guess my state of mind. I loved her so dearly and was so delighted to be with her again that it didn't cross my mind to ask where she had been living or how she was. All I could think of was my relief at seeing her again.

She mentioned that Dad had recently discovered her current address and was back living with her, so she wouldn't be able to stay with me too long. I looked into her eyes and could see the fear she harboured inside her. Although she loved me, the fear she had of my father which had dominated her life was so great that she felt it was imperative to get back before he realised she had gone out. She was only a young woman herself, and when I saw the terror and pain she was experiencing I made up my mind there and then that I couldn't and wouldn't let her endure any more suffering. The time had come for something to be done once and for all. Mum gave me her address and I promised to see her very soon. We kissed each other goodbye and I squeezed her as I cuddled her. She blew me a kiss and then waved as she approached the door, and after she left I laid back on my pillow. I knew I had to do everything within my power to ensure she wouldn't have to tolerate any more suffering and that I was the only person who could help her. I resolved to go and face my father and I would have to act promptly.

I was discharged from hospital the following evening, which gave me a chance to make plans. The next day I went along to meet Mum after she had finished work and this pattern continued for the next month or so. It was so good for us both to see each other again. Meeting her this way meant Dad knew nothing was going on, and I used to tell Mum my intentions. When the opportunity finally arose for me to confront my father, I went to see him at their home whilst Mum was there. Six months prior to this I had a tattoo engraved on my arm with the word "MUM". I was very proud of this, but my father straightaway caught sight of it and showed his disapproval. He had obviously been drinking before I had arrived and he was so incensed at the sight of me and my tattoo that he didn't hesitate to strike me. I was quicker than him this time and ran straight into the kitchen. My eyes veered straight at a knife on the kitchen table which gleamed in the sunlight. Dad followed me into the kitchen and I grabbed the knife in my hand. I told him quite categorically that if he ever touched me again I would kill him. I had never been able to speak to him in this way before and this time he didn't push his luck. He knew I meant what I said. He recoiled from me and went back into the other room. I was shaking because I couldn't believe I would ever be able to threaten him and I put down the knife. It worked though, and he never came near me again.

My plan was that Mum and I should go away together and completely distance ourselves from Dad. I reassured her that, together, we would have more strength and determination to conquer him than ever before. First of all Mum said she didn't want to go for she still feared that he would follow us, as he had done for so many years, but for my part I had reached the stage where he didn't frighten me any more, and I think Mum knew that, too. At last I got Mum round to my way of thinking and eventually we made arrangements and every detail was carefully planned as to what course of action we would take. In arranged to meet Mum the following Saturday morning at ten o'clock, so all that week I started collecting my belongings together and said goodbye to my friends who I had been living with. I left early that Saturday morning and set off towards the High Street to meet Mum, rather than for me to go to the house. More than likely Dad would still be in bed after drinking all night and sleeping it off. It was also easier for Mum to pack her clothes and personal belongings without him knowing what was going on. If I wasn't there it wouldn't arouse any suspicion, either. I was really nervous so I decided to get there early and, as I stood waiting, I noticed the time on one of the shop's clocks. It was only 9.15 a.m. and I had hardly any money on me, only about £9.00, and I had no idea how much Mum would have with her.

It was snowing very heavily and it was too cold to stand around for three-quarters of an hour, so I found a little coffee shop to seek refuge from the icy-cold weather. I chose to sit at a table near the window and put my suitcase behind my chair. As I sat down after ordering, the man who owned the coffee shop brought over my hot cup of tea. I was more interested in holding the cup to keep my hands warm than drinking what was in it. As I gazed out of the window I wondered what the future held in store for Mum and me. I was scared she wouldn't come at first. Perhaps she was too frightened to come, or what if Dad had seen her getting ready to leave and had stopped her coming? Perhaps he had given her a hiding into the bargain? There were so many possibilities going round and round in my mind as I sat watching the snow fall softly to the ground, covering the pavement like a white blanket. I glanced down at my shoes only to find my poor feet were red raw and freezing cold from all the standing around outside. The snow had seeped into the holes in my shoes, subsequently making my feet soaking wet. Before I had left the house that morning I put some paper inside my shoes in the hope of covering up the holes, but after all the walking and standing around in the deep snow the paper was now very wet and soggy.

There were not many people in the coffee shop so I slowly took off one of my shoes surreptitiously removed the paper, hoping no-one could see what I was doing or suspect anything. i screwed up the paper into a pulp and swiftly popped it into my handbag. I then did the same procedure with the other shoe. My shoes were still wet, of course, but not soggy any more.

My table and chair was so positioned that I would be able to see if and when Mum was arriving. I took another look at the clock and saw that this time it was almost ten o'clock. My stomach felt as if it was tied up in knots and I was beginning to feel uncomfortable and fidgety. I couldn't help thinking that neither Mum nor I had been very happy over the years, either when we were together or apart, but this time we really had to try to get away by ourselves, if only we could pull it off. Surely, by running away together we would be able to find solace and peace of mind.

I decided to get up and walk to the counter to order another cup of tea when I heard someone open the door of the coffee shop. I turned round to see who it was and to my delight it was Mum.

"Get me one, love" she said casually. She looked around the shop and then noticed my suitcase at the little table by the window, so she took another chair and placed it by the table. Before she sat down she put her suitcase next to mine and by the time she had settled herself I returned with the two teas. Mum picked up the newspaper which had been left on the chair before she came in, and opened it to the classified section to see what rooms were to let within the Harrow area.

She looked up at the date of the paper and she said, "This is last Wednesday's, but with a bit of luck not all the rooms will have gone. By the way, have you eaten yet, Ann?"

"No, Mum, I haven't," I answered.

Mum turned her head to look out of the window. The snow was getting worse. When she looked back at me she suggested me order something substantial to eat before we set off in that awful weather outside and, before I could answer, she had got up and gone to the counter to order us something to eat.

After we had finished our meal Mum continued going through the newspaper, marking off suitable rooms to let. I sat quietly, taking stock of the situation, and admiringly observed her face. Here she was, only thirty-eight years old and still quite attractive for age with her slim build and now dark hair. She had not mentioned Dad at all and, although I was dying to ask her how she had managed to slip out without him knowing, I thought it best not to ask and left it that she would tell me in her own time.

Just then, she looked up and smiled at me as if she knew all along what was going on in my head and she said, "Come on, cheer up, love. You'll see, it's all going to be alright."

I smiled back at her and put my hand on top of hers. I said, "Oh, I'm O.K., Mum. I just hope we can get somewhere to stay soon for I don't fancy walking around all day long in this," and I pointed my finger to the weather outside, but then I thought it sounded selfish of me. With that, I apologised to Mum and said that I didn't mean to moan but I was a bit edgy and so pleased she had managed to leave Dad and meet me. I went on to explain about the state of my shoes and that they were the only real reason I wanted to find somewhere - fast.

"Come on then, love," said Mum, reassuring me in her usual, familiar way. "Let's get you some new shoes. I've got about £40 or £50 on me and if we go carefully with it I can afford to buy you a new pair."

We left the warmth of the café and ventured out into the bleak, snowy weather. It was not letting up at all and it was bitterly cold. We went inside the first shoe shop we came across and I chose a suitable pair of shoes. We couldn't afford a pair of boots but what a difference the new shoes made! At least my feet were dry now.

We spent all that afternoon telephoning some of the people advertising rooms to let, and also walking round to those with just addresses given to see if they had been taken or not. By four o'clock that afternoon we still had no luck at all in finding a room. Each one we enquired after had already been taken, so we made our weary way back to the High Street where we had started off all those hours ago. We were both suffering from cold, wet feet due to the snow and it was now starting to get dark.

"Let's go into Woolworths," said Mum. "At least we'll be a bit warmer inside."

I was so cold by now I would have gladly gone inside anywhere so long as I could get the feeling back into my fingers and toes. I felt sorry for Mum for I knew she was getting worried that we had been unable to find anywhere to stay. I put my arm around her shoulders and said, "Don't worry, Mum. We'll manage to find somewhere to stay, some way or another," but even I was wondering what other way we could find a place to rest our weary bones. "I hope so, Ann," Mum said and we picked up our two suitcases and walked around Woolworths for about half an hour.

When we came out of the store Mum suggested we try looking at the big houses in the opposite direction from which we had been looking earlier that day, just in case someone had put up a notice board advertising a room to let. So off we set towards the end of the high Street where a clock tower stood opposite. As we walked past the huge clock tower. Mum suddenly stopped in her tracks. She had caught sight of a notice board in the window of one of the large houses. I followed her pointed finger and sure enough, there, just past the clock tower, was a board in the window with "ROOM TO LET" printed in large, bold letters. Thank God, I prayed, it hadn't gone like all the rest! I grabbed Mum's arm and, looking carefully to chèck there were no cars coming, we crossed the street with a scurry. We pushed open the front gate and rushed up the path. Mum rang the doorbell and we waited for somebody to answer the door. It seemed like an age, but was probably only a couple of minutes before an elderly lady opened the front door and stood in front of us. Mum introduced herself and told the lady we were enquiring about the room to let and we were so excited when she invited us in. We stepped into a warm and very large hallway. To my relief, the room was still vacant, so after Mum and the lady agreed on the rent we eagerly followed her upstairs. We climbed up and up three floors in all and we finally arrived at our destination. Our room was in the attic! The lady unlocked the door and showed us in. Mum settled up with our rent money and the lady bade us a pleasant stay. We put our suitcases down as we entered the room. It wasn't a palace, but ideal for us. We thanked the lady who then left us on our own. We both gave a huge sigh of relief and shut the door behind us.

23

CHAPTER FOUR

It was quite a large room and as I looked around I noticed a big double bed along one wall, and in the middle of the room stood a small table with two chairs. In one corner stood an armchair and alongside that was a small sink. A kettle, cutlery and crockery were on shelves above the draining board and at the side of the sink, on the floor, was a small paraffin heater. There wasn't much in the room besides these things but they were clean and tidy.

We were both glad to get in from the cold and Mum checked the paraffin heater to see if there was any paraffin in it whilst I put the suitcases on the bed. "We're O.K.," said Mum, "There's enough paraffin in it for a couple of days." Mum picked up the heater and placed it near the little table which stood in the middle of the room and then she lit it.

"It shouldn't take long to warm the room up," said Mum and then sat on the bed beside me. She asked me if I was alright, to which I smiled and nodded. "Well, it's not much, but I'm sure we'll be a lot happier here, don't you agree?" said Mum.

"Oh, yes, Mum, we'll be just fine," and I gave her a big hug.

Mum noticed the state of my clothes as I hugged and said, "Your clothes are soaking. Take them off before you catch your death of cold."

"Yours are no better," I replied, "The landlady said the bathroom was just along the hallway. I think I'll go and have a nice hot bath and then you can have yours."

By the time I returned to our room Mum had unpacked and hung our clothes up. It was already beginning to feel like home to me. Mum had her bath and I had two mugs of soup ready. We had bought a few items of food just in case we were lucky enough to find somewhere to stay.

I said to Mum, "This'll warm us up," and we sat on the chairs round the heater. "I'll pop out to the shops in the morning and get some groceries," said Mum, and started making out a list of the things we needed.

"We haven't much money so we'll have to go carefully until we both get a job."

"Don't worry, Mum," I said. "We'll start looking first thing Monday morning. I'm sure we'll be able to find some work without too much trouble."

"I sincerely hope so," said Mum. "I've only been able to pay two weeks' rent in advance."

With that, we dropped the subject and lapped up the luxury of feeling warm and at ease.

"Are you glad we're together, Ann?" asked Mum.

How could she ask such a thing, I thought. "Oh, Mum, you don't know how much!" and I got out of my chair so I could hold her tight. After a few seconds Mum pulled back and looked at me squarely in the eyes.

"I'm so sorry, Ann, love," said Mum so seriously.

"Sorry? Whatever for?" I replied, but of course I knew Mum was referring to Dad and all the times we had to be apart from each other. I knew it wasn't Mum's fault. How could it be when I knew how much she loved me.

I tried to console her by saying, "Mum, I'm just glad we're together," and I gave her a kiss on the cheek.

Mum lit a cigarette but I noticed her hands were trembling a little.

"What's wrong, Mum?" I asked. "Are you worried in case Dad finds out where we're living?"

"Not really," she replied. "I'm still a bit cold from being out in that snow all day. Anyway, by the time your father came in last night I didn't get to sleep till the early hours, and even then I kept thinking about our running away today so that was on my mind and I didn't get much sleep.

There was a small alarm clock near the sink. As I looked at it I could see it had gone past ten o'clock so I said, "Come on, Mum. Let's get into bed. We'll be much warmer there and I think we are both tired out."

Mum smiled and got up and got ready for bed.

As we lay there we chatted for a while until finally Mum fell asleep. I felt much

25

warmer now but, nevertheless, couldn't get off to sleep. I watched Mum for a while and was so pleased that we had managed to be together without worrying about Dad barging in in a drunken rage. The curtain at the window wasn't pulled properly so I could still see the snow falling outside. It felt so good to be safe and warmly tucked up in bed. My eyes looked to my handbag which was lying on top of my suitcase on the floor. It wasn't so much the handbag itself which occupied my mind, so much as what was inside it. I had managed to buy enough pills to last me a couple of weeks, so at least I knew there was sufficient supply and I didn't have to worry about buying any for a while. What I was worried about was how Mum would take it. I had never seen her take a pill for anything, not even a headache, and by God she must have had many of them in her time. I was so confused because I was happy and contented lying next to Mum, but concerned that she was unaware of what I was doing to myself. I still had a great need for the pills and, although I had tried desperately to stop taking them a couple of times, I found the after-effects so painful. As I looked at Mum I wondered if there was any need to tell her for a while. After all, we both had enough to worry about in the next few weeks, what with finding work and hoping Dad wouldn't find our whereabouts. There was no point adding to our problems by confessing I was taking pills. I decided that would be the best thing to do and with that I turned over and very soon I fell asleep.

We had a lovely long lie-in on the Sunday morning and spent the whole day relaxing. Apart from the fact we didn't want to do anything in particular, we couldn't go anywhere because of the bad weather and the lack of funds, so most of the time was spent chatting. Mum was interested to know what I had been doing since we had last lived with each other. I told her most of it - except probably the most important part - the taking of drugs. I knew I would have no option but to tell her soon because living a lie was almost unbearable. I wouldn't be able to keep up the pretence much longer and I was finding it difficult finding hiding places for my pills, let alone administering them whilst living in one room together. However, that Sunday I left it, and made up my mind not to tell Mum, for we were so happy and I didn't want anything to spoil that contented feeling.

The following morning we left early in search of work. I was very lucky inasmuch as the first shop I tried showed some interest in me. It was the little baker's shop not far from where we were living so I wouldn't have to worry about fares. The wages weren't much but enough to survive on till Mum could get a job, too. Mum didn't manage to find a job that day but it was decided that I would start mine the following Monday. By the time Wednesday arrived we were gradually running out of money and Mum was so worried about the situation.

She said, "I'm afraid we'll have to live on bread and dripping until the money starts coming in, love."

"Well, that'll be better than nothing," I said, trying to look on the bright side of things. "At least we've got a roof over our heads."

Poor Mum looked so depressed so I tried to cheer her up by saying, "I start work next Monday and you're sure to find a job before the weekend, you'll see. It won't be long before things improve."

Sure enough, when we went out job-hunting for Mum on the Friday morning, Mum was given a job in a restaurant in North Harrow. The following week flew by and by Sunday we were both fed up with eating bread and dripping. We had it for breakfast, dinner and tea but we were very happy there all the same. There was no worry about Dad coming in drunk and throwing his weight about and we could get up whenever we liked, and we fully enjoyed the wonderful feeling of freedom to do exactly as we pleased without Dad spoiling it for us. It was a completely new way of life for us both, one which we enjoyed every minute of. Mum would play a game and say, "What would you like for dinner today, Ann?" and I would reply with, "Er, I think I'll have steak and chips today," and Mum would put the bread and dripping in front of me which made us both roar with laughter.

Seriously though, by the time Sunday arrived, we were both pleased to be starting work the following day and were looking forward to a few more luxuries - especially FOOD!

I had only been at my job in the baker's shop a few weeks when Mum came home one night to eagerly tell me there was a job vacant at the greengrocer's opposite the restaurant where she worked.

She said, "If you apply for the job, Ann, at least we'll be working right near each other and it would certainly give me peace of mind to know you were only over the road if I needed to see you."

I was aware of how worried she had been about where I worked in case Dad had seen me. When we first decided to run away together we agreed there was no point in going to the other end of the country, as Mum had done that many times before and Dad had always found us, so this time we had made up our minds to stay in the same area. At least then, just in case anything really bad happened, we could call on the family, so all in all I was happy to apply for the greengrocer's job.

Fortunately, I got the job and was soon much happier, because Mum and I left the flat together and even managed to get the same lunch-hour and come home in the evenings together. Above all, our financial status was much healthier and naturally life was a lot easier for us. We managed to build our little room into a small home and we were happier there than we had ever been before. The snow had now completely gone and now it was spring. Besides all these wonderful changes, I was still secretly taking the drugs and, as far as I was aware, Mum had not found out or, if she had, she had not said anything to me. However, it was becoming increasingly harder for me to keep hiding them and there were so many times I wanted to talk to Mum about it, for I knew I was ill and yet there was nothing I could do about it on my own. I had found extra strength in the drugs and I didn't want to lose that feeling, no matter how happy I was being with Mum.

I was sixteen years old now, but I really didn't realise how sick I was becoming. There were so many times when I really didn't want the drugs to be such a major part of my life any more, but I didn't know how to survive without them. Things were gradually slipping out of my grasp so I decided that I would tell Mum all about it the following weekend. Strangely enough, though, the question of drugs cropped up a couple of days earlier. We were on our way home from work one night when Mum said, "When we get in, love, I want a word with you."

I was quite disturbed about this and asked what it was all about. It seemed important and I couldn't wait until we got indoors to find out what Mum was so concerned about. I hadn't seen her so serious for a long time.

Mum opened up her handbag and brought out an empty tube of the pills I was taking. For a moment I just looked at it but could say nothing. I had tried so hard hiding them the past few weeks and yet here she was holding one of them.

"Can I explain when we get in, Mum", I asked in a croaky voice.

"O.K., love," said Mum, and nothing more was said on the way home.

When we got inside, Mum put the kettle on and took off her coat and shoes. She laid the table for tea whilst I got changed from my working clothes into a skirt and jumper. There was the most awful silence, one which I'm sure many of you can acknowledge. It is a moment in time when two people feel slighted in a sense of mistrust and lack of truth from either party. One which seems to last hours and yet only five minutes has slipped by. I think Mum was waiting for me to bring up the subject, but I was trying to avoid it, because I knew how much I had hurt her by keeping such an awful secret from her and she undoubtedly felt betrayed, a feeling which I would never knowingly bestow upon her, the one person in my life whom I loved so dearly.

Somehow or another we managed to finish our tea but then Mum picked up her handbag again and brought out the empty tube.

"Ann, what exactly are they for and why are you taking them?" Mum asked. I put the book down that I had buried my head in since I'd sat down and knew this was the moment I had been dreading.

"Mum," I uttered apologetically.

"Hold it a minute," said Mum. "Before you tell me your story, I know what these pills are for. They're slimming pills and you can't be using them for that purpose because you are too skinny for starters. There's no reason you'd need anything like that so I would like to know the truth."

Her voice didn't sound angry but more concerned.

"O.K., Mum, I said, and I proceeded to tell her the whole story, right from the beginning. What I didn't tell her, however, was how many I was taking a day. My intake had gone up to fifteen or twenty a day but I told her it was only a few a day.

"What do you call a few, Ann?"

"Well," I said, "Sometimes it's eight." I tried my best to sound convincing and chose the number eight as a compromise, but I knew by looking at her face she was worried. I knelt beside her and said softly, "I can control them, Mum, honestly I can. They're not that bad, it's just that I need them for now."

I went on to remind her of the past and how they had helped me cope with my difficulties.

"I promise that when we are settled I will stop taking them. It shouldn't be that difficult, honestly."

Mum appeared satisfied with what I had said but nevertheless was still very worried, so I repeated my promise to her and also that I wouldn't be on them for ever.

I even got to believe the words myself, let alone Mum, but at sixteen I truly believed anything was possible, including coming off the pills, but how wrong I was to not only deceive my mother, but myself also.

Mum cuddled me for a while and then said, "I don't want anything else to happen to you, Ann, for you mean the world to me. We'll speak no more of it tonight, but I can't sit back and watch you kill yourself."

I knew then that she had realised I was taking more than I had admitted to because, if she had really believed me when I said I took no more than eight a day, she wouldn't have said such a thing. I just cuddled her and kept silent. I was just happy and relieved it was out in the open because when I was ready I knew I had Mum to help me come off them altogether.

Life carried on and, as far as I was concerned, I had never enjoyed life so much. Both of us were much more relaxed and, although I was still taking the pills, neither of us talked about it and put it behind us for the time being. I don't know if that was a good thing or not, but it suited me anyway.

One day, during our lunch-break, Mum pointed out a young man who was sitting near us at one of the other tables in the restaurant. He was one of the lads who worked at the Radio shop, according to Mum, and as I looked across to look at him I could see he was about thirty with fair hair. I wouldn't say he was terrific looking but he had a kind face. He must have noticed me looking at him, for suddenly he looked at me. I quickly turned away to ask Mum what she had mentioned him for.

"Well," she said, "I thought I'd buy you a radio as there isn't one in our room and there's no television either, and I spoke to him yesterday about it. He told me to pop in and have a look at what they've got in the shop."

"That's great. I'd love that," I said, and with that I looked at the clock in the restaurant to check on the time.

"I've got to rush. See you at the bus stop tonight, Mum." I gave her a quick kiss on the cheek and went back to work.

That evening, Mum said to me, "I'll tell you what, Ann, you go into the radio shop and choose which one you want. Go tomorrow if you like."

30

I gladly accepted and thanked her. It would be really appreciated having my very own radio here. The following day I couldn't wait for my lunch-time to come. I went straight over to the radio shop. As I opened the shop door the young man I had seen the previous day was near the front of the shop.

"Can I help you?" he asked.

"Yes, please. My mother works next door and apparently she spoke to you about buying a radio and sent me in to choose one, because it's for me really." "Fine," he said and smiled. "Come in and I'll show you what we have." His voice was soft and friendly and straight away I liked him. There was a young man in the back of the shop who was about nineteen.

He said, "Do you need any help, Tony?" and laughed cheekily at the fair-haired man, but he was refused his kind offer of assistance! I laughed to myself for, without sounding big-headed, I was quite a nice-looking young girl and I suppose, like all men, they were both trying to chat me up, but at least this way I had managed to find out the name of the fair-haired man. It wasn't that he had interested me that much but I did find him to be pleasant. I chose which radio I wanted and went in to tell Mum about it. I only had about ten minutes before I was due to go back to work, so I rushed to tell her I'd chosen one and said I had to go or I'd be late back to work. Mum said she'd leave work five minutes early and pop in and sign for it.

When I met Mum that night at the bus stop she had the radio with her. I was over the moon, for I loved music and dancing and it would be the first time I would be able to listen to my own music for weeks. I was so excited about it that as soon as we finished our evening meal and cleared away I put the radio on. Mum reminded me not to have it on too loud, in case it disturbed the people downstairs, but I'm sure she said it with a twinkle in her eye for she knew how much it meant to me.

As Mum stood ironing she said, "I think that young man from the radio shop likes you."

"Which one?" I replied, laughing and trying to show some modesty.

"The one who was sitting in the restaurant the other day. He asked me where you worked and if you had a boyfriend or not," said Mum. She went on, "But I think he's a bit old for you," and looked that 'motherly-concern-for-her-only-daughter' type of look.

31

"Come on, Mum, he can only be in his late twenties. Anyway, there's no problem because I've only seen him twice so I shouldn't worry." With that, I carried on listening to the music.

I noticed that during the next two weeks the fair-haired man happened to take his lunch-hour at the same time each day as Mum and I. He sat at the next table to ours as before when we were eating our dinner. Very soon he was sitting at our table, and I found out that he was the supervisor of four shops, and on the day I had gone into the radio shop to choose my radio he had just happened to be visiting the shop himself. We soon became friends and I used to pop into the shop during my lunch-hour instead of going into Mum's restaurant. She didn't mind and was quite happy to see me enjoying myself. The lads used to play cards in the radio shop so I started to join in with them. I now called the fair-haired man by his first name, and in a way wished he would ask me out. I could tell he was interested, but that was as far as it went.

One Sunday morning there was a knock at our door. Our landlady was standing there and told us there was a gentleman downstairs wishing to speak to me. At first Mum was alarmed and said, "I'll be down in a minute. Can you tell him to wait a little while, please."

Mum shut the door and started trembling. "It's your father, I bet," she said. "It's alright," I said, "I'll go instead. If it is him he might think it's just me living here on my own. You never know, it might work."

I knew Dad was only really interested in Mum, and if I was to go to see him he might accept it and leave without any trouble.

"What if he's drunk?" Mum said with a sudden worried thought.

"I'll worry about that," I replied, and before she could say any more I had gone. I had curlers in my hair and an old green coat draped over my shoulders. I could see the broad shoulders of a man through the window and Mum's words that he may be drunk went over and over in my head, so I hesitated a little. I had to open the door, because if it was Dad he would have pushed the door in, and the last thing we wanted was to get ourselves thrown out of our room by the landlady. With my hands shaking I managed to open the front door and, with a huge sigh of relief, there in front of me stood the fair-haired man, Tony.

"What do you want?" I blurted out rudely. Having worked myself into a lather thinking it was Dad I was about to be confronted with, and then seeing a friendly, familiar face, had made me edgy.

"Oh, I do apologise," I said with a sigh of relief, "I thought you were someone else."

His face seemed to drop so I went on, "No, my father may have called by. I thought it was him."

"Oh. I just wanted to return this to you," he replied. In his hand he was carrying a playing card. It was the Joker.

"You left it at the shop," he added.

I thought to myself, What the hell is he on about, and then I suddenly remembered I had taken a pack of cards to play in the shop on Friday, but I must confess I couldn't remember leaving the Joker card there or honestly caring whether I did or not. I didn't know whether to laugh or cry, just before I opened the door. I really had thought it was Dad and was so frightened and now, here I was, standing in front of a man with a Joker card in his hand." Thanks!" I replied. "That was nice of you."

All the while I was wondering what the hell was going on. I was still worked up, thinking it was my father at the door but, calming down, I realised how pleased I was to see Tony and not my Dad standing there. I thanked him once more as I took the card from his hand and went to say goodbye and close the door, but before I could do so Tony blurted out, "Would you like to go out tomorrow night?"

"Yes, that would be lovely," I replied. "I'd love to."

He smiled and walked back down the path and as I watched him I though to myself, Yes, I do like you, and with that I shut the door and went back upstairs. Mum was anxiously awaiting my return for she was still unaware if it was Dad at the door or not.

"It's O.K., Mum. We're safe. There's nothing to worry about. It was Tony."

"Who's Tony?" asked Mum perplexed.

"You know, the guy from the radio shop. He wants to take me out tomorrow night," I said.

33

"Are you going?" asked Mum.

"Yes I am. I rather like him. You don't mind, do you, Mum?"

"No, love," said Mum with a smile. "As long as you enjoy yourself, Ann, that's all that matters."

From that time on Tony and I started to date regularly, and gradually we fell in love. I knew I would have to tell him about my illness one day but I was getting used to living day by day and, once again, I put it aside. The following months completely changed my life, for Mum and I were happy and now I had Tony. Nothing seemed to spoil it and I could have gone on forever, but it wasn't meant to be.

Mum and I decided to look for a bigger place to live and, as money was now coming in, we would be able to afford it. We found a flat in West Harrow, the owners of which were a lovely Irish couple who were kind to us. We settled in and enjoyed having more than one room to live in. We had now been together for about four months and life had a new meaning and fresh beginning for us. Naturally, we were still worried about Dad ever finding us, but it didn't seem to matter so much for, as time went by, we learned how to live freely and got more used to his not being around.

One Friday night, however, I had to work late so Mum had gone home well before me. I was to go out with Tony later that evening and I didn't think I'd have much time to get ready, so as I looked at my watch as I walked up to the front door I was pleased to see I still had a couple of hours to get ready. I knew Mum would have my tea ready so there was no big rush. As I walked up the stairs, unbuttoning my coat, I stopped halfway because I thought I could hear a man's voice. I froze for a moment. I couldn't mistake that voice - it belonged to Dad. I had to somehow put a brave face on and prepare myself to meet him, but I was still petrified of him. I was really more scared for Mum and I knew I had to walk into the room to confront him, but it was easier said than done. My heart was pounding as I whispered to myself, "How on earth did he find us?" I knew I had no option but to enter the room where he was, as Mum was obviously on her own with him, and as I walked in I saw my father standing there as large as life as if nothing untoward had happened. What's more, I could see that terrible look of fear was back in Mum's eyes again. I didn't know what to do. Everything was kept on an even keel and I tried to make polite small-talk, all the while trying to sort out in my mind the best course of action to take. In the end, I simply said in a calm voice, "Oh, don't forget we have to go to the shops, Mum," and by some

34

unbelievable chance my father fell for the ruse. I can't really remember if he smelt of drink or not, but all he said was, "Alright, I'll wait here. You won't be long, will you?"

Mum and I answered together, "No", simultaneously and walked out of the room as if nothing was afoot, and shut the door behind us. As soon as we were outside the house we ran with all our might.

We kept on running and I felt physically sick, as, I suspect, did my mother. My first thought was, where could we hide? As we passed an alleyway I grabbed Mum's arm and we ran a little way down the alleyway, then stopped, pressing our bodies up against the wall. It was evening, so of course it was dark, something which was in our favour. I was hoping that it was dark enough for Dad to fail to see clearly. I don't know how long we had been sheltering there, it seemed like an eternity, when suddenly I saw my father's silhouette at the end of the alleyway, not facing our direction, but looking all around him. I saw that he knew what we had done and turned my face to the brick wall, praying, not even daring to look at Mum, although I knew that she was pressed right up against the wall next to me. Both of us did not dare to make a sound.

After a while we heard my father's footsteps walking away but we continued to stay where we were, immobile, for a while longer, just to make absolutely certain that we were safe. After what seemed a lifetime we stealthily managed to return to the flat.

As soon as we got indoors Mum sat down and started to sob uncontrollably. I, too, was shaking from the shock of him finding us but I knelt down by Mum's chair and tried to console her.

"Come on, Mum," I said softly, and I held her close. Thinking back, it had been so much worse for her and I knew how terrified she was that he might come back later that night. After a while she calmed down a bit and I made her a cup of tea.

"Wait there, Mum, I won't be long," I said. I'm going down to have a word with the landlady," and I slipped out the door.

I went downstairs and knocked on their front room door. I told the couple all about my father and the predicament we were in. They were so concerned and sympathetic and after I had told them the whole story the husband said, "Now don't you worry about a thing, love. Just tell your mother from me that there is no way your father will step over this threshold again." I thanked him and bid them goodnight. It was very kind of him to say such a thing, but as I walked back upstairs I knew we would have to find somewhere else to live. Although they were a lovely couple they really didn't know how much trouble my father could cause, but for the time being at least we were safe. Before I could open the door to our room I heard a knock at the front door. My heart began to beat so fast and I could feel such horror overpowering me. I looked towards the front door and could see the figure of a man standing there, knocking. I leant back and thought, Please don't bring trouble, Dad. Mum opened the door to our room and came out to the top of the stairs to see what was going on.

"Sssh, someone's at the door," I whispered, and saw Mum's face turn white.

We waited for our landlord to answer the door and a voice said, "Hello, is Ann in, please?"

I sighed with relief. It was Tony after all. With all the trouble and comings and goings of the evening I had completely forgotten all about my date with him! The landlord had met Tony before so without hesitation he shouted up the stairs, "Ann, your boyfriend's here for you," and then he went back into his living room.

"Come up, Tony," I shouted and took Mum back into our room. I told Mum quickly what the landlord had said before Tony came in, because I hadn't told Tony about Dad before and what he was like. I loved Tony and thought he might well be put off seeing me any more if he knew what my father was like. But now I had no choice, not now that Dad had found out where we were living, and I knew I had to tell Tony the truth. I didn't want to leave Mum on her own that evening, just in case Dad came back, so I just told Tony Mum wasn't well and could we make it the following evening. Tony accepted this and stayed for about an hour before going home.

That night I just could not sleep, neither could poor Mum. I could hear her moving about and I was well aware she was worried about Dad coming back. I hated him so much, I thought, as I lay there. Why couldn't he leave us alone? Since I had been living with Mum the pill intake had kept at the same level. Although I couldn't stop taking them I was a lot happier and so didn't need to increase the dosage. However, the happiness we had created over the past four months had been shattered in one evening, and I was once again scared of what might be in store for us. For the first time in months I found myself turning to the drugs again for renewed strength. I was determined that Dad would never get near Mum again and the pills would give me the courage and determination to stop him. I knew in my heart it wasn't the answer, but for the time being it was the only answer I had for solving the problem I was now confronted with. How on earth Dad had found our address I didn't know but I did know that if he had managed to find that bit of information out then he would also find out where we both worked, and that worried me. We needed the money we earned to live on. And then there was Tony - I had to tell him, for knowing my father, he would no doubt find out about him, so I had to warn him to be on the safe side. I couldn't risk Dad hurting Tony also. As I lay in my bed I thought about Tony more deeply. I had only known him a few months by now but I had learnt from him that his background was completely different from mine. He was the only child to his parents and had had things fairly easy, so how would he take learning about my Dad and the way he was? I had never met his family and it didn't worry me that much as we had not been going out together that long, but the fact still remained that I had left him in the dark about my father. To think of it, we really hadn't spoken very much about our families but just enjoyed each other's company. I hated Dad already, but if he did anything at all to spoil my relationship with Tony I would have hated him even more, if that was at all possible.

The following day Mum and I went to work and that evening Tony and I dropped Mum off at her mother's house on our way out, which made me feel much happier as I hated the thought of her being on her own, in case Dad made a return visit. We arranged a time to pick her up later that night and Tony and I went off to a pub for a quiet drink. Tony soon sensed something was on my mind as we sat together in the cosy corner of our local, and asked me what the matter was. "Nothing!" I replied, which is the worst thing you can say when the other person knows darned well there *is* something wrong.

"Well, you're a little bit quiet tonight, Ann, and I want you to be able to share it with me. I might be able to help you, you never know," Tony said, with a caring arm around my shoulder.

"We've had some problems at hope, that's all, I replied.

"Then don't you think you'd better tell me about them? I hate seeing you like this."

For a moment I thought to myself, Should I just go ahead and tell him everything, including the drugs, or just about Dad? The chances were I might lose him one way or another anyway, so it was in for a penny and in for a pound. If I told him everything at least I wouldn't feel I had been cheating him or deceiving him.

I went into the whole background of my life, all about my Dad's drinking and violence, about my brother, Mum and the life we had led and, above all, about my drug addiction. I found it so much easier to tell Tony than I had ever imagined and felt like a great weight had been lifted from my shoulders. After I had finished telling him everything he was very quiet for a while. "Well," I said, "Aren't you going to say anything?"

Tony replied, "It makes no difference to me whatsoever about your father, but I am worried about your health. How many of these pills are you taking a day?"

"A couple," I quickly retorted, lying through my back teeth. I went on. "I can come off them whenever I want to. It's just that I need them for the time being to see me over this bad patch."

"Are you sure?" asked Tony, looking really concerned.

"Of course," I replied, and we dropped the interrogation.

I couldn't help saying what I did. I had been so used to lying to Mum about how many pills I was taking that I had no option than to lie to Tony to keep my story the same. I was getting myself in deeper than ever but I felt I had to protect myself somehow, and in a way I felt I was protecting them from the truth. Tony was still looking very apprehensive and I felt there was something else he wanted to say. After a couple of minutes he said quietly, "If it's a night for speaking the truth then I had better tell you my secret." I was taken aback. What on earth had Tony got behind his back that I didn't know about?

He went on to say, "I want you to know I really love you, Ann, no matter what, but.....the fact is, I'm married!"

"Married!!" I exclaimed, and sat there with my mouth open. Married? Impossible, I thought. There I was, worried sick about telling him about Dad and everything, but to me this was far worse. I had never asked him before if he was married or not because the thought never entered my head. When a guy asks a girl out for a date, and the relationship then blossoms and they fall in love, surely there's never a thought of whether he or she is already married. Another thing, he always managed to have lots of free time to take me out whenever we wanted. Perhaps I was ignorant enough to think there was only me in his life. The mere suggestion of him belonging to somebody else made me feel betrayed. I had enough problems at the moment without adding to them and I could well do without this additive right now.

"Let's go," I said to Tony, getting up to leave the table. The tears were ready to flow and I wouldn't or couldn't cry in front of so many people. I walked out to the car with Tony behind me. He unlocked the car door and I got in. Everything was collapsing on top of me, my whole world was turned upside down and I burst into tears. What with the events of the previous evening, and now having just learnt I was going out with a married man, was too much for me to bear. Tony sat there quietly until I gathered my senses once more. I wiped my tears away and turned to look at him.

"You'd better take me home," I said, sobbing.

"Please don't be like that, Ann. My marriage is finished. I love only you," Tony said.

I didn't know whether to believe him or not and said to him again, "Just take me home, please. I don't want to talk about it any more."

"I don't want to finish it, Ann. I would have told you before but I was waiting for the right moment, and obviously this wasn't it. I'm so sorry," Tony said, and with that put his key in the ignition and started the car up.

We picked Mum up from her mother's as arranged and I kept very quiet in the car all the way home. When we arrived home Mum got out and went indoors.

"Ann, please don't finish it," said Tony.

I loved him but I just couldn't think of anything but him having a wife. What chance did I have with my problems?

I said to him, "No, it's better we finish it now because I just can't cope with all this at the moment." I got out of the car and ran inside, shutting the front door behind me.

"What's the matter?" Mum asked, as she could see my eyes were red from crying.

So I told her what had happened and I had to put a show on as she had enough on her plate for the time being, and I tried to convince here I wasn't that upset. I didn't tell her about his being married, but that we had had a row and split up.

"I like him, but that's all, so I've told him I don't want to see him any more. "I went on to ask how she was feeling now and, although she said she was better now, she thought it best that we move on because she feared Dad would keep coming round and we couldn't have that.

I agreed totally and said, "We'll start looking for a new place next week, Mum. It shouldn't be too difficult to find somewhere suitable. I'm going to bed now. I'll see you in the morning."

I gave her a goodnight kiss on the cheek and went to bed. I couldn't get Tony out of my mind and kept thinking, Why me? I thought I had found myself a really nice man and he turns out to be married. That word, 'married', seemed to stick in my throat. Apart from the fact that I was upset about Tony, although I didn't want to let on so to Mum. I was much more worried about the prospect of moving again and that was far more important as both Mum and I had to be safe. I felt so mixed up. Would total happiness elude me for the rest of my life? I fell asleep telling myself not to wallow in self-pity so much.

The next few weeks Tony was always on my mind but I saw nothing of him. I knew I was very much in love with him and it hurt me so not to be with him any more, but it had to be that way as far as I was concerned. Once again, I turned to the pills and they helped me cope with the trauma I was experiencing.

One evening, Mum said to me, "Ann, Tony came in to see me today at work." My heart skipped a beat.

"Did he?" I eagerly replied. "What did he want?" praying it was to do with me. I had missed him, but I had deliberately stayed away from the restaurant, making excuses to Mum that I was working for extra money during my lunch-break.

"He told me he was married," Mum said, "But it is you that he loves. He wanted me to have a word with you because he wants to see you so badly." "I told him we were going to move soon due to your Father and he offered to help us find somewhere to live. I really don't think you should get involved, though, Ann," said Mum. She went on, "He is married with children and I don't want to see you getting hurt."

"I know he's married, Mum, and that's exactly why I've been avoiding him. The trouble is I do love and miss him so much. I don't know what to do and I must see him, Mum, I'm sorry."

Ever since Mum and I had been together on our own we had confided in each

40

other. Mum knew me inside out and all my anxieties and desires - except the whole truth regarding my daily intake of pills. I didn't want to make a habit of lying to her about anything else so I thought it best to tell her exactly what my feelings were regarding Tony.

Mum agreed to let me see him once she was convinced I was sincere about him and that I knew the full facts. I asked Mum if she was annoyed that I should want to see him again, and she couldn't help but understand how I felt. It was just that she didn't want me to get involved and hurt any more than I had been up until now and that was all she was worried about. I assured Mum it would be alright and that I would handle the situation sensibly. I promised to keep a level head and Mum said that was just as well, because Tony was going to pop in tomorrow lunch time for my answer!

I said, "OK, could you ask him to come round tomorrow night to see me, Mum, please?" I didn't want to break up his marriage and I was quite satisfied to just see him now and again, but at sixteen I could not realise the hurt the whole situation could bring on other people if things got out of hand. I could only really think of today and not the future, and to me a tiny amount of happiness was not too much to ask for at this stage in my life, surely. Tony came round the following evening, nice and early. I was still in the bath when he called, so Mum invited him in and whilst I was getting dried and dressed she had a chat with him. I was ready by 8.30 p.m. and was a little nervous as I opened the living room door to see him for the first time since we had split up. I was so pleased to see him, as I think he was to see me, judging by the look on his face.

Tony and I left to go out for the evening and as I got into the car Tony said to me, "Thanks for coming. Where do you fancy going?

"Let's go where we went last time," I replied, so off we went to the same little pub as before. There was very little or no conversation on our journey there, for it was still a bit strained between us and awkward. When we arrived at the pub we settled ourselves down at the same table as the last time we visited it. When Tony returned with our drinks he asked me if I had heard any more from Dad, to which I replied, "No, thank heavens." I could sense Tony was nervous and trying his best to avoid the subject of his being married, so I brought it up for him!

"Tony," I said quietly, "I've accepted you are married now and, although it still hurts, I am pleased we're together again. The main thing is, in no way do I want to be the cause of a broken marriage, but at the same time I am in love with you. So, if you want to see me now and again, I'll accept the situation for what it is.

You know I've many problems at the moment which I've got to sort out and I really can't take on any more, so if you do have a problem with your marriage, leave me out of it. I can't and won't take on your problems as well. I've given this matter a lot of thought and have come to the decision that if you still want to carry on seeing me we shall just enjoy what we have, and maybe we can keep what we have between us as it is.''

Tony spoke in a soft voice, "But don't you want any more than that, Ann?"

"At the moment, no," I quickly replied, and I really meant it, for I was contented with what little happiness I had, for the time being, anyway. I finished my drink and Tony told me my Mum had had a word with him to make sure I wasn't hurt in all this, and he assured me he gave her his word. "I wouldn't hurt you for the world, Ann, I mean it," he said in all sincerity, and I believed him.

By the time we left to go home we were both a lot happier. It was now three weeks since Dad had come round to pay us a visit but we were still on edge. We knew it wasn't the last we'd seen of him. We had managed to find a boarding house with a room to let and decided to move in there. We paid our respects and showed our gratitude to the kind couple who had been our landlord and landlady at the last place and explained why we were leaving. We told them we had fully enjoyed living in their house but it was now time to move on. They said that they understood and were sorry to see us go as they had enjoyed having us there.

CHAPTER FIVE

We had only been living in the boarding house for about one month when the man who owned it asked Mum if she would like to manage it for him. Mum was highly delighted with the idea, for it meant not only did we have a bedroom but also a sitting room with a small passage leading to a tiny kitchen. we both continued working and running the house as well, which was good therapy for us as it kept our minds pre-occupied. There were four lads living at the boarding house, two of whom were male models, and we all got on fairly well. Once again, we settled down with no fear about Dad coming back, but it was to be a short-lived period of relaxed and trouble-free days. One Saturday I finished work early, which gave me a chance to do some shopping on my way home and still have enough time to get ready to go out with Tony. After Tony had mentioned to me about his pending divorce a couple of weeks ago, we had not brought up the subject again, and that made me happy because I just wanted to forget it. I had had a successful afternoon shopping and was very cheerful as I got the bus home and looking forward to my evening out with Tony, but as I unlocked the front door I could hear Mum crying. I slammed the door shut behind me and rushed into the kitchen once I had established from which direction the crying was coming from. The door was ajar and as I pushed it open there was Mum, sitting in the armchair. One of the young lads had his arms around her and as she had her head bent forward, she had what looked like a cloth in her hands and partly covering her face. I knelt down beside her and lifted her face. No one had to tell me what had happened to her nor who did it. I knew only too well. There was a large cut above Mum's eye which was bleeding badly, her eye was red and swollen and it was obvious she had been hit struck a blow by someone with a large fist. The young lad had tried his best at administering first aid by putting plaster across the cut, but it had only slowed the bleeding down very slightly. I hurried out to the first aid cabinet to fetch some more plasters while the young lad kept a hold of Mum, who was still trembling and sobbing. I took the cloth away from her, which I then realised was the kitchen tea-towel, and I applied a clean face towel instead. I wiped the blood away as best as I could and put on a larger plaster across the wound. Her eye was still puffy and swollen and she was still shaking. The young lad got up and went out, returning two minutes later with a large brandy.

"Give her that," he said as he offered Mum the glass. "It will help calm you down."

"Thank you, love. You're very kind," I said and held it for Mum to sip. I asked the young lad if Mum had told him what had happened and he said,

"No, she'd only been in a few minutes before you got here."

"Are you feeling a little bit better now, Mum?" I asked. I was shaking myself but with anger, not pain, and if I had any notion of where that father of mine was at that precise moment I would have killed him without hesitation. After she had composed herself a little, Mum was ready to talk. "I had gone out shopping in the High Street when suddenly he came out from nowhere. He grabbed my hair and punched me a couple of times in the face and then ran off, leaving me on the pavement."

"Did anyone see what had happened or help you?" I asked.

"No," she said. But, as I got myself up from the floor I noticed a car parked a little way up with a man sitting at the driving side. I ran up to him and asked him to take me home. He was very kind and wouldn't take any money from me. My head was hurting so badly I just wanted to get back here to safety," Mum said, and started crying again.

"Come on, Mum," I said, putting my arms around her, "Let's get you into bed," and with that I helped her undress and put her to bed. "Try and get a bit of sleep, love. Nothing is going to happen to you now, so try to stop worrying." I turned out the light and shut the door quietly behind me. I swore if it was the last thing I did, I would kill him.

I went back into the living room and promptly swallowed a pill. I just couldn't handle it. We had found some contentment in our lives and somehow I had managed to put behind me the memories I had regarding Dad's violence, and was now of the opinion that he couldn't do us any more harm. Then I remembered the state Mum's face was in and I realised what a fool I had been. He wasn't the sort of man to go quietly, he would always find some way of getting back and he proved that today. I made myself a cup of tea and lit a cigarette, then sat down to gather my senses. I was so angry and determined that he was not going to get the better of us. I decided that when Mum got up I would discuss it with her. The last thing I wanted to do was to upset her, but I felt something had to be done about Dad, but exactly what could be done and how to go about it, I didn't know. Even though I was angry, like Mum I was terrified of Dad. Tony came over before I woke Mum up and I told him all about what had happened. "I know you told me about your father, Ann, but I never dreamt he was as bad as this. I really didn't realise he was that evil to do such a wicked thing to your mother. Why didn't she call the Police?" he asked.

"I'm going to have a word with her when she gets up and see if I can persuade her to charge him with assault. I got her to rest for a little while because I thought it would do her good." I paused a little, then said, "Do you mind if we stay in tonight, I can't leave her in the state she's in and go out enjoying myself. I wouldn't be able to stop thinking about her, anyway." "No, love. Your mother comes first," said Tony in his usual caring way. I made a fresh pot of tea and gave Tony a cup, then took one in to Mum. She was just lying there and I could tell she hadn't slept at all.

"Are you OK, Mum?" I asked.

"Yes, thanks, love," she said. She sat up a little and asked if it was Tony I was

44

speaking to in the living room, which I assured her it was.

"Come on, get up and come in with us, mum," I said, helping her to get steady on her feet.

As Mum entered the living room in front of me I could see Tony's face as he caught sight of her. For a split second he had a look of shock but very quickly composed himself, and got up to help me guide her into the armchair.

"I think you should go to the Police, Mum," I said. "If you don't he's going to think he can get away with it."

Her reaction was exactly as I had expected. "What's the point, Ann?" she replied. "I've called the Police before about him but nothing came of it."

"Well, maybe they couldn't do much then because you were living with him at the time, but surely now they can do something. Look, I'll tell you what I'll do,"and I turned to Tony and said, "Tony, will you take me down to the Police Station?"

"Of course, if that's what you want to do," he said.

"I knelt down to Mum and softly said, "You stay right here , Mum. I'll have a word with the Police and see what they can do. I won't be long."

I got up and put on my coat then, giving her a peck on the cheek, told her not to worry and that I wouldn't be very long.

When Tony and I arrived at the Police station there were no other civilians there apart from us, which I was very pleased about because I didn't want to have everyone else overhearing my problems. I pressed the bell for assistance and waited until someone came. After only a few seconds a policeman appeared.

"Can I help you, miss?" he asked.

"Yes, please," I replied. "But is it possible to speak with someone privately in case someone comes in and hears what I have to say?"

He went to see if there was anyone I could speak with in confidence and asked us to take a seat. We waited for about ten minutes, at the end of which time a door to the side of the desk was opened and out came a tall policeman. He asked us if

45

we would like to go into his office, so I walked in and sat down. He shut the door behind him before he seated himself at the opposite side of his desk and proceeded in asking me what he could do for me. I told him the whole sequence of events. He listened intently to what I had to tell him and said, "Well, I'm afraid there's not a lot I can do. Where does your father live?" I gave him the address and he assured me he would pay my father a visit to have a word with him, but he stressed that, unless they caught him actually hitting my mother, there was very little they could do. He went on, "Unless your mother makes a charge against him and takes him to court, which I,m sorry to say most of the wives we see are too scared to do, our hands are tied." I understand what the Police officer was saying in that, very often, the fear of what the husband will do after his battered wife has brought the subject up for the Police to deal with, and then taken him to court, far outweighed her anxieties. She would always dread being beaten up again as part of his revenge. I knew my mother would be in that situation because she was far too frightened of Dad to go to court.

The Policeman went on to say, "I'll tell you what, though, miss, always call us if he bothers you again at all."

I got up and thanked him. Despite the fact I had not got anywhere, at least the Policeman was kind and sympathetic, and not once did he give me the impression I had wasted his time.

Tony was sitting outside waiting patiently for me all this time. He got up from his seat and asked, "Everything alright, love?"

I told him everything the policeman had told me and Tony went on, "Well, the problem is that they can't do much unless they catch him in the act or causing trouble at the house. That's a fat lot of good to us." He was a bit angry after seeing Mum's badly beaten face, as it was something he had never experienced before and it had made a marked effect on him. He added, "I just hope one day he'll have a go at me and he'll find himself in court so fast, he won't know what's hit him."

Tony suggested we get back to Mum to see if she was alright on her own. On our way home I told Tony that I could kill my father for what he had done to ruin our lives. With any luck, he might not find out where we were living at the moment, and that was a blessing in disguise.

They were famous last words and something that wasn't to last for long. When we arrived back home I told Mum all about my conversation with the policeman

46

and was pleased to see she looked a bit better than when we had left her. I asked Mum what we would do if he ever found out where we were living. Would we have to move again?

"No, love," she said. "Not unless you want to."

"No, I like it here," I said.

Mum said, "Right then, we shall stay as long as the landlord lets us."

Our landlord seemed to be happy with the way Mum had been running the house and we very rarely saw him, so if there was going to be a problem resulting from Dad's turning up and upsetting thing, we could hopefully cope with it without the landlord knowing about it. I was glad Mum had decided to stay where we were as I was now beginning to feel tired of having to run and hide from Dad, although of course I would have done so for Mum's sake if that was her wish.

For the next six months things went fine. We had settled down again and life was improving much more. Mum and Tony had not mentioned the pills, but I was still taking them. At least my daily intake had not increased for some time, and they continued to make me feel I could keep my head above water. The incident with my father was now forgotten and Tony and I were seeing each other regularly. By now he had decided to separate from his wife, but still lived under the same roof with her and their children. This made life somewhat difficult for him so, although we were seeing more of each other it wasn't as much as I would have liked but knew I had no option but to put up with it.

Tony's mother ran the R.S.P.C.A. centre in Hillingdon and one day I asked Tony if he would be able to get a dog for me. I had already asked Mum if she minded and she said it would be a good idea. So, one evening, Tony turned up with a young dog. She was only about a year old and her owners didn't want her any more, and had taken her to the R.S.P.C.A. to see if they could find a home for her. As soon as I saw her little face I fell in love with her. She was only a mongrel, but to me she was the most beautiful dog I had ever seen. All through my childhood I had never been allowed to have any pets and had always wanted a dog of my own and now here she was. I called her Sally and everywhere I went she came with me. mum even allowed Sally to sleep at the side of my bed at night.

One evening, mum and I were sitting in the back living room. Mum had just made us a cup of tea and brought it in from the kitchen. We sat chatting when, suddenly, Sally got up and went to the back door. I followed her, wondering if she wanted to got out to the garden, but then she started barking.

"Shut up, Sally," I shouted to her. "What's the matter with her?" Mum asked.

"I don't know. Just ignore her," I said, and went back to my armchair and cup of tea.

Sally carried on barking so I had to get up again to see what was wrong. It was so out of character for Sally to continue barking so long. I put my cup on the table and walked over to the back door where Sally was. I bent down and patted her on the head and said to her,

"For goodness sake, Sally. What's all the commotion about?" and I went closer towards the door. We didn't have a curtain up so I could see right out to the garden. I looked down at the lock and as I unlocked it I was startled to find there was a man crouching down outside. I knew instantly it was Dad, jumped back, and promptly fell over Sally.

"Mum, quickly, get David!" I called to Mum. david was one of the young lads staying at the house at the time.

"Dad's outside!" I screamed, and quickly picked myself up from the floor. We both rushed towards the living room door, thinking he would try to get in by the back door. We stood in the hallway and by that time David came rushing down the stairs saying, "What the hell's going on?"

I explained my hysteria and, no sooner said than done, he went through the living room and into the kitchen, leaving Mum and me in the hall. Sally was still barking like mad and I feared her safety.

Five minutes later David returned. "It's O.K.," he said, "He's gone. If he comes back give me a call and I'll sort him out," he said.

He gave Mum a big hug and said to her, "Come on, he won't try anything with people in the house, surely." Mum just smiled.

Very cautiously, we walked back into the living room and I checked the kitchen door to make sure it was locked. Sally had calmed down now and, although I still felt uneasy, I was relieved he had gone and that there was someone else in the house and that we had a dog to protect us.

The following night when Tony came round I told him what had happened and he asked me how Mum was from this latest upset. I said she was alright now but that it had very much unnerved her. I added,

"Mum didn't seem too bad today, considering, but I'm frightened too because he's found out where we live, and I know he'll be back."

Tony asked me if I had called the police but I told him I didn't consider it necessary. The fact is, Dad didn't actually do anything and because of that I knew there was nothing the police could do.

I was far more frightened than I let on to Mum and Tony and, instead of showing it, I took a couple of extra pills to make me feel better. At least they helped take the edge off for the time being. Now that Dad knew our address he could be back anytime and that was an awful thing to know. It was like living on knife's edge, waiting for the enemy to attack at any time. It caused unrest and Mum and I had to be on our guard at all times. It was good that Mum and I worked opposite each other because it meant we left home in the mornings together and most evenings we came home together. The only thing was, I didn't want to go out in the evenings and leave Mum on her own. It was alright if one of the lodgers was in, but even then I didn't feels settled in my mind. I am so fortunate in that Tony understood my predicament completely and agreed that we should stay in every night during the weeks that followed. This arrangement certainly eased , my mind on that score but the waiting was wearing me down. It was almost like an animal lying in wait for its predator to swoop down on its prey.

I was so uptight about the whole situation that my intake of pills had increased dramatically. I knew my father only too well, and that at any time he could come and shatter our peace once again, and the waiting for it to occur was making me so jumpy and irritable. This didn't go unnoticed by Tony, naturally, who, after showing an abundance of patience, said, "Look, it's no use worrying to the extent that it will make you ill, Ann. If and when your father comes round, all we have to do is to call the Police and they will deal with him. You are worrying yourself silly before anything has happened."

It was very reassuring that Tony should sympathise as he did. I never intended to involve him so much in our problems, but I was glad he wanted to be and I thanked him for being so wonderful about the whole thing.

"Ann, I love you, and your problems are mine as well, it's as simple as that," He said.

It was time for him to go home so I got his jacket for him and walked to the front door with him. We stopped in the hallway and Tony held me close to him. "Come on, love," he said softly. "I doubt it very much if your father will come back here again, so stop your worrying, O.K.?"

He had his back to the front door so that meant I was facing it. There was a small pane of glass at the side of the door and, and as Tony kissed me goodnight, there was an almighty crash. I looked up and could see a hand come straight through the glass! Tony immediately jumped out of the way and, as I stood there in wonderment, I watched the hand vanish. I guessed it was Dad's hand but for a few seconds I was too shocked to move. The only thought I had was, "You bastard, why can't you just leave us alone!"

"Mum rushed out and held me because I was shaking like a jelly and crying. She knew how much strain I had been under for the past few weeks and she was just as worried as I was.

I assured Mum I was alright but as I looked at her I felt that, for the first time she and I had been living on our own together, I didn't feel I was the strong one any more and I was glad to have Mum's arms around me.

After smashing the glass Dad had run off somewhere. My father was an extremely strong man and built like an amazon, so no one in their right mind would take him on. However, he was scared of the Police and he must have known we would call them. We weren't on the telephone so Tony went out and rang the police from a call box and Mum and I tried to compose ourselves by sitting down in the living room.

The Police came but told us that there wasn't much they could do except keep an eye on the house and that they would pay him a visit. It was the same old story, unless they caught him in the act there was very little they could do once he had vacated the scene. If they had seen him committing an act of violence or causing damage to the house where we lived it would be different. Tony stayed after the Police went, but I told him he had better go home because I knew he had to be up early next morning and it was now very late.

"Only if you're sure you will be alright," said Tony.

"Yes, love, you go, and thanks for staying with us," I said and I saw him to the front door where we said goodnight.

When I returned to the living room I gave mum a kiss on the cheek and told her I was going to go to bed, if she didn't mind. Mum said that she had calmed down a bit by now and asked me if I was alright. I sat back down beside her. I could sense she was worried sick about me and I didn't want that. She had enough on her plate without have to worry about me, so I just smiled and said, "I'm fine, Mum. Dad will soon get fed up with coming round here, you mark my words," and after feeling I had convinced her, I went off to bed.

As I lay in my bed I knew I was kidding myself about Dad. There was no way he'd give up that easily, but in a way I was glad the waiting was over for I knew now what to expect, whereas before I really didn't know if he would return to cause havoc or not. I felt exhausted, even the extra strength the pills had provided me with had disappeared. I started to cry as everything crowded in on me. Why us, I kept asking myself. I wasn't so concerned about myself, for I had the love of Mum and Tony and I was happy with that. I was worried about my increasing addiction to the pills, but without them I felt I couldn't fight Dad and I was well aware that they were making me feel so ill all the time. I tried not to let outsiders see but I knew in my heart what they must be doing to me. I felt remorse for all the lies I had told Mum and Tony about the amount of pills I was taking daily and I desperately wanted to tell them the truth. I couldn't tell them the truth, though, because I knew only full well they would nag me to come off them, and I just couldn't cope with that and the threat of Dad's returning at the moment. I was so hooked on the pills by now that I felt my life depended on them and realised that if I had been happy I would never have had to take the damn things in the first place. I lay for hours that night going over everything in my mind. I was so depressed and hated Dad intensely for what he had done to us and wondered what he had in store for us next.

It didn't take long for me to find out what Dad had up his sleeve. In the next few weeks he came round to the house on a regular basis, always very drunk and argumentative. We couldn't inform the Police because as quickly as he appeared he went away again, but whilst he was present he frightened Mum and me so much, and we didn't know what else to do.

One day, David, one of our lodgers, came up with an idea to try and help us put a stop to Dad coming round any more. My father always came through the back garden now and David decided to wire the garden in zig-zag fashion, so that father would have to trip over one of them and it would be a form of warning system to us. If it worked, and he fell, he would surely make a noise and we would be bound to hear him. So, the following evening, David rigged up his invention and when he had completed his work in the garden he came indoors.

He said to Mum, "Now, just in case he's clever enough to miss them all, which I very much doubt because it's getting dark now, I'll take a bucket of water up to my room and if he makes for the back door I'll get him that way." We thought it was an ingenious idea and were grateful for David's interest. His bedroom was at the back of the house so he had a clear view of the back garden. He invited us up to see what would happen if Dad came round that evening so we eagerly followed him upstairs and sat down to wait for our bait. It was some minutes before I thought he might not come that evening, but I didn't have to wonder about it for long because very soon I caught sight of him at the bottom of the garden. Whenever I saw my father I felt intimidated and it was no different that night, even though it appeared we may have upper hand. In a way I felt ashamed and embarrassed on that evening because whenever Dad had caused trouble before we were usually on our own, but now David was watching and that made a lot of difference. As we sat there I kept looking at David, wondering what he made of all this. I knew he wanted to help us but I still would have liked to have known what was going through his mind. The next minute my attention reverted back to Dad again and it was as if I had been hypnotised as I sat watching him. I was totally amazed for, somehow or another, he managed to step over each and every trip wire. Whether he cottoned on to what was going on or not I'm not sure, but by the time he reached the back door, and was standing immediately below David's bedroom window, he had missed every single wire! David couldn't believe his eyes either and looked at Mum and said, "Did you see that?" He held up the bucket of water and held it out of the open window, intending it to go all over Dad's head, but to everyone's astonishment it missed him completely, and it was as if he was so drunk he didn't realise what was happening. Dad turned round to face the back of the garden and staggered back down it, once again missing all the wires. It was unbelievable, but deep down I was glad it was over. It was somewhat out of character for Dad to just walk away and I feared retaliation. It was also enough that Dad liked to cause trouble, but to see him make a fool of himself as he had done in front of somebody he didn't know, hurt me and from that day on I vowed I would never involve anyone else. If anyone was to fight Dad it would be me, only me.

CHAPTER SIX

After that night, Dad kept right away from us for which we were truly grateful. I still had that underlying fear that some day he would turn up out of the blue, but it was a good few months before he showed his face again.

Having had no news at all of his whereabouts, we were beginning to all feel more settled in our lives but, as for me, I still relied upon drugs. One Saturday after I had finished work I went to the chemist to collect my pills. I looked towards the shelf where they were always on display for sale but, to my horror, they had gone. I tried to console myself by telling myself they must have had a change-around in the shop and they had put them somewhere else.

I walked up to the counter and said to the assistant, "Excuse me, please. Could you tell me where my usual pills are? I don't see them in their usual place."

The shop assistant knew me well and to which pills I was referring but to my utter amazement the girl replied, "Oh, they've been put on prescription now. You'll have to get them through your doctor from now on."

I tried to act calm and thanked her, but inside I was going to pieces. As I walked out of the chemist I was in a state of shock. What on earth was I going to do now? There was no way I could manage without them and the only way I'd be able to keep taking them was to get them with a prescription. All the way home that evening i was in a whirl. By the time I got home I didn't feel at all well and felt like going straight to bed. Mum asked me what the matter was but I bluffed my way out of it by saying it was nothing much but I thought I had a cold coming.

"What shall I tell Tony when he comes?" asked Mum, a little concerned.

"Don't worry, Mum," I said, "He said he wouldn't be around till later tonight so I'll see him then. I just want a little lie down," and with that I went to bed.

I knew there was very little choice I had but to accept the situation. The pills were now off the market and I wished I was dead, I knew there was no way I would be able to cope and tried to be rational about it, but it appeared that everything was against me. At that moment I hated the world and God.

Since we had moved to our present house I had kept notes in a diary which I was

53

given as a present. It was incredible how it helped me to write down my thoughts when I couldn't talk things over with Mum or Tony, and it was easy for me to express my inner feelings by putting them all down on paper. My diary was very private and personal to me and, in a way, a life-saver. Instead of bottling everything up I wrote everything down in it, putting it back in a secret hiding place so nobody but I would know it existed.

As I lay on my bed I picked up my little diary and started to read it. I flicked the pages until I came across the part where I had written how much I hated the pills, and that was exactly how I was feeling right now. I bent down to pick up my handbag from the floor and took out a tube of pills. I always had a week's supply in hand and I sat up to count them out. I had just about enough to last me until the following Tuesday. I was in such a quandary. What on earth was I going to do after next Tuesday when they had all gone and I'd no longer be able to stroll up to the counter and buy however many I liked, whenever I liked. I started to shake and burst into tears. I couldn't go to Mum about it because she had never liked pills of any description, and certainly disapproved of what I was taking. Mum had never dictated to me concerning them but, then again, I couldn't go to her for help this time. I wondered if Tony would be able to help me. No, he hated them too, just as much as Mum did, so it would be no use telling him.

Just then there was a knock on my door and Mum walked in.

"Tony's here, love," she said. "Are you sure you're well enough to go out?" she asked.

I was a bit flustered, and as I answered Mum I tried to look busy so that she wouldn't suspect anything was wrong, nor that I had the pills on my bed and my secret diary. I was put out because I had been interrupted, and it was obvious. I apologised to Mum for being tetchy and asked her to tell Tony I would be out soon. I rushed round putting my things straight and made myself presentable.

I didn't mention the pills to Mum or Tony at all that evening as there was no point, there was nothing they could do and I felt I had already given both more than their fair share of worry. I honestly believed I could find a solution myself.

When I came in from seeing Tony later that night, Mum was already in bed asleep. Sally was sitting at the door waiting for me to come home. She was always pleased when anyone came in and wagged her tail happily. The problem I was facing, regarding the pills and how I would be able to continue taking them, was still very much on my mind. After I said goodnight to Tony and he left to go home I decided to take Sally for a walk. Maybe I'd be able to come up with the answer as I walked with her. Hopefully, I'd be able to see the situation in a different light and come up with a solution. I took hold of Sally's lead and she became so excited as she loved her walks. I checked that my front door key was safely in my pocket and Sally and I set off, shutting the door quietly behind us. It was well past midnight and the streets were empty. Normally I liked the peace of the night, but I couldn't feel serenity this night because I was so worried about not being able to get any more pills. Surely, there must be somebody who could help me, I thought. Both Mum and Tony were out of the question because then they would realise how much I needed the pills and that wouldn't do.

Just then Sally started tugging at her lead. I stopped to let her spend a penny and as I waited I looked all around me. It was a clear night and the moon made everything brighter and shiny. After a couple of minutes Sally was ready to continue our walk and, as I turned to pull Sally to come with me, I noticed a board which was mounted upon the garden gate near to where we had stopped. I had never noticed this board before and this time was curious as to see what it said. I went closer and saw that it had the word 'Doctor' printed on it and underneath the doctor's name were the times of his surgery hours. I looked up at the front door and noticed a small box alongside it. Printed on the outside of the box was the word 'prescriptions'. My imagination was working overtime. I wondered if, by any chance, there would be somebody taking the same pills as I and had a prescription made out for them ready for collection. I should be so lucky, I thought! I started to tremble at the mere idea. I knew what I wanted to do, but had never done anything like this before and the whole thing scared me stiff.

All of a sudden, Sally started barking, which made me jump. I pulled on her lead and patted her on the head.

"Ssh, Sally," I whispered, and looked once again at the box. I plucked up enough courage to open the lid of the box and took out all the prescriptions from within it and stuffed them quickly into my pocket. I walked back home as quickly as my legs would go, dragging poor Sally behind me. I wasn't sure if anyone had seen what I had done, and I knew if I was found out I'd be in so much trouble, so when I arrived back home I shut the front door behind me and gave a sigh of relief. I got undressed as quickly as I could and got into bed and then laid out all the prescriptions on top of the bedclothes. I read each one in the hope that one of them would be for the drugs I was taking. To my dismay there was nothing at all of interest to me. I flopped back on my pillow. I had never done such a dishonest thing as this in my life before and was feeling bad about it. Having said that, however, I was very disappointed that I didn't find what I was looking for. *Now* what do I do, I thought? I was getting tired now and put the prescriptions away in my handbag and settled down to sleep.

When I woke up the following morning I had forgotten all about the stolen prescriptions, but very soon I rallied round to the stark reality of it all. The mere suggestion of my doing such a thing made me feel sick and a nervous wreck. I had got myself into this mess and somehow or another I had to get myself out of it.

All that day I was like a bear with a sore head. Mum and Tony must have noticed my dreadful behaviour but, thankfully, didn't question me at all. The stolen prescriptions remained in my handbag until the Sunday evening when I went to bed. I took them out to examine them closely. I had only two days to go before my pills ran out and, as I looked at the prescriptions in front of me, I thought they were my last hope, but what exactly, I wasn't quite sure. There must be something I could do with them to get me my drugs. It is amazing how strong-willed a person can become when they want or need something that badly and I was getting desperate and paranoid about not being able to get my drugs. I had no alternative but to take the matter further and the idea came to me when I noticed a big gap below an item on one of the prescriptions. If I was extremely careful I might be able to write down the name of my drug in that gap and if I could copy the style of handwriting of the doctor who had made it out, nobody would be the wiser.

I rushed to find a pen and a piece of paper and started to copy the doctor's handwriting over and over again until I was satisfied that it was virtually the same. I sat up until the early hours until I got the writing perfectly the same and when I was ready I copied it on to the prescription. It looked just as if the doctor had written it himself and I was very impressed with my efforts. The biggest challenge was yet to come, of course, and that was when I would take the prescription into the chemist to be made up. Would he be able to tell if I had forged part of it, or would it be good enough to go unnoticed?

I left for work early on the Monday morning, making some excuse to Mum that I had been asked to do some overtime. I hated lying to her and of course what I intended doing now was far worse, but I had got this far and there was no turning back. I was frightened and ill with worry, but it way my only hope. I got to the chemist before they opened. It meant that I might be a little late getting to work so I had an excuse ready just in case. As I waited for the chemist to open my heart felt as if it was in my mouth. My head was thumping as I feared the chemist would notice the prescription I was about to hand over to him had ben tampered with. I was really sweating as I paced outside the shop. After a couple of minutes I heard the key turn in the lock and then the bolts undone.

"Good morning!" said the man, smiling.

"Good morning," I replied in a shaky voice. "Er, can I give you this?" and I passed the prescription to him. He took it from me and looked at it.

That's it, Ann, I thought to myself. You're in trouble now, he's looking at it too long. He knows there's something wrong with it, I convinced myself. I wanted to run but my legs just didn't want to move.

The chemist smiled at me and said, "If you'd like to wait for ten minutes I'll do it for you now."

"Couldn't you make it five?" I urged him, and walked out of the shop. I had to for I was literally shaking. I thought to myself, That was a stupid thing to do, he's bound to wonder what on earth is wrong with me. I stood still once I got outside the shop and gave myself a good talking to. "Compose yourself, Ann, for goodness sake," I heard myself saying. I managed to calm myself and walked back into the shop. To my relief the chemist didn't appear to have noticed my peculiar behaviour and told me my prescription was ready.

I thanked him and, with the pills in my hand, walked out and went to work.

From then on it became easy, perhaps too easy, to repeat the procedure. Naturally, I never let on to Mum or Tony as to what I was doing and, as we hadn't heard from Dad for some time, as far as they were concerned, things were looking up. If only they knew!

I continued to take a handful of prescriptions from the box as I had done the first time but after a few weeks I was finding it more difficult. The whole situation was making me feel ill, and there were times when I even wished I was caught in the act. It would have to be something like that to make me stop. My wish was soon granted, for one day, whilst I was at work, I had a visit from the Police. I was asked to go down to the Police Station where the Detective Sergeant wanted to have a word with me. I was expecting something like this to happen, but also glad they had gone to my place of work and not to my home, so at least I was able to keep it from Mum and Tony. My boss asked me what it was all about and I told him it was about an accident I had witnessed.

I was so terrified about going to the Police on my own that I made up my mind to tell Mum and Tony all about it before I went. So, after work that evening, I put Mum in the picture and told her everything. She was terrific and did her best to calm me down before Tony arrived. He, too, showed such strength and support for me and they both came with me to the Police Station. I had been given the name of the Detective Sergeant whom I was to ask to speak to and was shown into his office. Mum and Tony waited outside for me. The gentleman at the desk was in his forties and as he say me enter the room he got up and invited me to take a seat.

"Hello, you're Miss Pinkham, I understand," he said. He had a friendly approach and had obviously sensed my feeling awkward and embarrassed. He went on, "It's alright. I'm not going to bite your head off!"

He had a kind face and smiled. He added, "But I must ask you a few questions, and I must ask you to be honest with me because I want to help you. If you don't tell me the truth I can't assist you."

I still wasn't quite sure why he wanted to see me. I had an idea it was concerning the prescriptions, but I wasn't going to mention them unless he asked me outright. His hand went down to the drawer in his desk and he carefully brought out a handful of prescriptions and put them in front of him. I thought to myself, I knew it! and was glad I had come clean by telling Mum and Tony beforehand. In a way I was also pleased I had been found out. I had told no-one how ill I was feeling, and now it had been brought to the notice of the Police I hoped I could get help.

"Did you write on the prescriptions?" the Detective Sergeant asked me.

"Yes," I replied, bowing my head.

There was no point in denying it and he seemed such a pleasant man.

He asked me why I had done such a thing and I told him the whole story. All the time he sat quietly, listening and waiting for me to finish. He didn't interrupt me and, because he came across as a friendly, caring man, I found it so easy to talk to him.

As I came to the end of my tale he picked up the prescriptions and flicked through them.

I concluded by saying, "I can't lie any more. I just can't live without the drugs,

58

and without some form of help I feel I'll have to carry on stealing the prescriptions. I'm sorry, but that's how dependent I am upon them."

He looked up at me in astonishment. "Are you being completely honest? You know it's a crime to forge and steal, don't you?"

I nodded, feeling ashamed on one hand and bitterly sad on the other.

"Yes, I know it's wrong and I realise the trouble I'm in but that's how it is."

He got up from his chair and rubbed his chin with his hand.

"Look," he said, "Will you pop in here at the same time tomorrow and in between time I'll see if I can get you some help. I can't promise you but I'll try."

I shook his hand and thanked him. As I came out of his office, Mum and Tony stood up, looking worried sick about me.

"Come on," I said, "I'll tell you all about it in the car going home," and I could see the relief on their faces.

The following evening, instead of my going to see the detective sergeant at the Police Station, he came to me at home. He told me he had found someone who would help me and made me promise not to forge any more prescriptions. With the knowledge that someone would try to sort out my problems, I promised and felt as if a great burden had been lifted from my shoulders. Hopefully, in the next few days, someone would come to see me and it would be alright. After the detective sergeant left, I knew it would be hard to keep my word. I had tried before and hadn't succeeded, but that had only been for a day and I could vividly remember the pain then. I only hoped he could find help for me soon. I had only enough pills for one more day and I was glad that the day after would be the weekend, which meant I wouldn't have to go to work. I used to work most Saturdays but this Saturday was my day off so I had two full days to come off the pills.

All day Friday I tried to put it behind me and Mum and Tony both promised to help me as much as possible, for which I was truly glad to hear. On the Friday evening Tony took me out for the evening. When he took me home later that evening, just before he left me, he said that he would be round the following morning. Both he and Mum knew I would more than likely not be well, but exactly how much unwell I was to be no one could foresee.

When I woke up the following morning I didn't feel too bad but by the dinner time I started vomiting. I kept being sick right up until the late afternoon, by which time I couldn't stop shaking either. Mum insisted I went to bed as I was in a terrible state. Tony hadn't arrived yet, I don't know what had held him up, but in a way I was pleased he wasn't around as I felt so ill and really didn't want to see anyone, but just curl up in bed. Tony finally arrived early evening and Mum explained to him how I had been all day.

"Sorry I'm late, love," he said to me, as he popped his head round my bedroom door.

"How are you feeling?"

I burst into tears. I couldn't talk to him as I felt so awful.

With that, Tony came right into my room and sat on my bed, holding my hand.

"I can't stand the pain any longer," I sobbed.

"Come on, you can make it," Tony said reassuringly and he put his arms around me.

"I'll stay the night with you," Tony said.

"But won't it create problems for you at home?" I had to ask.

He replied, "No, it'll be O.K., don't worry."

I knew things weren't too good between his wife and himself but I still didn't really want to be the cause of the break-up. I am not the sort of person who would want to hurt anyone, let alone his wife, but on the other hand I was glad he was staying the night.

However, I didn't get a wink of sleep that night. My whole body was racked with pain. I had taken the last pill on the Friday evening at 6 p.m. and by Sunday morning I would have given anything to have another pill. Tony and Mum both knew this, and Mum had cried during the night as she held me close to her, cradling me in her arms. She just couldn't sit there and bear to see me in so much agony. As she held me she said softly,

"If professional help doesn't come soon for you then...."

Mum didn't finish her sentence but stopped. She just held me closer and Tony sat the other side of me.

By the time the morning came the sickness was not so bad but my body was still hurting. As I lay in my bed all I kept asking was, Why me? Why me? I didn't ask for the pills and I didn't ask for the pain I was suffering. The tears rolled down my face and I could hardly move. Mum and Tony had no sleep the previous night either but, nevertheless, Mum got up and made me a slice of toast and tea.

"Come on, love, it will settle your stomach and maybe ease the sickness," Mum said softly.

I took Mum's advice as I could see they were both worried about me. After I had finished the tea and toast Mum suggested I try to get some sleep and beckoned to Tony to follow her out of the room.

I could hear them talking in the other room as I lay there but my head was hurting too much to concentrate on what they were saying. Despite the fact that they were speaking quietly to each other it sounded loud to me so I put the pillow over my head and that blotted the noise a little. I kept thinking of the detective sergeant to whom I had given my word and I didn't want to let him down, but on the other hand I couldn't keep up with the pain. It was getting too much to bear, and I knew what I had to do as I had no alternative.

I got out of bed quietly, having remembered that there were some old prescriptions hidden at the back of one of the drawers in my dressing table. My hands were shaking as I held them, for I knew it was wrong, but I also considered it wrong for me to be put through so much pain and agony. I put the prescriptions in my handbag and, luckily enough, I had already written the drug I wanted on them otherwise there was no way I could have done it that day.

I crawled back into bed, knowing I couldn't get any of the prescriptions made up until Monday. I just hoped I could hold out until then and manage to change one at the chemist without anyone realising how ill I was. It was only the fact of knowing I was going to get the pills the following morning that got me through that Sunday. Mum had already informed my place of work I wouldn't be in till the middle of the week, so my job was safe. Tony stayed with me till late Sunday evening and Mum had managed to get a couple of hours' sleep herself, but by that time my bottle had gone. I sat on the settee shaking all over and, as I looked at them, I told Mum and Tony, "It's no use. I can't do it. I can't go through another day without them. It's no use arguing with me, I am not going to have this pain any longer!'' And I went on and on about it.

Mum got up from her chair and came over to me, putting her arms around me. She looked over at Tony and said to him, ''There must be something someone can do for her. I can't see her suffering like this.''

Tony got up and knelt down beside me, holding my hands which were trembling even more than ever now.

He suggested that he would go to see a doctor tomorrow as things were getting out of hand. By this time my body was jerking in the most violent way and the pain was intense. I couldn't bear it any longer, it was hurting too much. I kept muttering, ''No more, no more.''

''Come on, love,'' said Mum, ''Let's get you back to bed.''

It was getting late, so Tony came into my room and said he would be back in the morning as soon as he could make it.

''No,'' I said. ''Make it the afternoon.''

Although I had told them I couldn't take any more I hadn't told them what my dishonourable intentions were regarding the prescriptions in my handbag. I decided it would be best to tell them after, for I knew if I were to tell them now they would stop me,

I never thought the following morning would come. I watched the clock on the hour every hour until daylight. Mum was very reluctant to go to work, but I persuaded her I would be alright on my own. After a lot of convincing she got herself ready and when I heard her slam the front door behind her I dragged myself out of bed. I took a look at myself in the mirror and had a fright. I looked absolutely terrible and knew I had work to do. My hands were still shaking terribly as I tried to put a bit of make-up on, but I managed it somehow. I slowly got dressed and finally was ready to put my plan into action. I looked up at the kitchen clock which said it had just gone past 9 o'clock, so that meant the chemist would now be open for business.

As I walked down the road all the promises I had made to everybody, including myself, had gone out of the window. All I could think of was taking those damned pills, and that by dinner time I would no longer be in this wretched pain.

The thought of being in trouble with the Law didn't concern me, only to get rid of the pain I was in. I was given the pills without any bother and went straight back home with them.

Almost straightaway I felt much better, and I carried on that way for a couple of months until I had used up the last of my secret supply of prescriptions. Not once did I consider contacting the detective sergeant to tell him no-one had been round to see me. It may have been that I thought he didn't care after all or was too busy. I know now that I was wrong to take that attitude for he was so nice when I had first met him.

It wasn't long before I was to meet him again, however, for one day when I went into a different chemist with a prescription I suddenly felt a hand on my shoulder. I turned round and, to my horror, saw it was him.

"You had better come along with us, Ann," he said quietly, and I had no choice but to leave with him and his constable. They drove me to the Police station and ushered me into the same office I had been in before. They told me to sit down and they left no doubt in my mind that this time they meant business. I was filled with morose and self-pity.

As the detective sergeant sat down at his desk he told me he had sent for someone to fetch my mother.

"I'm sorry, Ann, but this time I have got to charge you," he said. I could tell he really was sorry by the tone in his voice, and that made me feel a little bit better, for I had done it solely because I was ill and not because I was a criminal. He asked me why on earth I had carried on stealing and forging since our last meeting and I explained that not a soul had come to see me with a view to helping me cope with my situation. His face dropped in disbelief and I could tell he was angry that no-one had been to see me.

"I'm sorry, Ann. I didn't know, but they'll get a rocket from me, mark my words. This makes me feel worse for charging you, but it's my job and I have to abide by the rules." He showed such compassion, but his hands were tied.

"What will happen to me now?" I asked.

"Well, you'll have to go to court first of all and it will be up to the magistrate to decide what punishment you deserve. I'm afraid you'll have to stay here tonight."

This part shook me, for I had never been in such a position before and it terrified me.

"Come on, you'll be alright," he said, trying to calm me down.

There was a knock on the door and a policeman walked in.

"Her mother is here, sir," he said.

"Thanks," the detective sergeant said. He looked at me and told me he would give me ten minutes with my mother and that was all he could allow us. He added that Mum had been told exactly what was going on and why I was there, and with that he left the room. A few seconds later Mum entered the room and held me close. She said, "It's not fair, it's not fair."

"You've never done anyone any harm," she said.

Mum held me at arm's length and looked at me. "Don't worry, love, I'll get you a good solicitor. You are a sick girl and they will see that for themselves, so nothing will happen to you, I promise."

Those ten minutes went far too quickly and soon it was time for Mum to leave. I asked her to tell Tony and kissed her goodbye.

When I was taken to court the following morning Tony was already there with Mum at his side. I wasn't permitted to speak to them but Tony smiled and gave me the thumbs-up sign. I felt a little better knowing they were both present to give their support. As I stood in front of the magistrate the detective sergeant stood up and read out the charge sheet. He then went on to explain how I had got into such a mess and that nobody had been to assist me with professional advice. The magistrate listened very carefully and, when all the evidence had been given, he said, "It is a very serious offence." He faced me and continued to say that he could understand the reasons why I had done it, but I would have to go to Holloway Prison for one week to have medical reports made out on my case. As I looked towards Mum and Tony tears rolled down my face. I didn't want to go to prison and was so frightened.

On my way to the Police cells I couldn't really believe all this was happening to me. I wasn't at liberty to see Tony or Mum after that for I was to be sent straight to Holloway.

Despite the fact that I was petrified of the thought of being in prison, once I arrived there, I found everyone was very kind to me. I got on well with the other girls and luckily the week went quickly until I had to return to court. During my time in prison I had to see a doctor from a special hospital. His report was read out by the magistrate and, after doing so, she looked up at me and told me I was to go to a hospital in Shenley with a view to getting me cured of my drug addiction. She went on to warn me that if, for any reason, I should appear before her again, I would expect to be given a stiffer sentence. I met Mum and Tony in the hall outside the courtroom and they both hugged me. "I've got your clothes in the car," Mum said and tried to give me a little smile. "They said you have got to go straight to the hospital," she said, still hugging me.

I was so relieved to be free for, although it wasn't too bad an experience in prison, it wasn't all that good, either. I had a lot of time to think whilst I was in there. I hated Dad for putting me there, albeit indirectly. I couldn't help but blame him entirely for the position I had found myself in. I tried to shake it off and reverted back to the present. I was just pleased to have both Tony's and Mum's arms around me.

We came out of the courts, holding hands, and as we walked along the street we heard a loud shout. In absolute horror I turned round and saw my father trying to cross the road. He was waving his arms about, trying to attract our attention. How the hell did he know where to find us? I wondered. Apparently, my photograph had been in the papers and he had seen and read all about me.

Tony grabbed my arm and said, "Quickly, this way," and, with Mum in tow, we managed to get into the car and away before Dad could catch up with us.

I was shaking like a leaf with fright and Tony tried his hardest to console me. "He can't get you now, Ann, you'll be out of the way for a little while, somewhere he won't be able to find you." he said.

Yes, but for how long? I asked myself. I tried to calm myself down by reminding myself that I was free and that I wasn't going to allow my father to spoil our day. We had all been through a traumatic time with me being sent away, and Tony and Mum were worrying how I would cope. We had a few hours before we reached the hospital to enable us to unwind and put things into perspective.

Whilst I stayed in hospital I had the best treatment available, and they managed to cure me by gradually reducing my intake of the slimming drug I was addicted to until I was on none at all. For the first few months everything went considerably well. I saw Tony every day and at weekends I used to go home to see Mum. There had been no word from Dad since that day outside the courtrooms and I wasn't so worried about Mum's safety because Tony used to pop in and see her during the week. Apart from that, Mum had the lodgers living there, so there wouldn't be much Dad could do to her with them around.

One day the doctor came to see me whilst I was in hospital. I had been there about two and a half months and I was beginning to feel much better and showing signs of improvement.

The doctor said, "Ann, your father is in my office and he would very much like to see you."

I swallowed hard and all the old feelings came charging into my body once more. It was too early in the day for Tony to come to visit me and without him I knew I was completely on my own. I said to the doctor,

"I don't want to see him, I'm too frightened."

The doctor knew full well what my reaction would be but he had to tell me all the same. The doctor said he would tell Dad what I had said, but added that he couldn't stop him from coming to the hospital. I looked at the doctor in despair, and asked, "Does that mean I've got to see him?"

"No," he replied, "But if you agreed to see him just the once he might not come again."

"Do you mean to say he's been here before?" I asked.

The doctor confirmed this was true, that Dad had been at the hospital a few times but the doctor had told him they didn't think it best for me to see him just yet, in case it interfered with the treatment they were giving me.

He went on to say that if I agreed to see Dad this time it might satisfy Dad's curiosity and that the doctor himself would be in the same room as us anyway. He also told me that he would only b allowed to stay for ten minutes anyway, so there was nothing to fear.

Reluctantly, I agreed, but I wished Mum and Tony had been with me. I appreciated the doctor's concern but he wasn't my family, whom, I knew I could lean on, and in a way I was too scared to argue with him.

66

As I followed him to his office I suddenly realised that this was the first time I would be seeing my father on my own. In the past Mum had always been with me, and the very thought terrified me. I felt I wanted to run, but instead I carried on walking behind the doctor. I had been so good regarding complying with everyone's wishes since I had been admitted to hospital that I had been taught how to cope without the drugs, but right now I felt I was back to square one. It was if I had forgotten everything and all the hard work and effort on the part of the hospital staff and myself were gone. All I wanted now was to take a handful of pills and how I yearned for them.

The doctor pushed open the door and there in front of me sat Dad. All the horrible memories of the past, and the hate I felt for him, built up inside me in that split second. He got up from his chair and walked over to me with his arms out-stretched. He took me in his arms and as he cuddled me I thought to myself, "You rotten bastard." I couldn't help it, I just hated him so much. I stood there rigidly with no emotion of either direction showing. He was so blind to the fact that I found him repellent and repulsive so naturally he had no idea what he had done to make me feel that way.

I could smell the drink on his breath and clothes but thought it best to be wise and not say anything which might upset him. I hated him, but I also feared his just as much. Those ten minutes seemed a lifetime to me and because I felt so frightened of him I didn't really hear or take any notice of what he was saying to me. I just kept looking at the clock on the wall behind him, praying for the minutes to go as quickly as possible.

Eventually, the doctor told Dad he would have to leave. Without any argument Dad got up and said, "Yes, of course." He then looked at me and said, "I'll come again to see you, Ann," and he gave me a hug.

Not if I can help it, I thought to myself and the doctor saw him out.

I flopped down on the chair, knowing I could never go through that again. The shock of it all suddenly hit me and I started shaking. I heard the door go, which made me jump. I turned round to face the door but it was only the doctor coming back in.

"Are you all right?" he asked.

"Well, I wish you hadn't suggested I see him," I replied.

67

"Is it alright if I go now?" I asked, and with that I left the office.

I was so angry that I had to go through that experience and I was still trembling as I remembered Dad's last words, "I promise to see you again."

Those words kept going over and over in my head, haunting me. Tony was due to visit soon and I couldn't wait to tell him what had happened.

I always felt safe with him and I felt sure he wouldn't let Dad near me again. Ever since my admittance to hospital I felt safe from harm, but it had all changed now. Now that Dad had shown up he could do so again at any time and I felt intimidated and vulnerable. I knew I had to stay at the hospital, so I couldn't up and go.

I told Tony all about it and the dreadful effect it had on me so he made an appointment to see the doctor. The doctor told us both that I would not have to see Dad again if that was my choice. However, the fear didn't leave me and that night I couldn't sleep for thinking about it. I was so distressed and restless that the nurse rang the doctor who, in turn, gave her permission to give me some strong sleeping pills. After taking the pills I felt the fear slowly leaving me and was so relieved that I was given them because I found they gave me strength. To be honest, they gave me the same wonderful feeling as the slimming pills that I was in hospital to be cured of. Was there any chance of. Was there any chance that I had found a substitute pill which would take away the pain and anguish of life? I may have been cured of one drug but by some fluke they may have prescribed a different drug which I could very well become addicted to. I didn't care what the name of it was or what it's purpose was, just as long as they took the edge off my despair.

Although I was an in-patient, I had a lot of freedom and was permitted to come and go as I pleased. There was no problem regarding going out to the shops or seeing Tony, or anything else that I wanted to do. Obviously I had to be back in time for my evening meals and let them know where I was, but I was more or less a free agent.

I liked the effects the sleeping pills had on me and made up my mind that if they were going to make life easier for me to cope with, then I would plump for them. It was so incredibly easy to get them and this time I didn't have to forge any prescriptions, because all I needed to do was to tell the nurse I couldn't sleep and the doctors wrote out prescriptions for them. They were private doctors so I had to pay for the drugs but that was no problem either. I used to make up excuses to Tony whenever I needed the money and he gave me whatever I asked for without hesitation.

I didn't like doing it but it was the only way I could escape the fear that was eating away at me. After six months I was now still living at the hospital, but half of the time I was there, and the other half I was at home.

It was during the latter part of this period when I became pregnant with my first child. I was both surprised and delighted at the idea of having a child of my very own. I hoped Tony would be as happy as I was and, come to think of it, would Mum be able to accept it?

I wondered how I would tell the doctor and what his reaction would be. There were so many questions I wanted answered. The baby was not planned but I was so thrilled that I didn't really care what anyone thought. I had missed two periods so I had a pretty good idea I was pregnant and had the task of telling Tony he was about to be a father again; after all, he already had three children by his wife.

The time came when I knew I had to tell him and, when he took me back to the hospital one night, I was a bit quiet. When the time was right, I said, "Tony, I've got something to tell you. I'm pregnant and I want to keep the baby, so before you say anything I thought I'd let you know how I feel." It all came out just like that in one breath. I was praying he would agree with me to have the child. For a moment Tony looked stunned and didn't say a word, and I suppose I couldn't blame him really, for it came as such a surprise to both of us. We had never planned anything like this. He turned to look at me and still remained silent. This was driving me mad so I said,

"Aren't you going to say anything, then?" and his reply was,

"Oh Ann, I do love you. Of course I want our baby, but what on earth's your Mum going to say?"

"Don't worry, I'll tell her," I said and with that he gave me a kiss and I got out of the car and called out "Goodnight" as I entered the hospital doors. Telling Mum was the least of my problems, I could manage that alright and I felt sure she would welcome a baby of ours, but I found it so difficult to face the doctor. After giving it considerable thought, I decided that night to inform the doctor in writing. I sat at a table and wrote the letter to him. I was completely honest in that I found it easier to write as opposed to telling him face to face. I addressed the envelope and went to bed. The following day was a Saturday and I was due home, so I pushed the letter under the door of his office. On the way home Tony was a bit

69

nervous. He was worried about what Mum would say about the baby and I couldn't blame his concern. I knew Mum loved me and would do anything for me, but this was a different matter. To tell her she had a grandchild on the way, in the circumstances its mother and father were in, might not go down so well. When Tony and I arrived home I told him to vanish for a while to give me a chance to have a word with Mum on my own.

I sat down and told Mum to sit next to me as I had something important to tell her. I told her I was expecting a baby, and at first she said nothing.

The first thing she said was if I wanted the baby and I said, "Oh, yes, Mum. I want the baby so much," and Mum looked at me and smiled. She leant over to me and gave me a big cuddle and in a way I knew she was pleased with my decision.

That night Mum said she was thinking it might be best for us to find somewhere else to live, as Dad knew our present address and, now that the baby was on its way, it would be better if we could find a house of our own. The pregnancy went well and, although I was still on drugs, I felt contented in the knowledge that very soon I would have a child of my own.

Mum found a lovely house in South Harrow that she liked and, whilst I was in hospital awaiting the birth of the baby, Tony helped her move and life looked good for all of us. On July 13th, 1962 my first child was born. The nurse laid my beautiful daughter in my arms and I cried with joy. The first thing I did was to examine her little pink body, making sure she had all her toes and fingers. She was perfect and I was so happy. I was very tired after the delivery but, as I looked down at my baby, my only prayer was that her life would be blessed and that it would mean a much smoother sailing than mine. I held her close and whispered to her so many promises. I had so many plans and ambitions for her and wanted her to know how much I loved and wanted her. That night Tony and Mum came to see her for the first time. Like many fathers, Tony didn't have much to say but looked admiringly at his new child, whilst Mum was over the moon. As she picked the baby up I could tell she was looking upon her as her own daughter. I didn't mind for I knew Mum had missed out on my early years, due to Dad causing problems, and as my baby lay in Mum's arms I was pleased she had a grandmother who had so much love to give to her.

I was nineteen, going on twenty now, and the hospital staff were marvellous. When it was time to take our baby home I had everything I could have wished for. That is, apart from one thing and that was the fact that I couldn't stop taking the drugs. I had been able to obtain them quite easily and was addicted completely once more. By this time Mum and Tony had found out I was back on drugs and, although they didn't like the idea, there was very little they could do to stop it.

CHAPTER SEVEN

One day, quite unexpectedly, my brother appeared at our front door. We were delighted when he said he'd like to stay with us as now we seemed a complete family. The only thing missing was dear Sally. She had passed away whilst I was in hospital. I really loved that dog and she was a good friend to me. The next twelve months sailed by and as Dad hadn't shown his face for some time everything was at peace. That is, everything apart from my drug addiction. The pill intake grew steadily and I couldn't find enough doctors to help me so I slipped back to forging the prescriptions again. I honestly didn't want to keep taking the drugs and yet I couldn't survive without them and it was during this period that I tried to take my life on more than one occasion. I would accumulate pills and swallow the whole lot, whereupon Mum would find me sprawled out on the floor and rush me to hospital. This was particularly hard on her, and I hate myself now for doing it, for she had gone through hell herself, yet she couldn't agree to see me wasting my life and dying. She also helped me try to get back to normal and even I made the effort by saying to myself, "Ann, you've got to go on, got to fight," but I always returned to the view that I didn't want to live, I wanted out. I often put the gas on and simply lay there in front of it to inhale the fumes and on one occasion I can remember putting the gas on and placing a pillow in the oven. I put a row of photographs beside me of Tony, Mum and baby Karen. I took a couple of sleeping pills and lay perfectly still, but Mum and Tony found me in time.

Today I am glad that I survived, but at the time I felt terrible. Nothing ever seemed to come easy and I was constantly fighting so much, whether it was with Dad or the pills. As the final straw, Tony and I were starting to have problems, too, for, although he was still attentive and gave me some support, the fact remained he was a married man.

It was around this time that justice caught up with me and I was found out regarding my forging prescriptions. Once again I appeared in court and this time

71

there was no pity shown. I had been given many chances to be cured and none of them had worked so there was no alternative. As I stood in court this time I was sentenced to Borstal and, as it was just two days before my twenty-first birthday, I was devastated.

As I left the courtroom and was shown to my cell I thought of the judge's words as he sentenced me. Two years seemed a lifetime but I didn't know that if I showed good behaviour I could expect to get out a lot sooner. However, I could only think of it being a full two years and, as I sat alone in my cell, I just cried and cried. I couldn't bear to think I'd be away from my baby that long. My daughter was now thirteen months old and she had given me such happiness, even though I was drugged up with pills. What would Mum do, and would Tony wait for me? All these thoughts went through my mind as I sat there waiting for the police to take me to prison.

The key went in the door and the warden said, "Come on, they're ready for you."

She spoke sharply to me so I got up quickly because she frightened me a bit. I didn't really want to upset anyone and did as I was told. I followed her outside the building to where a big black van was parked. I learned later that it was a black maria and as I climbed up the steps to get in I noticed even my distressed state the row of small doors with mesh on the windows. The policeman who had taken me from the warden showed me which compartment to sit in. There was a small wooden seat and I sat down on it. The door shut and I heard the policeman lock it tight. As I looked at the partition in front of me I noticed there was writing on it. It read, "I was here, 1963," signed, "Kathy".

The words had been scribbled in felt pen. I looked down at the floor and thought how clean it looked. I sat there sobbing my heart out with the magistrate's words, "Two years!" ringing in my ears.

As I sobbed, I heard a gentle male voice trying to console me, saying, "Hey, it'll be O.K. It's not as bad as you think. I've been inside before and you'll be surprised how quickly the time goes." He seemed so young and yet reassuring, and somehow it comforted me. I thanked him and he said, "Believe me, I know. You'll get through it alright, you'll see."

He made me feel a little bit better and made me realise I wasn't totally on my own.

Suddenly, I could hear another man's voice call out.

"Ann!" Is that you?" he inquired.

I knew instantly it was my Dad. Out of all the courts in England and of all the black marias, he had to be in mine! Believe me, I wasn't laughing at the time, far from it. All it did was to bring back flood of memories of when I was fourteen and a half, that crucial stage in my life, and my fear of him was being instilled in my body yet again. I still believed my father was capable of harming me, despite the fact that there was wire mesh between us, that the doors were locked, and that there were police officers present. What could I say, except,

"Yes, Dad - it is me."

As I hadn't seen my father since his visit to me in hospital I couldn't believe that he had found me again. Fancy him being in the same vehicle, under similar circumstances! He kept calling out my name and for a moment I thought fate was saying to me that I hadn't suffered enough yet.

My father shouted out, "Don't worry, Ann. You wait till I get out! I'll see your mother and Tony and tell them I'm not having my daughter behind bars!"

There I sat, ashamed that I had put myself in a position where I was about to serve a prison sentence, and equally ashamed of my father, who did not know it was *he* who was the reason behind it all, and it was *he* who had driven me too far and consequently put me in this sorry situation. I held my hands over my ears as I sat in my little compartment. I could listen no more - I had had enough. There can't be many people who can't wait to get to prison, but that's exactly how I felt at the time! Anything, so long as I could get away from my father again. At the time the irony of the situation was not apparent to me. I simply prayed that we'd reach my destination as soon as possible, so I could be locked up, far away from the man I had been terrified of all my life.

I was in such a state by that evening that I went berserk inside my prison cell. I started breaking up everything I could get my hands on. I shouted and yelled at the top of my voice and was promptly taken to the prison hospital where I found the staff to be kind. Having said that, it wasn't precisely the most desirable of places, of course, but there was no alternative.

On my twenty-first birthday I spent all day in the workshop. One of the wardens came up to me with a posy in her hands, saying to me,

"Ann, would you like to see your family, they are waiting outside to see you?

That is, of course, if you promise to be on your best behaviour.''

As the posy was from my daughter I was overjoyed, and eagerly agreed to control myself in order to see Karen and the others. I was taken to a special waiting room for visitors where Tony, Mum and my little girl were all waiting. They had sent me so many flowers that day, bunches and bunches of them, which only proved to me that my beloved family hadn't forgotten me. My mother, naturally, was very upset, as was Tony, for until this time we had been such a close-knit family unit. Nobody knew for sure how long I would be behind bars, although I had already resolved the previous day that I would try my best not to aggravate the situation, but that I would be an exemplary prisoner. I didn't realise how much the effort would take it out of me at the time, but soon learned during the months that followed. Tony, Mum and Karen were asked to leave after half an hour and I continued my stay in Holloway for another week.

In that short time I made friends with a girl called Chris, and soon discovered that we were both waiting for our transfer to the same borstal, Bullwood Hall. I had two major problems to face at this point: being able to cope without drugs, which was a terrible ordeal in itself, and not being allowed to smoke. For me, the latter was highly trying, as I had, and always have been since then, a heavy smoker.

The day arrived for us to be transferred to borstal. Chris and I managed to cadge a couple of cigarettes from the lady who accompanied us on the journey there and were both terrified when we reached our destination, as we didn't know what to expect. On entering, we were shown into a huge hall which had rooms going all the way around the top of the landing, with stairs climbing to the landing itself. There was a large dining room to one side of the hall and I stood still for a moment, trying to take in the vast size of the building. I don't precisely how many girls lived there at one time, but would hazard a guess at forty or fifty.

In spite of being upset about the predicament I was in I knew I had no option but to face up to reality and that I would have to somehow or another pull myself together. Chris and I were shown to our rooms and it was then, and only then, that I truly realised that my sentence had commenced.

Over the months that followed, Chris and I tended to stay with each other as much as possible and found comfort in our friendship. The first couple of weeks went quite smoothly and I soon managed to get into routine. I was always polite and friendly to everyone, as is my nature, but unfortunately not everyone reciprocated. On one occasion I was walking across the landing towards my room when a girl came up to me and, for no apparent reason, started hitting me. I knew I must not retaliate, for I was frightened that a brawl might put a stop to my coming home earlier than planned. There were no wardens anywhere near us, so all I could do was let her carry on attacking me, until eventually someone became aware of the disturbance and the wardens swooped down to investigate the commotion. They helped me back to my room whereupon I panicked, hoping that I had not hit the girl back in self-defence, but they assured me that I had no need to worry.

After a while I learned the reason why the girl had attacked me. Owing to the fact that I was being civil and sociable to everyone since I had been there, I was totally ignorant of the fact that some women are lesbians. Never having come across lesbians before, I could not have guessed that my friendly nature was being interpreted as attempted seduction of my attacker's girlfriend.

After the news about the girl beating me up had spread throughout the building, all the other girls seemed to show me more respect, simply because I had not hit back, and that attitude took much courage. It isn't easy to just stand there and permit a total stranger to beat the living daylights out of you and refrain yourself from retaliating. I don't mean to sound self-righteous about this, but all the girls knew my only interest was to get out of that place as soon as possible to be with my child, Tony and Mum. If I had been stupid enough to show my anger and, in consequence, fight her back I would have made things very difficult for myself and I would have been put back to square one.

In time the aggressive girl came to apologise to me and the incident was over and forgotten and, generally speaking, my stay remained smooth and without many traumas until the day I was freed. I shall never forget the date, it was the 8th April, 1964 and it couldn't come quickly enough.

Prior to my leaving, I was taken to the matron's room, where she told me that I was one of the few girls who had ever been allowed out of borstal so early, which was purely due to my good behaviour and self-control. In total, I spent seven long months in Bullwood Hall, but am thankful that it was not a longer sentence as it may well have turned out to be. It was a period in my life which opened my eyes to different types of people in our society whom I may never have come across had I not been there with them. On the whole, my stay in Bullwood Hall was somewhat straightforward, but there was one other memorable incident which took place one Saturday evening. We used to have recreation downstairs in the big hall every Saturday evening, when we were allowed to play records and dance to them. On this particular night, I happened to be standing near the stairs. As I watched all the others enjoying themselves during this social evening, I suddenly heard an almighty scream. It sounded as if it was coming from one of the rooms

75

above. A warden who was on duty that evening was standing near to me and she also heard it, so we both tore upstairs to investigate.

She and I were the first to reach the room from where the screaming was coming. We barged open the door, only to find that the girl inside had tried to attract attention to herself by lighting the piles of newspapers which surround her. In the process, her nightdress had caught alight, and she subsequently suffered third-degree burns. Without hesitation, the alarm was raised and the fire fighters and police were on their way within minutes. Whilst the fire was being extinguished the wardens allowed some of us to go and console the poor girl until the ambulance arrived. The wretched sight of that girl's face and limbs will stay with me for the rest of my life.

It is awful when we consider the things we put ourselves through, for the poor girl had only wanted to attract attention to herself for reasons that were unknown and obviously very private to this troubled girl, and yet the burns which resulted would remain with her for the rest of her lifetime. On the day I was to be released I sat on the stairs in the big hall feeling very excited and glad to be able to wear my very own clothes for the first time in seven months, instead of that awful uniform. Tony was unable to come up to drive me home so my Uncle Bill came to collect me, bringing with him both Mum and baby Karen. My baby was now about twenty-one months old and I couldn't wait to see how she had grown.

I was incredibly excited as I sat waiting for them to arrive and, to make matters worse, they were late. When I saw my mother at the door I burst into tears. I really broke down at the sight of her for I had missed her so much. We walked out of the building towards my uncle's car. I sat in the back where my little girl was sitting. She looked even more beautiful than last time I saw her and had grown so much. She was more like a proper little girl now rather than a baby, I longed to cuddle and kiss her, but to my horror she didn't recognise me at all. I had been away from her for such a large part of her short life that I was a perfect stranger as far as she was concerned. Initially this hurt me very much, but once I remembered I was going home and a free woman, I tried to make the best of it. After all, it wouldn't take me long to get back into the swing of family life and hopefully Karen would grow to love me and know me as her mother again. I was so looking forward to catching up on lost time and very soon ceased feeling upset but pleased to be going home.

CHAPTER EIGHT

Tony had arranged to rent a house for us to live together so I was taken straight there. He had left his wife permanently by now and we were able to set up home together for the very first time. For some reason unbeknown to me, my father had stopped coming round to see us and had almost completely vanished from our lives. Years later, we heard through the grapevine firstly that he had been very ill, and then that he had passed to spirit. Apparently, he had tried to get Mum to visit him during his spell of illness, which I understand may have been cancer, but the damage had already been well and truly done and my mother refused to go. No one knows for sure how or where he died. Anyway, peace was restored once again and after a rest I got a job that I really loved. It was at a garage in West Harrow and was good money because it was shift work. If I happened to finish my shift early in the afternoon, little Karen would run down from the top of our road to meet me, while Mum waited and watched us. On the whole, life was pretty good at this stage. My memories of the time I had spent in borstal were gradually fading, although those of the pills were not. To have to face up to the world without them was extremely difficult for I had found it much easier when I was behind closed doors in borstal or in hospital when no-one could hurt me and I felt safe. Strangely enough, I had no ill-effects each time I was admitted to hospital or when I was in Holloway and then borstal when it was impossible for me to have drugs. However, my father had taught me that it was a different world outside the sanctuary of a hospital or any other type of institution and finding myself open and having to face the outside world was a terrifying proposition. It wasn't long before I felt the desire to start taking drugs again so I started taking pep-up pills which I bought over the counter at the local chemist.

I soon found them to be not very strong, but I took them anyway, only to find that they just weren't strong enough for my needs.

I had put on a lot of weight during my stay in borstal, so one day I plucked up the courage to visit a general practitioner, saying that I wished to diet and that I had been prescribed slimming pills in the past for the same reason. The doctor was very obliging and gave me a prescription without hesitation. Little did he know what he had done. That was the start of my becoming addicted to them again.

It was quite easy for me to obtain repeat prescriptions from him, and then from other doctors, and I found it much easier than before to get the pills without having to forge them. This time I had become more cunning, as I vowed I would

77

never go back to prison, and so I found several different doctors who agreed to take me on as a private patient. As the saying goes, money talks. Very soon I was seeing three doctors a week, which made it even easier to obtain repeat prescriptions, and each doctor was unaware of what I was up to. This pattern was to become part of my life in the years to come.

Tony was waiting for his divorce to be finalised and not long after I came out of borstal I felt I really wanted another baby. I became pregnant that same year and continued working at the garage. We then moved into a flat in Welldon Crescent, Harrow. My second pregnancy was well on the way when we learned that my cousin Joyce and her husband were having problems with their marriage. They had two small children, a son, then aged two and a half, and a daughter of six months. I had always envied Joyce her lot in life since she seemed to have everything that I had never had. Although she had lost her mother at an early age, and she hadn't seen her father for years, she nevertheless always looked well-groomed and attractive and wore lovely expensive clothes. She and her husband lived in a beautiful flat and she was adored by her near-enough perfect spouse. When we heard that she and her husband were having personal problems the news came as a complete surprise and a bit of a shock, to say the least. One morning, in the following March, I was in our flat with Karen whilst Mum was out shopping, when there was a knock at the door. When I answered the door my Uncle Eddie was standing there, asking to see my mother. When I told him she was out he said that he would pop back later and stressed there wasn't anything for me to worry about. Two hours later he returned to speak to my mother and announced that my cousin Joyce was dead.

He had the presence of mind not to tell me when I was on my own that morning because I was carrying my second child and he feared I might go into shock from hearing the news on my own. Joyce and I were not only cousins but we were also quite close friends. She had been found early that morning, having committed suicide. It was a terrible shock, for although I had known that Joyce was having problems, I never imagined that she might not be able to overcome them. That same day I vowed I would never be jealous of anyone again, and I never have been. Nobody knows what goes on behind closed doors, do they? I also vowed that if I had another daughter I would name her Joyce after my cousin. Joyce was only twenty-two years old when she died and my youngest daughter was born on 1st May, 1965, two months later.

Even though we were feeling the sadness of Joyce's untimely death, we now had two little girls, a tremendous joy to us all. In my eyes my family was now complete and I was happy, despite the fact that I was still suffering from ill-

78

ealth. For the first time in many years I felt at peace for Dad, God rest his soul, vas no longer around to intimidate or pressure us and I had two beautiful daughters. We lived in the flat for about eighteen months and I went back to work at he garage whilst Mum stayed at home to look after my two children. I was able o cope with my job and the drugs at the same time, for the drugs had now •ecome a major part of my life, since I was so used to taking them and totally lependent on them.

n time we moved on once again, this time to a bigger flat which was situated in 'inner Road and we lived there for three years. The girls were growing up now, Karen being six, but little did I know there were clouds on the horizon. The make •f slimming pill I was addicted to was being withdrawn from the market but I ound out that a new sleeping pill was available on prescription. I acted on this iece of information straightaway and got prescriptions from general practitioners or the new drug by paying privately for them. In no time at all I was hooked and 1ere was no difficulty in acquiring them, just as I had got away with it for some ears now.

Ve lived in our large flat until I was twenty-seven. Mum continued to look after 1e children whilst Tony and I went out to work. We had our ups and downs, like 1l families, but my drug addiction was taking its toll and my family must have one through hell as a result of my illness. Mum and Tony were well aware of 'hat I was doing to my body and that there was no hope of my ever coming off rugs. It was my way of existing, living from day to day, and they coped with the ituation so well, accepting me for what I was. They had to contend with changes f mood, tantrums and although I hated myself for it, I had no intention of topping taking drugs as, apart from that side of things, we had a relatively settled nd organised routine. I had got over the idea of attempting suicide as I had done 1 the past and took each day as it came.

lowever, one morning my mother woke up feeling very ill. She had suffered a 1assive stroke in the night so we rushed her to hospital and for the next four 'eeks she fought with all her might. The doctors told me that the only reason 1um had had such a severe stroke at her age was owing to the beatings she had 1dured years ago. Mum had a very strong willpower, something which was 1ade clear to me one afternoon when I went to visit her in hospital. She could ardly see and yet she was sitting up, trying to pretend she was reading a book as 1e waited for the doctor to come to examine her. She was equally determined to 3me home to the two children she absolutely adored.

sent Mum many flowers during her stay in hospital, but on one occasion I

decided to choose something really unusual so I ordered blue carnations, just t
make a change. Four weeks later Mum was allowed to come home. The doctor
gave her a walking stick for support but as she walked out of the door she threw i
away. It took her many months to get back on her feet, and from that time on sh
had several periods of illness, but, being a woman with such a strong constitutior
she fought them all.

After Mum was well on the road to recovery, Tony and I continued to find i
increasingly difficult to surmount our problems and we were going through
rough patch. We decided to break up, since I felt at the time that it was the bes
solution. We needed some breathing space away from each other and I move
into a house near to the garage where I worked. On reflection, I now blame th
drugs, for they made me do so many strange things, including leaving Tony.
used to say very hurtful things to him, things which I would never say had I nc
been under the influence of drugs, but I blurted them out before thinking what
was saying.

I took Mum and the children with me and we stayed there for a whole year.
was whilst we lived at this house that I met an American. I had no idea at th
time what I was letting myself in for but, like many people, I thought the gras
was greener on the other side. What I didn't know was that history would repe:
itself. I fell in love with the American - he was so full of fun, laughter, life - an
shortly after meeting him I decided to live with him. Mum thought it wasn't
good idea for all of us to go, so she stayed in the house and I looked in every da·
keeping an eye on her and the girls. When I went to live with my American,
was as if the clocks had been put back. He beat me up senseless, although
didn't fully realise it at the time because, along with the drugs, I was now drink
ing as well.

I lived with him for about five months in all and then he wanted to take me
Spain with him for a holiday. Tony was still in the shadows, he never did want
part from me completely, and many a time he and Mum had to collect me fro·
the hospital following a beating I had sustained by my American. Yet, despi·
their desperate attempts at trying to make me sense and leave him, love is blin·
and at that time it was the last thing I wanted to do. They begged me not to go t
Spain with him for they could see him for what he was, but I wouldn't listen.

I started going to spiritualist churches in the area on the odd occasional Sunda·
and I happened to go to one the week before we were due to fly out to Spain. Th·
medium came to me and advised me not to go because I would live to regret i
Even then I refused to heed advice and, as I came out of the church, I insisted

my friends that I still intended going as it was the first chance I had of a holiday in my lifetime, and so I chose to ignore what the spirit world had told me. If we only take their advice when it is given, but we rarely do, I'm sorry to say.

Before I went to Spain, Mum, the children and Tony decided to live together again for Tony's mother had died, leaving him a house in Long Lane, Hillingdon. I set off for Spain with my American. Perhaps I was arrogant or selfish at that time and thought I knew best, but I very soon found out the hard way that I should have listened to everyone who tried to put me off going. We had only been there for a day and a half, maybe two days, when my American went berserk. He beat me senseless and even tried to strangle me until I passed out.

The following morning I awoke to find myself sprawled out across the sofa. I don't know how, but I managed to pick myself up and made for the bathroom. I was all aches and pains and found it difficult t walk but when I looked at my face in the bathroom mirror I was horrified by the sight of me. I was so scared I ran out to see the people whom we had briefly befriended on arrival and they helped me to catch the first plane back home. Tony met me at London Airport at five o'clock in the morning. I was in a terrible state by the time I reached the airport. Half my hair was missing, I was black and blue and in desperate need of drugs as I had been unable to take my usual daily quota. Tony took me straight to the doctor, who prescribed sleeping pills, and then Tony shepherded me back to the house in Hillingdon. It was there that I steadily relapsed into sickness and depression until the time came when I felt that I could no longer cope.

I tried to commit suicide by taking large overdose and was rushed to hospital and put on open order. The doctors there told Mum and Tony that if I didn't pull through by seven o'clock that evening then I wouldn't make it at all. Looking back, I think I must have had an extraordinary amount of help and support, not only from the people in this world, but the next one, too. Sheer hell is what Mum and Tony were going through and I shudder when I think it was all my fault. They didn't deserve the life they lived with me, including all my attempts at taking my own life, half-hoping they would find me in time, not to mention my black moods and screaming fits. I was a most tiresome, unpredictable and difficult person to live with, but it was all superfluous for they knew deep down it was the drugs that gave me the Jekyll and Hyde characteristics. They say you always hurt the one you love, and that is so true.

I spent a whole month in hospital following the last failed attempt at suicide and when I came out Tony and I decided to get married. I was twenty-eight by now and Tony's divorce had been finalised. We had overcome our problems and now

81

he was free to marry me. We were both very happy with our decision as we fel
ready to commit ourselves to each other and seal our love properly.

We lived in Long Lane for a few years and when I was better I went back to
work. I was still a drug addict as I found it quite easy to get the pills I needed
repeating the pattern of paying two or three independent doctors each week for
repeat prescriptions. This kept me going, but it wasn't long before I was becom
ing terribly ill again. As I look back I see that all I was doing up until then was
imitating my father. The only difference between him and me is that at the time]
didn't see the thin dividing line between physical violence and mental cruelty
and didn't realise what I was doing to my family as a result.

I gradually became more and more desperate, praying to God that I wouldn'
wake up each morning. If only I could die - it would stop all the misery I was
causing. It was a vicious circle, for the more misery I could see I was creating, so
the more pills I took, and the more pills I took the more misery I was inflicting or
my loved ones. I would be fine for a few weeks, or even a few months, but ther
Tony and Mum would see the warning lights and keep a close watch on me in
case I would try to do anything rash again. I woke up very early one morning and
I vividly saw two nuns praying at the bottom of my bed. I lay there looking a
them, hardly daring to move, put my head under the sheets and went back to
sleep. I told Mum and Tony when I eventually got up, but they thought it was my
imagination or a dream I'd had. That was the very first time I saw spirit. Al
though it came unexpectedly it didn't really frighten me, if anything they seemed
to have a calming influence on me. It didn't really make much of an impression
on me at the time, but when another incident occurred which concerned spirit
took more notice. It happened a year after my cousin Joyce died and it was the
first time I was fully aware of spirit being around me. I had had a dream that
Joyce was at the front door. When I went to answer it we ran into each other'
arms, crying.

When I got up the morning after my vivid dream I told my mother about it and
she said that she had heard crying all night long. She went on to add that th
crying was so loud that she had actually gone to all the bedrooms to see who i
was who was obviously so upset, but upon investigation found us all to be fas
asleep. Every night for a week Mum was tormented by the crying noise, but onl
she ever heard it. Mum had never believed in there being a spirit world, bu
nevertheless called in a priest since her nerves were in shreds. The priest came
and carried out an exorcism and Mum confirmed the crying ceased after that.

Many years later I learnt that it was Joyce telling us that she had been ver unhappy towards the end of her life. Apparently even the priest thought this may be the case, which is something to think about.

The girls were now growing up fast and I was rapidly becoming more sick when we decided to move just down the road to another house. I was finding it increasingly difficult to move my hands and fingers and had to ask my eldest daughter to write a cheque out for me one day because I found it hard to hold the pen, let alone write the words on it. The pills had taken their toll and yet I was still working. My boss knew I was a sick woman yet he didn't know exactly what was wrong with me. My daughter Karen was now coming up to fourteen. At the time I had no idea how awful it must have been for her to have a mother swaying from side to side at the top of the stairs and not permitting her to have friends in her own home. My mother always used to make sure that I was either in bed or otherwise out of the way before Karen brought anyone home. My youngest child, Joyce, still didn't realise anything was amiss, that is, enough to know the reason behind it all, but must have wondered why her mother was different from the mothers of her friends. As Karen was the eldest, it was she who was at a more vulnerable and impressionable age. She had her first boyfriend at fifteen, at a time when I knew I was desperately ill and yet could do nothing to stop or correct it, even though I could see the terrible effect it was having on my family. I would lie in bed, doped up to the eyeballs, demanding Karen's time and attention. I knew in my heart that I loved her, and yet here I was showing her up, embarrassing her in front of her friends. The situation was degenerating and eventually I found I couldn't go out to work any more. It was then that Mum decided the best thing to do was for her to take the girls away to live apart from Tony and me. I was so drugged up at the time that I didn't have a clue what was going on, although I had a faint idea Mum had to do something like this. There was no way my girls could carry on living under the same roof as me, but it did hurt so much. I was not in a position to do anything about it, however, for all the social services had been to see my mother and consequently put the children under her care, anyway. It was the right thing to do for them.

CHAPTER NINE

Tony and I sold the house and bought a mobile home in Denham. Mum and the kids settled into their new home but I didn't like being away from the girls and Mum. I knew there was no other way whilst I was so ill. The decision to make the break almost broke my heart, for it was almost as if half of me had been taken away, leaving me shattered beyond belief. There was nothing I could do as I realised the girls were growing up fast now and I had already affected the eldest child to detrimental proportions. Whilst we lived in our mobile home I didn't see Mum or the girls every day, much as I would have loved to, for I knew it would do them more harm than good. The youngest one was at school anyway and the eldest out at work, so I couldn't have seen much of them anyway, so I decided to visit them at Mum's house on Saturdays only. However, every time I turned up Karen would turn her back on me, even if she had a friend with her. She would make it abundantly clear that she wanted nothing to do with me and this treatment hurt me so badly. I tried everything I could think of to win her back, including money. On the day we received the money from the sale of the house we went to the bank. I felt I had to give the children something of it, so straightaway we drew some money out to give to them both. When we arrived at Mum's house we found both girls were at home but Mum was out shopping. I had one thousand pounds in my pocket and I quite openly admit I was trying to buy Karen's love and attention, but that day I made up my mind I would try anything.

As my youngest opened the front door she smiled at us and I knew she loved me by the way she looked at us, and for that I was truly grateful to God. She, along with Mum, had tried so hard to help me and had never turned her back on me.

The Easter holidays had just finished and as I walked in I remembered how my youngest daughter had given me an Easter card. On it she had signed her name on the bottom of it and had forged her sister's name so that I would think that both of them had sent the card. However, I knew only too well how bitter my eldest daughter was towards me for I had gone all through that with my father. All of these thoughts went through my head as I walked into the living room. Karen was sitting on the settee reading a book.

"Hello," I said.

There was no reply. I know I should have been used to her attitude by now but nevertheless it still hurt me. As I sat down I said to Joyce, my youngest, "Here is £500 for you. Put it away safely in a bank account. Your grandmother knows I've given it to you," and I handed over the money.

Looking over to Karen, I quietly said to her, "And here's your £500."

No other words were spoken and I had to get up and go before I started to cry.

Karen hadn't even looked at me, let alone take the money from me, so I said before I left,

"Joyce, give this to her, please," and with that I gave her a kiss and left. Tony was sitting in the car and knew the instant he saw the expression on my face that I was far from happy.

"Don't try to buy her," he said. "You'll have to wait till she's ready."

"That's easier said than done," I replied, feeling choked up inside. I just couldn't explain how I felt and how could a man possibly know how I felt, after all, he had never given birth to a child so he couldn't really understand the magical bond a mother has with her child.

As he drove I sat in silence. Would she ever understand that I had never meant to harm her?

But would any of them realise that? As I looked at Tony I was thinking about him and Mum regarding their accepting me for what I was, but as far as the children were concerned it was a different matter. I had had enough, so much that I couldn't be hurt any more, but equally, I realised I couldn't let those kids get hurt any more, either.

When we arrived back home I sat Tony down in front of me and said to him, "I can't go on, Tony," and the tears filled my eyes.

Tony looked at me, worried sick for he had known me to attempt suicide before and didn't want to experience that again. I could tell his concern and said, "Don't worry, I don't want to take my life but I wish God would take me instead. What point is there is me being here?"

I was feeling too selfish to realise that Tony loved me and needed me. I went on, "I feel I desperately need help but I don't know what sort of help."

Tony looked up at me. Both he and Mum had tried everything within their power to help me, but to no avail. How could he help me just that little bit more now? Tony had always tried to help me find the pills I needed but the family had taken it the wrong way, thinking he was doing me no good at all by aiding me to get them. Owing to his determination in helping me in whatever way I wanted had eventually broken down the strong friendship he had always had with Mum, and they were now not on the best of terms. Tony was the only one who could keep tabs on my actions and a tight control over the pills I had in my possession. It would be the only way he could prevent me from killing myself. I felt sorry for Tony to have to go through this with me, and I felt sorry for the others, too. All I had ever done in my life was to bring pain to my loved ones and I couldn't see an end to it in the future.

As I sat there with my hands covering my face, a thought came into my head. Perhaps if I went to church I could get some help or guidance there. Anything, as long as I could change the look on my daughter's face every time she saw me and take away the hate she felt towards me. Looking up, I said to Tony, "Will you take me to church?"

He looked so surprised for it was something I had never asked him to do before.

"Oh, please, Tony," I begged him. "Will you take me to one now?"

"Yes," he replied, "But which one do you want to go to?"

Tony didn't have the faintest idea which church I wanted to go to so I told him to take me to a Roman Catholic church, but I didn't care which one, I just felt I needed to go.

Tony got up and went out to the car. I got my coat and before I knew it I could hear Tony tooting the horn of our car to let me know he was ready. I quickly checked I had the keys to the door safely in my handbag and walked out, shutting the door behind me. It was a cold evening and not the best of nights to go out in, but I was determined to go to the church no matter what. I wasn't quite sure what it was I was searching for and I am sure Tony didn't know either but whatever else I felt I needed to pray. We drove around the streets for a little while until we came across the church. Tony pulled up outside and asked me, "Do you want me to come in with you, Ann?"

"No, I'd rather go in on my own if you don't mind." I leant over to him and gave him a kiss.

"Stop worrying about me, love. I just need to go into the church for a short time, that's all," I said.

Hugging me, Tony said, "I just hope you find what you are looking for," and he smiled at me.

86

I said, "I hope so, too," and with that got out of the car.

As I walked up the stone steps towards the doors my stomach was churning. I wondered if I was being silly and if the priest would understand my predicament. All manner of thoughts went through my mind, but most of all was the thought of my children and the impression I had on them and their attitudes towards me. We had been one united family for years and now it was divided. I couldn't get the look in my eldest child's eyes out of my mind and I sincerely hoped the priest would be able to help me.

As I pushed the door open I could see many people kneeling in prayer inside the vast church. The priest was in the distance and it was evident that he was carrying out a service, so I moved quietly towards the back of the church, finding a tranquil spot for me to sit and wait for the priest to finish. I felt so cold as I sat there and where I was sitting it was very dark. I shivered for a moment as I was so scared, not of the church itself but of the priest, and yet I didn't know why. I had been brought up in the Catholic faith so I knew there was nothing to be frightened of, but it was now the first time for many years since I had been to church and this would be the very first occasion when I had actually spoken to a priest in person. I pulled my coat round my trembling body and hoped the service would soon be over.

Eventually, as the service came to a close, I sat and watched the people get up from their pews and walk past me to go out. One lady smiled at me so I smiled back but my mind was on the priest. He came down from the pulpit and entered a small room at the side of the church. I got up and walked towards the small room. The door was open and I could see the priest taking off his robe over his head. I knew I shouldn't have imposed upon him but I was so desperate that I barged in and didn't bother to knock or ask permission to enter.

"Yes, can I help you?" he asked.

I don't know what came over me during the next couple of minutes, whether I had rehearsed what I was going to say to him too many times and had confused myself by doing so, or whether it was a combination of the pills and the help I needed with them, plus the fear I had of losing my girls forever, being to much for me to bear. I rushed into the room and knelt down in front of the priest, crying like a banshee.

"Please, please help me!" I wailed. I tried to explain my circumstances to him in between sobs, but emphasising the fact that I was frightened of losing my girls more than anything. That was more important to me than the other problems I faced at that moment of time and the more I tried to tell my story, the more tears came.

His curt answer cut through me like a knife.

"Do not be a silly child. Go home to them and they will forgive you."

He made the sign of the cross above my head and said he had to go. I thanked him and slowly got up off my knees. I felt totally numb as I walked out of the little room, through the church, and as I approached the church doors I stopped. I turned round and looked back towards the altar where a large figure of Jesus Christ on the cross stood high and magnificent.

"Thanks," I mumbled under my breath and, to be perfectly honest, wondered what the hell I was doing there. I was so angry for it was almost as if I had been cast aside.

As I reached the door I vowed I would never kneel to another human being on this earth. I pushed the door open and the cold air hit me once again. I wrapped my coat around me to keep me warm and from where I was standing I could see Tony. He had seen my shadow through the doorway and had already got out of the car, and was now standing at the foot of the steps, looking up at me. He very slowly walked up the steps towards me whilst I just stood there, holding my coat close to me. Perhaps I had gone inside in the hope of finding a miracle, maybe hoping someone or something could show me the way, but instead I felt more lost and more confused. I felt no warmth or comfort whatsoever but was left to feel cold and numb. I felt Tony's hand in mind as he said to me, "Come on, love, let's go home."

When we got to the car Tony looked at me enquiringly.

"Has it helped you, Ann?" he asked as he unlocked the car door on my side.

I leant forward to open the car door and got in. Tony walked round the back of the car and got in his side. He didn't push the issue but just started the car. I couldn't answer him, mainly because I didn't have an answer. I didn't really know what I was expecting when I went into that church but I certainly did think I would have had some kindness and consideration of some degree shown to me. Silently, I thought back to seeing the cross with Jesus Christ on it and said I was sorry, for I hadn't meant to take it out on him and I knew it was very wrong of me. I had

88

never been a religious person but I had the greatest respect for God and His son so I felt I owed them an apology. However, I was still feeling very bitter and angry, mainly at myself for putting myself in that position, only to be hurt yet again.

I sat in total silent until we reached our mobile home. I had been hurt deep within my whole being and I just wanted to be left alone.

"Do you mind if I go to bed?" I asked Tony as soon as we got in, not wishing to appear rude.

All Tony said was, "I presume it didn't help then."

I turned my head away as I could feel the tears coming again.

"No, it didn't," I cried, and with that went to bed.

As I lay in my bed I thought about what the church had taught me in that God was always with us. Well, where were you tonight, God? The question remained unanswered for after I had asked my question I fell fast asleep.

The following morning nothing was said about the visit to the church and I tried to put it all at the back of my mind, but the one thing I couldn't forget about was to stop, or try to stop, taking the wretched pills. I had discussed the matter the previous evening before we had gone out and we both decided it best to visit a doctor the following day to tell them of my drug addiction. After breakfast we set off and managed to find a lovely lady doctor who was willing to take me on as her patient. She warned me that she was going to let every doctor in the area be aware that she was treating me so I wouldn't be able to go to any other doctor for pills. I accepted this as I so wanted to prove to my family that I could make good and maybe one day take that look out of my daughter's eyes. It was almost like they were haunting me. I had tried so many times before, as you know, to come off the pills and had always failed, but this time I knew either I had to make it or die, for I was very ill. I was losing weight and slowly wasting away but, besides that, I was almost losing my family and certainly my eldest daughter. I knew I had to get better before I lost my youngest daughter also and had to try to win back the love of Karen. Although deep in my heart it would be a battle I had probably lost already, I was willing to give it a try and was not going to give up now.

So, slowly but surely, I started coming off the pills. It was very difficult and there were days when I would have willingly loved to have died. If it hadn't been for the support of Mum and Tony I would have given in easily. Mum telephoned me every day and Tony was always with me. The battle was hard and there was a time when I couldn't handle it and I got some pills and tried to take my life. I was pulled out of it in the nick of time and went back to trying to cut down. One Sunday, I had had a really bad day when I found the effort of coming off the pills was too much to bear. I lay in bed that morning wondering Why couldn't I just leave this earth or was that too much to ask? Every time I had attempted taking my life in the past I had always been found in time by Mum or Tony, no matter how clever I had thought I had been, so I knew there was no escape for me to die that way. I was so unhappy but, more than that, I was making my family desperately unhappy and it was apparent to me that it wasn't worth having me around any more to increase their unhappiness. I know that I was feeling particularly sorry for myself that day but I just couldn't help it and no matter how hard Tony tried I couldn't snap out of it.

"Come on, love, I'll tell you what we'll do today," he said.

"We'll go to a different church tonight and see if that helps you at all. We haven't been to a spiritualist church for years and there's no harm in trying. What do you think? You never know, you might even get a message that will cheer you up and give you some hope to carry on. You've come this far and I can't bear seeing you like this."

As Tony said, I hadn't been to a spiritualist church for a long time, but after the last visit to a church I felt it pointless to turn to God again.

"No, we'll leave it," I said to Tony. "I've really given up hope in turning to the church for help and advice after what happened the last time."

As I looked at Tony I knew he thought I was going to give up trying to come off the pills.

"Look love," I said. "I don't want to go backwards, but I feel so unhappy because every time I try to come off them there seems to be an obstacle in my way and I can't see me ever making it."

"Well," said Tony, "It's no good having a go at you, Ann, we've all tried that in the past but even if obstacles are there, surely you've got to try and get over them."

"But I'm tired of trying," I said. "All I seem to do is hurt everyone around me,

90

including myself."

I shrugged my shoulders in despair. I was too depressed to argue any more.

"Well, said Tony, "I'm going to the spiritualist church tonight so it's up to you whether you want to come or not."

He was well aware I hated being on my own so I said to him, "O.K., I'll go. Look, it's just a bad day for me but I still want to come off the pills."

He smiled and said, "I'm glad, Ann. Think of the girls."

That's all I keep doing, I thought to myself. I had never told anyone how much it hurt me to think of them so much so Tony didn't know how much his last statement meant to me.

The day dragged by and by the time we had to get ready to go my head was aching. I felt dreadful but I had to make the effort for Tony's sake. As I walked into the living room Tony asked me if I was going to put some make-up on. I was taken aback by this as I very rarely used make-up and said so. "Well, it's only that you look so pale and your eyes are red from crying," explained Tony.

I agreed and went back into the bedroom. As I sat down in front of the mirror I noticed how my face was looking drawn and, as I started putting my face powder on, I suddenly thought how old I was looking. I was only thirty-seven years old but the face looking back at me looked at least ten years older. I quickly powdered my face and got up. I felt depressed enough, without that!

When Tony saw me he told me I looked a lot better, thank goodness.

We left with plenty of time to spare before the church opened so we took a slow ride. I sat quietly with Tony asking me now and again if I was feeling alright. I would have replied "Yes" but inside me I felt far from alright. As we drew up outside the church I felt like saying to Tony, "Take me home", but I kept quiet. We were still a bit early so we sat in the car. I lit a cigarette and looked at the small church, wondering to myself what was the point in going inside. My mind went back to the Catholic church and that as I had received no help there why should I receive it at this spiritualist church? As I took another puff from my cigarette I remembered the times I had been to a spiritualist church before. It was always on those occasions that I went purely to receive messages from the other world about the future and what it had in store for me. The churches themselves had been unimportant to me.

I must confess that I had never before thought of turning to God directly, and when I did I felt I had been rejected. As I looked back at the church again I felt there was no point in seeking help there in case I was turned away as before. As we were sitting there I noticed lots of people going in so I looked at my watch. It was 6.25 p.m. and Tony said to me, "Come on, love, we had better go in before they start the service which starts in five minutes."

I leant forward and put my cigarette out and said, "O.K." and got out of the car. I waited for Tony to lock the car and as I waited I thought how cold it was and yet the weather that day had been hot. Maybe it was me, I thought, as I wrapped my jacket around me. We walked into the little building and I could see how packed it was. We managed to find two seats at the back of the church and sat down.

The service commenced promptly and the medium was introduced. She was a lady in her fifties or sixties and she appeared to be very pleasant. My mind, however, wasn't really on what she was saying, nor anything else that may have been going on around me; I could not snap out of my depression. After the prayers, hymns, healing silence and address, the medium stood up to give clair-voyance to the congregation and by this time I was at my lowest ebb. All I could think of was Would someone please tell me I am going to die soon. I could feel the tears welling up in my eyes so I just bit my lip as I didn't want people to see my crying. I was sitting near a window and I started to look out of it. Suddenly, a voice was saying, "I'm talking to you, love." Tony nudged me and as I turned to him I could see the medium standing in front of me. I had been in a daze and hadn't heard her. Even as she was talking to me my mind went a blank, but the words I had been thinking about came back into my mind and without thinking I just stood up, tears that I had kept at bay whilst I had been sitting there suddenly started to flow, and I interrupted her. With the tears now flowing down my cheeks I simply asked,

"Please can you tell me when I am going to die?"

I heard Tony gasp and I knew instantly I had made a complete fool of myself. I got up and rushed past Tony and out of the church to the car, forgetting that he had locked it. I couldn't go back to ask for the keys so I decided to walk up the road a bit.

Just then, I heard Tony call out,

"Ann, wait!"

I stopped in my tracks and turned round. As I watched him walking towards me I felt so ashamed for showing him up in front of all those people, and as he reached me I apologised to him for doing so.

"Come on, it doesn't matter," he said and as we walked slowly back to the car I said to him that I really should go back and apologise to the medium.

"I agree," said Tony, "But I'm sure she understands."

As we reached the car people were coming out of the little church and a couple of them came up to ask me how I was feeling now. They seemed genuinely concerned and both of them asked us to go back into the church for some tea. Tony agreed that it would be a good idea so we started to walk back in.

As we entered the doorway I stood still.

"Come on," said the lady, "Everyone in there has a problem or is worried about something or another and they all understand."

Her words gave me much comfort and I followed them in. It didn't take me long before I found the medium and, taking her to one side, I told her how sorry I was to behave in such a manner, and I hoped she would understand. She put her arms around me and gave me a kiss on the cheek.

"You are amongst friends now, my dear," she said softly, "And God will help you. You will see that in the years to come, I can promise you that."

I thanked her and went to sit down next to Tony, who was talking to some other people, and my eyes went round the church itself. As I took stock of the people within its walls I felt this time no one appeared to be standing on ceremony but were sympathetic to my plight, or at least they showed some interest and tried to anyway. Most of the people there had made me feel that I was not on my own in my distressed condition and that they, too, had at some time or another experienced my grief and pain in their own fashion. No one appeared to be in a hurry to leave, nor too busy to spare the time to show me they cared. Everyone in that little church seemed to care and my mind went back to the Catholic church where I was given the distinct impression that nobody cared, least of all God, and yet here, in this small, modest church, I had found friends and a door which was forever open, and no gold or glitter on show. It had no priest dressed in fine robes in too much of a hurry to listen but a whole body of people with one mind, all with the same belief that God Is Love, and that is the key to life itself.

There was such a beautiful atmosphere within the church and, although it was just a very small hut, not even made of bricks and mortar, it caressed me, making me feel secure and protected by all the love that was filled within it. There was an altar table at one end which was surrounded with fresh flowers and some candles. There were piles of blue hymn books neatly stacked after the service and an old piano to one side of the church which also had vases of flowers on top of it. The tables were covered with clean, lacy tablecloths and there were more vases full of flowers everywhere I looked. The walls were full of pictures of Jesus Christ and the main centrepiece was a simple wooden cross. As I looked at the cross I felt that God had not left me after all and that I had found Him again.

When we were on our way home, Tony asked me if I was feeling any better. "Oh, yes, love, much better," and yet somehow I couldn't tell him why. Everyone had kindly made me welcome and I felt as if a great weight had been lifted from my shoulders. For the first time in my life I felt I had found a haven, a sanctuary, where I found hands held outstretched to give me the help and support I so badly needed, and I grabbed them as tightly as I possibly could with both hands.

I continued to come off the pills but found I couldn't stay in the mobile home any longer, it was driving me up the wall, so we relocated to a house back in Hillingdon where we still live to this very day. The uprooting marked a turning point in my life. When we returned to Hillingdon I was down to only four pills a day, for in the past six months I had decreased the dosage from twenty pills daily to four, and I was able to take up work again and gradually find my feet. By this stage Karen was tentatively communicating with us again which was marvellous, for at least it was a step in the right direction and this pleased me beyond words. The family as a whole was beginning to close ranks just as before, even though we were still living in separate houses. We were all trying very hard to pick up the pieces, but nobody wanted to try harder than me. Although Mum and Tony knew I had managed to reduce my daily intake of pills, I don't think they honestly believed it possible for me to be completely cured. In my own heart, I never thought it possible either, but at least I was finally on the road to progress and beginning to feel partly normal again after such a long time. I had been to hell and back and had dragged my family behind me all the way, but I was now able to see the light at the end of the tunnel at last and hoped all was not lost. I was realising, too, that I had a chance of regaining my daughter's respect and I didn't want anything to get in the way to prevent that from happening.

We came back to live in Hillingdon in August 1979 to settle down, but I was still terrified of life. I didn't really know what direction I was heading for, nor if I really wanted to come off the four pills completely or to stay on them as a maintenance dose. As far as I was concerned, four pills a day didn't seem as bad as twenty. I was coping much better with Mum having the kids with her and I enjoyed going to see them so, in a way, it didn't seem as if we were really separated at all.

It was basically the drugs that had warped my path, I know that now, yet I think coming to this house made it easier on me somehow. I still wasn't quite ready to reject the pills completely because until this point I hadn't won any battles. On the other hand, I had the two most beautiful daughters in the world, the best mother anyone could ever wish for, and a gem of a husband who had proved his life for me a thousand times over. I had been such a bitch to them during my trials and tribulations and he was, and still is, a tower of strength to me. All of them had stuck by me, but what had I done for them in return? What could I do for them now? That was the burning question. I had often wondered about that for, whatever I had done in my life, I had done it with the best intentions and for all the best possible reasons. I would never have deliberately put them through hell had the drugs not overtaken and ruined my life. I loved them all far too much for that. People could quite easily say to me, "Well, nobody put the pills into your mouth. You did it, nobody forced you?" I started to believe that it had all been fated from the very beginning. I began to realise that even more clearly once I had learned that my God had kept me alive for a purpose. At this stage, however, I was completely unaware of what that purpose might be, no idea whatsoever.

As I mentioned earlier, we moved into the house in the August and in the September, to my utter amazement, I found I was pregnant. The doctors did not want me to have my baby since they feared that I would not be able to handle both cutting the dosage of drugs and the pressures of having a new baby, and they argued that I should have an abortion. I wasn't at all sure about this, as I wanted both the baby and to be cured of drugs. Tony and I decided to ask a good friend of ours, who happens to be a medium, to consult the spirit world for us to ask their advice. The spirit world do not order us, but they are here to help us and they agreed with the doctors, and, as I have now learnt that everything is fated, after listening to both sides of the story Tony and I made the decision to go ahead with the termination. Looking at our two lovely daughters I could see the misery I had inflicted on them and, even though I was partly cured and wanted to keep the baby, I couldn't possibly put a third child of mine at risk, and so I went ahead and had the pregnancy terminated.

The following months were spent settling down in our new home, visiting Mum and the girls, and life had seemingly returned to normal, even my health was now much improved.

Little did I know that in the following Spring something would happen that would completely change the whole course of my life.

CHAPTER TEN

I woke up startled one morning and looked around me. Something had woken me up but what it was I didn't know. I looked over at Tony, only to find he was blissfully sleeping. I looked at the clock and found it to be too early to get up so I lay back down, trying to get back to sleep again. Whatever it was that had woken me had now vanished from my mind and all I wanted to do was to snatch some extra sleep. The next thing I knew was Tony shouting in my ear, "Ann, wake up!"

With my head in its usual position under the pillow, I shouted back, "O.K.", but really wishing he would just go away. Dragging myself out of bed, I walked into the bathroom and, as I washed myself, I suddenly felt, for some unknown reason, as if something or someone was with me. I turned round from the basin and had a good look round. Of course nothing was there so I turned back and carried on washing. I could hear Tony shouting at me to hurry up as he wanted to use the bathroom.

"I've finished!" I replied, and dashed into the bedroom to get dressed. Damn, I thought to myself, as I caught my tights. I could see the ladder running so I quickly found another pair and started to put them on. As I looked at my watch I thought, Good, I still have plenty of time before Tony drops me off at work. When I got downstairs I made q quick cup of tea and sat down to read the paper. Tony was still upstairs when I heard him shout out again, asking what the time was. I called the reply up to him and continued to read the paper. Just then, the feeling I had experienced in the bathroom was back. Looking up from the newspaper I looked around me and a shiver went down my spine and then I felt cold.

I got up and called up to Tony, "Tony, are you coming down yet?"

He said he had finished getting ready and that he'd be down in a minute. I felt a bit foolish but I didn't want to be on my own in the room. When Tony came down the presence had gone and the feeling I had had gone, too. I smiled to myself, thinking, You're going do-lally, Anne, and shrugged it off.

As we drove to work I was thinking about how life was getting much better since we had moved from the mobile home. My eldest daughter and I were on better terms now and I was very close to my youngest. I was still down to only four pills a day so, on the whole, things were much improved for me than they had been for a very long time.

When Tony pulled up outside where I worked he said he would see me later for lunch. We often took a ride down to the river which was not very far from where I was working. I used to take something to eat for when we got there and it made a pleasant break in the middle of the working day. I told Tony I'd be ready when he came to pick me up and I watched him as he drove away.

We were very busy at work that day and the time went quickly so by the time Tony came for me that night I was glad to get home. When we pulled up outside our house and whilst Tony put the car away I let myself into the house. As I entered the hallway I felt sure someone was in the house and the feeling I had that morning was back again, but this time much stronger. I took my time, hoping Tony was coming.

"What's the matter?" he asked and as he stopped next to me I whispered, "Ssh, I think there's someone in the house."

"Hang on, I'll have a look," Tony said in a quiet voice, with a look as if he guessed I was imagining things. He popped upstairs and then took a look all around downstairs, then he said, "It's alright, you're just imagining it."

"Sorry, love", I said, as I put my things down on the settee. Walking into the living room, Tony asked me what made me think there was someone there.

"I don't know," I replied.

I hadn't mentioned my odd sensation that morning as it didn't seem that important, but the feeling I had then was now back. Tony didn't pursue the subject so I pushed it to the back of my mind. Having said that, I was convinced I had not imagined the presence of someone or something and the coldness that I felt that morning and now. I turned the fire on.

"For God's sake, Ann," Tony said when he saw what I was going.

"You can't be cold!"

"Yes, I am!" I retorted, but I didn't tell him why.

The following morning everything was fine and the incidents of yesterday were completely gone from my mind and Tony had arranged with me to pick me up at lunchtime from work as usual. I bought a few sandwiches from the Baker's across the road and a bottle of drink ready for when Tony arrived. Sure enough, Tony came for me dead on time and we took the old familiar route to the river. It was a lovely day with the sun shining. I was glad of the break as we had been busy again that morning at work. Tony was talking about what had been going on at his place of work that morning and, as I listened to him, I had already started eating one of my sandwiches for I was starving and couldn't wait till we got there. By the time we reached our usual spot I had finished my sandwiches and teasing Tony to give me one of his because I was still hungry! We started to argue over it as to who needed it the most, but it was all in fun.

We parked the car when we got there and I laid my head back. I felt good for it was nice to get one hour off and relax. Tony had some papers from work with him and was looking over them. I just sat there enjoying the break and was looking out of the window at the river which ran along my side of the car. It was only a small section of the river but nevertheless it was very pleasant. On the other side were swans sitting on the bank, enjoying the sunshine, and they made a beautiful, peaceful setting.

I turned to look at Tony, only to see him engrossed with his paperwork, so I looked at my watch and saw that we still had plenty of time so I was not unduly worried. I looked back at the river, but this time, to my amazement, the view was entirely different from what I had seen before. What I had seen a few minutes ago was now not there, but I could see a different river now, one which had a bridge. A young boy of about eight or nine was walking across the bridge, kicking the sides of it with his shoes, and as he reached the other side of the bridge he found a tin can which he began to kick about. It was almost as if I could read his mind; he was so annoyed. At first I couldn't make out why he was so angry and then I soon realised that it was because his mother had bought him a new suit and the trousers were short. He was annoyed about them being short trousers as all his friends were now in long trousers and he wanted to be like all the others.

I watched the scene for some time, feeling a little bit sorry for the young boy, for I knew how children can be cruel when another child is set apart from the rest of the gang.

Suddenly I was conscious of hearing Tony talking, but it seemed so far away. The scene of the little boy faded and I was now able to hear Tony clearly.

"Sorry, Tony, what did you say?" I asked him.

"Never mind, it wasn't that important, but where were you. You seemed to be miles away."

I didn't answer him straight away because I wasn't quite sure what I had just witnessed was true or not. I had never seen such a clear picture as that before and yet I knew I had definitely seen it and it wasn't my imagination. Also, I was puzzled as to who the young boy was. If I told Tony I knew he wouldn't laugh at me, for he isn't that sort of person, and he would listen to what I had to say.

I waited until he started the car and then I said, in a casual voice, "Tony, I've got something to tell you. I've just seen something which I don't quite understand but can I tell you about it?"

"Of course you can," said Tony, not having an inkling as to what I was about to tell him! I proceeded to tell him the whole story, wondering if it made any sense, not only to him, but maybe to me, also. After all, I had never in my life experienced anything like it before, and Tony, with his enquiring mind, could possibly have the answer. After I finished telling him everything Tony didn't say anything straight away. In fact, I was surprised, I'm not sure why, but I thought he would be able to come up with a simple explanation, instead of which there was a moment's silence. After a few minutes he asked me where and how I had got all this information from regarding the scene. My immediate reply was, *"They* told me."

I was surprised myself with the answer I gave, let alone Tony!

"What do you mean by *they* told you? Who are *they* and why did *they* tell you?" demanded Tony.

I was puzzled and thought about it for a moment, and then I said to him, "How do *I* know?"

I was getting more and more confused by Tony's attitude and questions and annoyed with him because I had told him a simple story and expected a simple explanation. Instead of which I was getting the third degree and getting a bit fed up with it all.

"Was there anything else you saw?" Tony went on.

"No, not really," I replied. "Just what I told you, that's all."

By this time I was so mixed up for I had never known Tony to behave like this before. He stopped the car so I said, "Come on, Tony, I'll be late back for work."

I knew the other girl at work wouldn't be too annoyed if I was late back as she could have as long a lunch-break as I did, but I didn't like taking advantage of her good nature.

"Do you realise what you have just seen?" asked Tony.

I thought to myself, How would I know? It was now beginning to be a complete mystery, and I knew Tony so well and that something was up for him to make me late back at work and to be so persistent. I asked him what was bothering him and began to wish I had never spoken of what I had seen.

"I had better tell you," said Tony. "When I was eight or nine years old my mother bought me a suit as you described, and the bit about the river with the bridge going across it happened to me exactly as you told me. On the day in question *I* was wearing the new suit and it was *me* who you saw kicking the tin can in anger. Every little detail you described to me was true, right down to the last detail, and yet when I asked you how you knew all this, all you said was that *they* were telling you. Is there no more? I can't make it out at all."

"Tony, I really do not know how I know, I only know what I saw, that's all. Why I said *they* were telling me I don't know either as I don't even know who *they* are!"

By now I was very annoyed as I really didn't understand what was going on. I could understand Tony's question, but I didn't know the answers, which made it all so frustrating. I shrugged my shoulders and said to Tony, "Just forget it.

Maybe somewhere way back in the past you had once told me something about that incident when you were a young boy and I had remembered it."

I knew that was not true, but by now I was well and truly fed up with the questions Tony was asking and eager to return to work. I knew I had not convinced him but he started up the car and took me back to work. I made my apologies to the girl for being late and she smiled, saying it was alright with her and that she didn't mind. With that, she picked up her bag and said she would see me later. I was glad to be on my own and, as we were seldom as busy in the afternoons as the mornings, it gave me time to think over what I had seen by the river and it scared me for I had never experienced anything like it before.

For a split second I thought of the pills. Coming off them after all these years was hard, but could it be they had caused me damage to my mind? Then again I knew what I had witnessed and there was no reason why I should have doubted it for it had been so clear and, remembering what Tony had said, it was also a past event that was true. I could not honestly remember Tony ever telling me the story and, even if he done so, why on earth should I remember it then when other things were far more important to think about.

When my work colleague came back after her lunch-hour I decided to try to put it all at the back of my mind and get on with my work, and hoping that nothing like that would occur again.

Tony picked me up from work that evening as usual and nothing was mentioned about the events of that lunch-time, which I was glad about. We went round to visit Mum that evening to see her and the girls and we stayed for an hour before going home. When we got in I prepared all that I needed for work the next day and then sat down to watch television for the rest of the evening. I had only been watching television for about half an hour when, suddenly, the feeling I had had the previous day returned. I shivered and Tony must have noticed for he said to me, "Are you feeling alright, love?"

"Yes, I'm fine," I replied, and he continued to watch the television. I didn't want to bring up the subject of the previous day, nor what had happened during the lunch-break, so I just carried on in silence.

Just then there was a knock at the front door. Tony got up to see who it was. I turned the television sound down for I was intrigued to know who it was at that time of night. I could hear a man's voice talking to Tony but couldn't make out what was being said. Tony popped his head round the door and said, "It's alright.

I've left my car lights on, that's all,'' and with that I heard the front door shut.

I got up to turn the sound up when suddenly I heard a voice call my name. I knew it wasn't Tony calling my name, for he was out in the street turning his lights off, and yet I heard someone call "Ann" quite distinctly.

Good God, Ann, I thought to myself, you *are* going round the bend! and I turned the television up quite loud. I heard the front door open and Tony walked in asking what had happened to the television! There was a film on which we were watching so I told Tony he hadn't missed much and we continued to watch it.

Suddenly, I heard the voice call "Ann" again. This time I nearly fell out of the chair and it frightened me for I heard it so clearly. Who the hell was it? I knew it wasn't Tony as he was sitting quietly watching the television and anyway, it wasn't his voice. My concentration went right off following the film but I knew Tony was enjoying it so I decided that after the film finished I would tell him about it. By that time I had heard nothing else so I changed my mind and decided not to tell him after all. Perhaps it was my imagination after all. I just didn't know, but as all was quiet for the moment I kept it to myself.

That night and the following day everything was as normal so once more I tried to put it all behind me. That is, until we had settled down for the evening in front of the television when I heard that same voice again. That's it, I thought, I'm mot going mad, I can hear it, and with that I got up and turned the television off. Tony looked so shocked and asked what the matter was, so I explained everything that had happened regarding hearing my name being called the previous night and now again.

"I don't know what the hell's going on but I know I can hear someone talking to me," I told Tony, "And I know it's not the drugs causing this effect."

"Why do you say it isn't the drugs?" asked Tony.

"Well, if I told anyone else I was hearing voices they would obviously think it was the drugs that were the cause of it," I explained.

"Don't be silly," said Tony. "You only take four a day and if you were going to experience something like this you would have done so years ago when you were really ill and taking a large quantity of them. You can't say you are ill now on a small dosage of pills.

I went on to say, "Well besides that, I would really like to know what's going on. I know it's no big deal but it frightens me a bit because I don't understand and I don't know who the voice belongs to. I only know I can hear it clearly."

"What are the exact words that are being said?" asked Tony.

"I told you," I said impatiently, "Just "Ann," nothing else," and there's this feeling I have that something or someone is around me when the name is spoken."

"And nothing else?" Tony asked.

"No," I replied.

"Why don't you ask whoever it is speaking what they want?" suggested Tony.

He had always been interested in the subject of spiritualism for years so I trusted him, but I was scared. I didn't really want to know the answer to that one but I took notice of Tony and, sitting there quietly, I asked the burning question. I felt an idiot for I didn't know who or what I was speaking to. To my utter astonishment, I heard the voice speak again, but this time it said, "Hello, Ann,"then nothing.

I turned to look at Tony and said, "It's no good. All I'm getting is "Hello, Ann"."

I was somewhat uptight with whoever the voice belonged to and wished it would just go away and I said so to Tony.

"O.K., then," said Tony. "Let's both try to forget it and maybe it won't come back any more. I can see it's worrying you."

"Only because I don't understand," I replied. "I can honestly say I don't feel anything will harm me, but it's something that's never happened before and that's what's worrying me."

I paused for a moment and said, "Tony, you don't think I'm cracking up, do you?"

Tony smiled and put his arm around me. "Come on, love, let's wait and see if anything else happens," and with that we went up to bed.

As I lay in my bed I just hoped it was going to be the last time I would hear the voice again. I put the pillow over my head, my old habit of a lifetime, and went to sleep. I could only have been asleep for a couple of hours when I woke up with a start. I could distinctly hear people talking. The words were not easy for me to make out but very jumbled. I sat bolt upright and looked across at Tony who was fast asleep. The pillow that had been over my head was missing and in a fit of panic I leant out of bed to see if it had fallen down by the side, but I couldn't feel it so I got out of bed to see where it had gone to. I looked under the bed and felt all around the bed itself, even under the eiderdown. It was nowhere to be seen. Suddenly I looked up at the pulled curtains, but why I didn't know. However, to my amusement, I saw the outline of the pillow behind them. I was absolutely flabbergasted and wondered how the hell it got there!

The voices that had woken me up were now getting faint and I grabbed my pillow from behind the curtain and got into bed quickly, pulling it tightly over my ears. For a little while I was too frightened to go to sleep and was hesitant as to whether I should wake Tony or not. I decided against it as I thought if I kept on about it too much Tony would begin to think I was seriously ill or something. Then I had second thoughts about it as I knew Tony only too well and he would undoubtedly believe me.

By now the voices had gone completely and I managed to go back to sleep. When I got up that morning I changed my mind yet again about telling Tony and decided not to tell Tony what had happened during the night. I told myself that if I mentioned nothing at all in future maybe it would go away. I went to work that day feeling very tired, and it bothered me a little because I didn't understand what the voices wanted of me. Despite the fact I had promised myself not to think of it, I found it very difficult not to as the whole thing was new to me. However, I tried hard to get on with my work and at lunch-time Tony picked me up for our usual drive.

As the day went by I heard nothing more of the voices, which pleased me. I was beginning to feel much more relaxed and I hoped I had beaten it, whatever it was. If it meant that it had all been a figment of my imagination, then I had beaten that, too. The thing that came out of this which gave me the most satisfaction and pleasure was that, in all of this odd and unusual occurrence, not once had I turned to the pills. I had come this far and my intake was still only four daily, so the last thing I wanted to do was to increase the dosage and go backwards.

That evening, when we came home after visiting Mum and the girls, I prayed I wouldn't hear any more voices and I made up my mind to tell Tony about the pillow incident. I felt it was now the right time to tell him and, as it made me nervous just thinking about it, I needed his support, just in case it happened again. I explained what had happened the previous night and looked at his face, waiting to see what his expression would be and what his reaction would show. I so needed him to believe me, but would he? It certainly sounded so far fetched as I told him about the pillow being moved from my head to behind the curtain.

Thankfully, he did believe me and I was so relieved.

"You don't think it is my coming off the pills that's doing it, do you?" I asked Tony.

"Why should you think that?" he replied in a surprised manner. "You've never experienced anything like this before, so there's no reason to think it's them now."

"I know that," I said, "But what is worrying me is that I don't know the reason for it all, so I've got to put it down to being the pills."

"I don't think it is them," said Tony, "But I think I can come up with the answer. I think the spirit world is trying to make contact with you. In fact, since you started telling me about the voice saying "Ann", I was sure it was a spirit and I still think it is."

I knew a little about what he was referring to in that the voices may have belonged to spirit people, but it hadn't crossed my mind that they were trying to contact me, nor why. I still wasn't convinced that what Tony was saying was true. If his explanation was correct, why should they want to contact me?

"Let's forget it," I said. "Perhaps I won't have any more contact, after all, I heard nothing this evening and I was hearing the voice around this time last night and the night before."

By the time I got to bed that night I had heard nothing more, so that made me feel much better. However, at the back of my mind I felt it wouldn't be the last of it, a fact somehow I could be sure of. It wasn't that I had ever feared the voice, but it unnerved me as to why it wanted me and I certainly didn't want a repeat perform-ance of the previous night. The way I felt as I drifted off to sleep I felt sure I wouldn't.

I had never been a good sleeper so it took some time for me to get off to sleep and as I lay awake I had forgotten the experience I had been having as my mind thought of other things. Eventually sleep fell upon me and it seemed to me as it I had only been asleep a couple of minutes when, once again, I was woken up. This time when I heard talking the pillow was still in its rightful position over my head and had not been removed. Half asleep, I wondered if I was dreaming and turned over, pulling the pillow tightly over my ears. Sleep came across me once more until, yet again, I heard the voices, only this time they were a lot louder. No matter what I did with the pillow it made no difference, and so I decided to put both my pillows over my head, hoping they would block everything out, but instead the voices got even louder. I realised I was wasting my time trying to ignore them so I decided to listen to what they were trying to tell me and took both the pillows away from my head. I put my hands behind my head and just lay there. I could tell it was early morning because the light was coming through the windows so I looked at the clock for confirmation. Good God, I thought, it's only five o'clock! I was so tired as I hadn't managed to go to sleep until the early hours, and was then woken up at this unearthly hour. I was not amused, to say the least, but at the same time was curious as to what the voices were saying. There was no "Hello, Ann," this time but instead they seemed to be talking amongst themselves, like they did the previous night, only much louder this time. How I knew that I don't know, but I did know there was more than one person speaking. As much as I persevered I could not figure out what they were talking about but I could hear them, that much I knew! I was beginning to get fed up with it by now for, whoever *they* were, *they* were keeping me awake and by now I was getting not only fed up with it but upset as well. Since I had been coming off the pills it had affected my sleep. I had come to terms with that as I so desperately wanted to come off the drugs and that was one of the side-effects, but now I was being woken up early by voices which I didn't understand and that was difficult to cope with. I tried to remember what Tony had said the previous night about spirit wanting to get in touch with me and I thought, Well, if this is the way they were trying then I didn't want to know. At least this convinced me that it wasn't all in my mind anyway, for I knew now it was spirit or whatever else anyone wanted to call it. I was hearing the voices as clear as I had ever heard anyone in the living, just like Tony's, Mum's and the kids. They sounded like normal, ordinary people and for some unknown reason I knew I was as sane as anyone else, but I was far from pleased about it. If this was how it was to be I didn't want to know.

I put my hands over my ears and said out loud, "Please, please, go away, whoever you are, please."

But to no avail. They didn't appear to listen to what I was saying but continued talking instead. I had to get out of bed as they were driving me crazy when, suddenly, Tony woke up.

"What's the time, Ann?" he asked.

I looked at the clock. It was now gone six and I told him. Tony could tell by my face that all was not well and asked me what the matter was.

"Nothing," I replied, trying my best to conceal my true feelings.

I went downstairs and turned on the electric fire. I sat down beside it with tears rolling down my face. The voices were still carrying on talking. I just didn't know what to do as it was obvious they were taking no notice of me. I hadn't been downstairs more than five minutes when Tony came into the living room. When he saw my tears and the state I was in he demanded,

"What the hell is the matter?"

"They won't stop talking," I replied.

"You mean the voices?" asked Tony.

"Yes, of course I mean the voices," I snapped.

"Alright, calm down, Ann," Tony said, speaking quieter. Although he knew what I was talking about he didn't fully understand, as he had never heard spirit himself or seen spirit, but he knew I was in a bad way and tried to comfort me.

He sat down beside me and said,

"Come on, love, I'll make you a nice cup of tea. Perhaps if we talk about it or whatever, it might help."

We were both perfectly helpless, not knowing what to do in this peculiar situation. Tony made the tea and as I sat there I wiped away the tears and blew my nose. I felt so vulnerable and perhaps a little bit foolish as I knew no one else, including Tony, could hear the voices so it was hard for me to cope with on my own. I was well aware Tony believed me implicitly and I tried to explain fully everything that I was experiencing, but I was nonetheless feeling out on a limb. I was glad, however, that Tony accepted what I had told him, which helped a little. What if I had had a husband who pooh-poohed such experiences and showed no interest or concern? I was lucky he wasn't like that, but then again, would spirit

107

have chosen to speak to me if Tony had been any different? All these questions, and yet no answers.

When Tony came in with the tea he asked me if I was feeling any better.

"Well," I said, having composed myself enough to reply, "The voices seem to have gone." I moved my head from side to side, trying to listen, but the had gone and I was so relieved. I looked back at Tony and smiled.

"Yes, love, they've gone," I repeated.

"Oh, I'm glad about that," said Tony. "Was it that bad?" he asked in a way in which he almost daren't, or else didn't really want to, know the true answer.

"To be quite honest," I said, "They were driving me up the wall. I've been awake since five o'clock and up until now they haven't stopped."

"I think it's time we had a bit of help on this," said Tony.

A bit, I thought!

"We need all the help we can get!" I said, "But how?" I asked.

"Well, I thought of Derek Markwell the other night when you were first hearing voices, but I put it aside as I thought, like you, it might have gone away by now. It's time we gave him a ring, I think, don't you?"

Derek is a medium and a very good one at that. He had been a friend of ours for years and we knew he had a good reputation so we waited until a reasonable hour and phoned him. Unfortunately, he couldn't see us for a week, so as Tony put the phone down he said to me,

"Let's hope things will quieten down for a while for there is no one else I can ask."

I tried to put things into perspective and said to Tony,

"Come on, let's go out for the day and try to take our minds off it."

It was Sunday and there was no reason for us to sit around all day moping.

108

"Where do you want to go?" asked Tony.

"I don't care," I replied, "As long as I get out for a while."

I rang Mum to tell her our plans and that I wouldn't be round today, that is, unless she needed anything which she didn't, and I added that more than likely we would pop in that evening when we got back, or it if was too late, we'd see them the following day.

I must admit the day was a very peaceful one and I thoroughly enjoyed it. We managed to put our troubles to the back of our minds and we didn't get back till late and I even slept well that night. I heard no voices at all and the following morning I got up feeling wonderfully refreshed. As far as I am concerned there is nothing like a good night's sleep to put me in a good mood.

CHAPTER ELEVEN

The girl I worked with had Mondays as her day off and it was also a quiet day as far as the workload went, thank goodness. I had only been in an hour when I had finished all the paperwork and ready to serve the public. I was still feeling good after the happy day out we had spent the previous day followed by a good night's sleep. Despite all my trials and tribulations I am the type of person who still had a smile for everyone, whether I feel good or bad, but today I felt like smiling, after the experiences of the previous week when I felt upset.

As usual, Tony and I had our packed lunch by the river, but this time I made sure I kept chatting for I didn't want another episode like before. Fortunately, everything went well and, after our hour was up, Tony took me back to work.

It wasn't busy at all that afternoon so in between serving the customers I was able to sit and read a book. There was a stool near my chair where the other girl sat but, being Monday, it was naturally vacant. I looked across at the stool, wishing she had been there with me as we had always found something to talk about and I missed her company.

I got so engrossed in the book I was reading when all of a sudden I felt very cold, and yet the weather was warm and sunny. I shuddered and shivered and tried to concentrate harder on my book, draping my cardigan round my shoulders. As I did so, a customer came up so I put my book down and served him, after which I returned to my book. This time my thoughts were far from the story I was reading and I actually felt something or someone around me. I turned away from the window where I was sitting to look behind me. What it was I was expecting to see I don't know, but I had to look all the same. I knew nobody could come into the office as I had the key, but at the same time I was convinced someone was there, although I couldn't see anyone.

Good God, Ann, pull yourself together, I thought to myself and made an attempt to read my book once more, but my mind was not on it at all. It was almost as if I was waiting for something to appear before my very eyes, and as it happened I didn't have too long to wait. For suddenly, from out of nowhere, there was a shadow of a person. I could see it so clearly but I couldn't see who it was, but nevertheless, there, in the corner of my office, the shadow stood. I stared at it, then looked back at the window. I knew I had seen it as I had heard the voices but tried to block out what I had just seen. I looked at my watch to see if it was time yet for Tony to come and pick me up. In a way I had accepted the voices to a certain extent, but to see a shadow and accept that, well, that was a different matter altogether. It is very strange, but for some reason or other I didn't feel frightened or bothered with the shadow as I did with the voices. Maybe it was because I was seeing something in black and white, although not clearly, but I felt secure in its presence. I decided to take a second look at it but this time the shadow had gone and in a way I felt sad. Whoever it was, I didn't want them to think I didn't like them or, come to think of it, I didn't mind the voices either. It is just that I wished I had had more warning and also that they hadn't kept me awake half the night.

I sat for a while, thinking over what was going on around me when I heard a voice say, "Are you ready?"

This snapped me out of my deep thoughts and, seeing it was Tony, said, "Sorry, love, can you hang on for ten minutes?"

As a rule I would have had everything done by now and would be ready for when Tony came for me, so no wonder Tony looked surprised when I had asked him to wait for me. He did wait, however, and soon we were on our way home. We popped in to see Mum and the girls for an hour and then went on home. I told Tony about the shadow, but this time I didn't put any importance on what I had seen and it was almost as if I had accepted all of it without question or doubt, and

110

Tony had noticed this and remarked on it.

He said, "It is as if you have accepted what I said about spirit getting in touch with you, after all."

"Yes, I have. Why, I don't really know, but yes, I think I agree with you now, although I don't pretend to understand any of it."

"I'm sure you will in time," said Tony assuringly.

"I hope you're right," I said, "But if this talking continues I don't want any of it, I just can't cope if it means I have to lose my sleep at night."

"I understand," said Tony.

I had a question to put to Tony. "If they are trying to get in touch with me, why is it me they want and not you?"

I had to ask this because for years Tony had always been interested in spiritualism, whereas I had only ever gone to a clairvoyant to tell me my future, and the spirit world in general had never appealed to me.

"What does that matter?" replied Tony. "In my opinion you should feel privileged and honoured that they have chosen you to speak to. I would love to be in contact with them, you don't know how fortunate you are."

"Sorry, love," I said, thinking I may have touched a nerve.

"It's just that it is all new to me and, although we're not perfect, I would have thought they would have picked someone better than me, especially with my past."

"Ann," said Tony in his stern voice, "Stop knocking yourself. You were just ill and now you are getting better and that's all that matters."

I said, "Let's forget about it for now. I still don't know if they are staying or going so we'll take each day as it comes and worry about it later if necessary," said Tony.

"That's all well and good, but if they keep me awake tonight then I don't want to know," I said.

111

Tony nodded in agreement and as I got ready for bed downstairs I felt the same coldness as I had experienced at work that day. Once again I was aware someone was around me and whoever it may be I didn't want to scare them away, so I continued to get ready for bed. Tony was upstairs and in a way I was glad, for I sensed the spirit was pleased I was on my own. I sat down on the armchair in my nightclothes and for the first time I asked who it was, instead of them speaking to me first. There was no reply, which was what I half-expected and I'm not sure why, but I had a lovely feeling of security about me and I knew I had nothing to fear. Also, this time, I saw no shadow but I was aware, without doubt, there was someone there.

Tony came down and asked if I was coming up, to which I replied in the affirmative. Once again, I told Tony about what had happened and got into bed. Tony turned the bedside light out and said to me, "I hope you have a good night," and with that we both settled down to go to sleep. I say we both settled down to sleep, and this applied to Tony more than me for I heard him snoring within minutes of him shutting his eyes. It wasn't long before I followed him in the land of nod, however, which was most unusual for me, to fall asleep that quickly.

Yes, it was too good to be true, for once again, after a couple of hours sleep, I was woken up by the sound of voices. Each time I heard them they became stronger and clearer and this particular night it was no different. By the time morning came I was shattered but I knew I had to go to work.

By now Tony wasn't very happy with the situation for it was beginning to affect my health. I had come this far and we didn't want anything to stand in the way of my progress. He telephoned Derek and explained to him what was going on and told him that, since he had spoken to him last, things had gone from bad to worse. Derek told Tony he had the day off so he would be able to pop over that morning to see me. Without checking with me, Tony agreed.

"What about my job?" I asked when he told me Derek was coming over.

"Don't worry," replied Tony. "I'll pop down and see the girl you work with to tell her you are not very well," and with that he went out.

I felt very nervous as I waited for Derek to arrive, for he had not told us exactly what time he would come over and I didn't want to be on my own when he arrived. I 'phoned Mum to tell her I'd be round as usual that evening. I hadn't told her anything about what had been happening to me of late, not that I didn't want to, for I had always told Mum everything in the past, but I felt I didn't really know enough about it myself so I kept it from her until I was sure.

As I put the 'phone down I said out loud, "Where the hell are you, Tony?"

He had been gone a good half an hour and I really did want him home before Derek arrived. Just then I heard a car pull up and, looking out of the window, I saw it was Tony. I gave a huge sigh of relief and opened the door for him. Not long after, Derek arrived with his wife. He explained that owing to what Tony had told him over the telephone he knew exactly what to do. He told me he would have to perform an exorcism and that he would start by saying the Lord's Prayer and call upon his Guides to help me. He would need two glasses from which he would pour water from one to the other.

He carried out this procedure in every room and then once over my head. I must be honest and say I understood absolutely nothing about what was going on, but I trusted Derek completely and put myself in his hands. Everything seemed fine after he left but then again I didn't know what to expect or how I was supposed to feel. All I wanted was some peace of mind and I hoped that what Derek had done would help me to find that peace.

Tony could only manage to have the morning off so at lunch-time he went back to work. I knew Mum would be out and the children, too, so I decided to sit and have a quiet afternoon. There was nothing on television so I thought I'd read a book. I felt much more relaxed and confident since Derek had been so I lay on the settee, reading.

After a little while the 'phone rang. It was Tony checking to see if I was alright. I assured him I was well and told him I'd see him later and went back to reading my book. However, not long afterwards, I had that same feeling of being watched, that cold sensation coming over me. I slowly took my eyes away from the book and looked towards the kitchen door. The door itself was shut and between the wall and the door I could see a shadow. This time it was a bit clearer and I could see the outline. It was the outline of a Red Indian, despite the fact that it was only a shadow. I could see it much clearer than I had the previous day and I just sat still, staring at it. I didn't feel at all threatened or frightened by it. My first thoughts were, Where the hell did he come from and wishing I could see him more clearly.

I don't know for sure how long I stared at him but I do know I couldn't take my eyes away from him. Then, suddenly, as quickly as he appeared, he went. His form just vanished in front of me. In a way I was disappointed for since seeing the

113

shadow I had felt more at ease than hearing just voices, and I really didn't mind the talking so much except they just wouldn't leave me alone at night, and it was that which was making me ill.

I sat still for a long time that afternoon, thinking about all the events that had occurred in the past week. I had now fully accepted that I was in communication with the spirit world but the question was, why me? I know I had spoken to Tony about this but as far as I was concerned, with my past record, it just didn't make sense to pick someone like me for the job. I had always been under the impression from the time I had started seeing mediums that they called upon good people. Who knows, some of them may even have been holy, and I certainly wasn't that. I stopped thinking about that and began to think about what would happen this coming night. I still trusted Derek, but obviously the spirit had taken no notice. They hadn't left me and I didn't want to lose any more sleep, but although I was now seeing spirit, perhaps by having Derek round, they might stop talking during the night. That remained to be seen. Tony came home early.

"Are you going round your Mum's?" he asked.

"Of course," I replied.

"Well, I only asked, seeing you weren't well this morning," Tony remarked.

"No, I'm O.K., love," I said, and I told him all about what happened that afternoon. Like mine, his reply was to wait and see what happens tonight. By the time I got back from Mum's I was eager to get to bed for I was absolutely shattered.

I was in tears, however, the following morning, for in the night it seemed to me as if the matter had worsened. The voices were still waking me up and, although they weren't as loud in the morning as they were in the middle of the night, I had noticed that during the day I would hardly hear a word from them. It seemed they just wanted to chat at night to me.

Once again, Tony rang Derek, and this time he asked us if we would go to his house instead and could we make it that evening. Tony went to my place of work to explain that I was still unwell and would not be in for the rest of the week. He went off to work after that and I went back to bed. For some unknown reason I knew I could get a couple of hours' sleep without any interruption and I didn't. When I got up at lunch-time I felt a lot better, but I had made up my mind I didn't want to know the spirit world or anything to do with it whatsoever. I still had to trust in Derek and I hoped that tonight he would be more successful.

I had just made myself a cup of tea and sat down when I saw the shadow. I knew instinctively it was the Red Indian back again.

"Please go away, whoever you are," I said, addressing the Indian, and then turned my head away to look out of the window. I thought that by simply ignoring him he would take the hint and just go.

Just then I heard the words, "DON'T GO," so plainly. I had heard all the voices before, chatting to themselves, and only a few times had any of them said "Hello", but this was the first time I had heard a few words directly being said to me. I turned away from the window to look back to see if he was still standing there, but he had gone. Oh, well, I thought, at least he took notice of what I had asked.

I had a few things to do before Tony got home and I wanted to get everything done before we went to Derek's. I 'phoned Mum to tell her I was going out so I made up some excuse as I still didn't really want to tell her about it until Derek had managed to get rid of them.

As I put the 'phone down I heard *"Don't go,"* again, this time even louder. I thought I had better reply so I looked around the room to see if the Indian had turned up again, but I couldn't see him.

"Don't go where?" I asked. As I stood there in wonderment I suddenly thought to myself, thank God no one can see me! Here I am talking to thin air, but then again I knew differently this time and, although I couldn't see him, I could feel his presence in the room. On previous occasions I had only felt a shiver and then saw a shadow, this time I was well aware he was standing near to me in the same room but I couldn't see him at all.

"Don't go where?" I asked again.

"Man," came back the reply.

At least I was getting some response, but I didn't know what it meant. I had the sense to realise that he obviously didn't want me to go somewhere but I didn't understand the bit about the man. I played around with the words in my head for about five minutes when it suddenly dawned on me. The only man I was going to see was Derek, but surely he wasn't telling me not to see him. Derek had worked for the spirit world for years and this Indian was a spirit so why should he advise me not to go? Despite the fact that I couldn't understand him saying so for those reasons, it was the only interpretation I could come up with.

115

I had no intention of ignoring the Indian's warning, but I knew I needed some form of help, so I told the Indian this and it was my only hope of getting some peace of mind. By this time it was almost as if I had known the Indian for years and yet I had only met him twice and, although I had only seen his shadow, I knew he was a Red Indian. I had no idea what sort of person I was talking to or anything about him whatsoever.

Suddenly, everything went quiet and I knew he had gone. His presence was no longer in the room with me. I sat back feeling very strange, for I had been talking to a spirit I knew nothing about and yet it had happened so naturally. I felt no fear at all of him, nor of the whole unusual situation.

I had been sitting quietly for a while trying to digest what had happened when I heard the front door. I shot out of the armchair, having forgotten all about the time, and realised it was getting late. I was still in my dressing gown when I opened the door sheepishly, only to find it was Tony.

"Hello, love," he said. "How are you feeling now?"

"Well, I'm fine. Actually I've got something to tell you," I said, and continued to tell him all about the afternoon's experience. I finished by saying,

"I'll leave you to think about it and you can let me know your thoughts on it," and I dashed upstairs to get ready to go to Derek's.

When I came downstairs Tony asked me why I hadn't 'phoned him at work to tell him about what had been happening.

"Well, it didn't really bother me that much and I certainly didn't feel frightened by the spirit's presence. In fact, I felt quite happy with him," I admitted.

"But what about you being disturbed in the night?" Tony asked.

"Well, that I certainly don't want so I really do want Derek to remove it all, if at all possible," I said and with that we got our coats and left for Derek's house. We had arranged a time to be there and didn't want to be late.

On our way there I was thinking about how tired I was feeling and I would be glad when it was bed-time, but then I started thinking about all the voices in my head. Although I was tired I was apprehensive about going to sleep in the knowledge that I would more than likely be woken up as before. I just hoped Derek would be able to help and I told Tony so. He said, "Derek is a good medium, Ann, so I'm sure he'll be able to help. I know last time wasn't successful but maybe you'll have to see him again for him to get rid of them sufficiently."

I agreed with him and changed the subject. We were not far from Derek's house now, when all of a sudden I could feel the spirit was back. The feeling was almost overpowering and it was almost as if he was trying to take me over.

"Tony, he's here," I said in a soft whisper.

"Do what?" replied Tony.

"The Indian. He's here!" I repeated, somewhat annoyed that he hadn't cottoned on to what I was saying the first time.

"What's he want?" Tony asked.

"I don't know, do I!" I replied.

Tony tried to act calmly in the circumstances and told me not to worry for we would soon be at Derek's house. As I sat there I was feeling a little nervous for, although I had accepted the Red Indian being with me earlier that afternoon, he hadn't been that close to me. Now, it was almost too overwhelming with his presence and I could sense he was angry, which in turn made me feel nervous. I wondered what he could possibly be feeling angry about. Was he angry about me going to Derek's and, if so, why? Derek wouldn't hurt me as far as I was concerned but was trying to help me and I trusted him. Just then, the car came to a halt.

"Here we are," said Tony.

Thank goodness, I thought, maybe I can get something sorted out, but at the same time I was feeling sorry for the Indian, and, just as my emotions changed, so the answer suddenly came to me. What Derek was doing for me was taking the spirits away from me and I then realised that that was the reason the Indian didn't want me here. Why he wanted me to stay away from Derek and that meant I would have to leave straight away and go back home. Although the Indian hadn't said a word to me since his presence in the car I spoke instead, hoping he would understand. I carefully chose my words and said, "I'm sorry, but all of this is making me ill. I've just got to see Derek." I quite liked the Indian as he had done me no harm personally, but I found I couldn't cope with the chatting during the night,

117

and with that I got out of the car and hoped he would understand. Tony asked me if I was alright as he rang the front door bell of Derek's house.

"Yes, I'm fine," I replied, but all the time I felt I was not going to be able to get rid of the Indian. I could tell he was still with me even as Derek greeted us and showed us into his living room.

As I sat down the anger from the Indian was still with me so I tried to ignore him, but it was very difficult.

Just then, without any warning, I turned to Derek, bringing my hand clutched across my chest and said, "The Indian greets you."

It all happened so quickly and I felt embarrassed. Derek is one of the very best mediums we had ever met and I have always held the very highest regard for him, so it made me feel a bit of a fool.

"Sorry about that, Derek," I said apologetically, "But there is this Indian around me."

"Don't worry," replied Derek, "I understand. The Indian was greeting me as a friend but in anger."

I sat back for a moment in amazement. How did Derek know he was angry and I asked him how he knew.

"I have an Indian guide so I'm aware of the signs," explained Derek. "And I can assure you he is definitely not pleased with me."

I told Derek all about what had happened over the past couple of days and explained that I didn't mind it all happening during the day, but I couldn't keep up with not sleeping at night-time. Derek understood my problem but explained to me that, if it was meant for me to have spirit with me, then more than likely he wouldn't be able to help me. I accepted what he said and Derek performed yet another exorcism, but whilst he was carrying out the procedure the Indian came in stronger than ever and he wasn't happy. As I sat waiting for Derek to finish, I knew there was absolutely no way I was going to get rid of this spirit and Derek confirmed this.

"All we can hope for, Ann, is that tonight it might calm them down a bit, but I can't remove the spirit from you," said Derek.

I thanked Derek for trying and asked him a question.

"I would like to know if it's possible to tell me who the Indian is."

Derek replied, "Yes, he's your guide."

I heard mediums talk about their guides before and knew they were there for protection, but that was about all I knew about the subject.

"Is this Indian here to protect me, Derek?" I asked.

"Yes, he is," replied Derek.

As we left Derek's house all the thoughts I had had previously regarding the spirit world upsetting my sleep evaded me. Instead, I was concentrating more on the Red Indian. Somehow it made me feel good that someone was protecting me and on the way home, when Tony asked me how I felt and if the Indian was still with me, I replied,

"I feel fine, and the Indian has gone. Maybe what Derek has done will quieten them down a bit and hopefully that will be the end to the bad nights I've been having."

The Indian didn't come back that evening but in a way I was hoping that he wouldn't stay away forever. Deep inside me I knew it wouldn't be the last time I would see him. That night, as I lay in bed, I thought about what had gone on in the past weeks regarding the voices, followed by the appearance of the Indian during the past couple of days. I was glad I had gone to Derek who explained and confirmed that it was the spirit world communicating with me. At the same time, however, I felt a little bit sad for, although Derek had said he didn't really think they would go, I wondered if what he had done would work. As much as I was feeling ill from the lack of sleep, I had felt so at ease in the Indian's presence and I hoped my feelings would be correct in that it wouldn't be the last time I would see him.

As I turned over to try to sleep, I spoke to the spirit voices.

"Please don't keep me awake tonight. Please go away," and as I said those words my eyes shut. Suddenly, I saw a large window and behind that window there were many faces. I could see them so clearly but what struck me was how miserable these faces looked. I somehow sensed it was because of what I had just said. As I

119

looked back at them I felt riddled with guilt, so I felt I needed to explain myself.

"Look," I said, "I don't mind talking to you, but I can't go on without sleep. If you understand what I'm saying to you why don't you all try talking to me during the daytime, rather than during the night."

All of a sudden their faces changed and their expressions changed from looking sad to happy. I wondered why I hadn't tried talking directly to them before, but anyway I hoped it would work and I drifted off to sleep.

I was woken up again during the night after all, but the voices were much quieter and, although I was woken up a couple of times in all, I found it wasn't so difficult to get back to sleep again.

That morning, when I got up, Tony asked me how I had got on and I told him what I had said to them before I went to sleep. I admitted to him that it wasn't too bad for they certainly seemed to have quietened down a little.

"Well," said Tony, looking relieved, "Let's see how it goes in the next couple of days. I'm so glad you didn't have too bad a night."

I smiled at him for I was glad of his support. I'm convinced anyone else would have surely thought I was potty, but not Tony.

There was no sign of the Indian that day and, to be honest, I was a little disappointed. It would be the start of the weekend the following day and I was pleased I had been absent from work that week and that Tony would be home all over the weekend. That afternoon I went round to Mum's. I wondered whether to tell her what had been going on or not. I really wanted to give it another couple of days for I wasn't sure if they were staying or not. So far that day the voices and the spirit Indian had gone completely.

I had left a message for Tony to pick me up when he returned from work and time went quickly. It seemed no time at all before Tony turned up for me.

"I'll see you in the morning, Mum," I said, as I kissed her goodbye, and then popped in the living room to say goodnight to the kids.

Tony asked me how things had been that day. I knew he was referring to the spirit world. I told him everything was alright but that I had had no vision of the Indian.

120

"You sound a bit disappointed," said Tony.

"Yes, I am in a way," I replied. "I rather liked his presence."

We went out that night with some friends and I was pleased to be able to forget it all for a while. I had no problems that night for not once did I hear any voices, and I felt so much better the following morning.

The next day was a Saturday and I knew Tony was glad to not have to go to work till Monday.

Mum and I went shopping and when we got back I settled down to a quiet afternoon at home. Nothing was said about the spirit world since early morning and Tony put a film on for us both to sit and watch. It was a comedy which made me laugh a lot. All of a sudden I felt the Indian's presence. As I looked up I could see his shadowy form, but this time it was a little clearer to see. I could see he had his arms folded and I was very pleased to see him and told him so.

Tony noticed my attention had wandered from watching the film and asked me what the matter was.

"He's back!" I said excitedly.

"You mean the Indian?" asked Tony.

"Yes," I replied and Tony got up to turn the video off.

Tony asked me if the Indian was saying anything.

"No, he's just standing there," I said.

Tony sat back down and said, "Why don't you ask him who he is or something?"

"Like what?" I asked. "As far as I'm concerned he's my guide."

"Well, try asking him anything, just to see what he says," said Tony persistently.

I thought, Anything to keep the peace, so I looked back to where the Indian was standing. He just stood there looking back at me.

"Aren't you going to say anything?" I asked the Indian.

121

There was no reply, so I said to Tony, "He's not saying anything."

"We might as well finish the film then," said Tony, and he got up to put the film back on. I looked back at the Indian but he had gone, although I sensed his presence, and as I watched the television I heard the same voice I had heard the other day which said, "Hello Ann." I knew it was a man's voice speaking but it didn't belong to the Indian. I asked Tony to turn off the television as, for some unknown reason, I knew I was about to have a conversation with this spirit person. Tony was wondering what on earth was happening so I said, "Sorry, love, it's just that someone's here and I'm sure he's going to say something."

"Who's here? The Indian?" asked Tony.

"No, all I know is it is a man's voice." I said.

Tony sat there dumbfounded. Just then, the man whose voice it was stood in front of me. I could see him so vividly. He was smoking a pipe and as solid a human being as you or I.

The tension was obviously getting to Tony because he said, "Well, tell me what's happening to put me out of my misery."

The man told me to describe him to Tony. I heard him so clearly and so I told Tony all about the man and how he was dressed, and that he was smoking a pipe.

Tony looked flabbergasted and asked me to describe the man again, as if he wasn't believing what he had heard the first time. I carried out his wishes and after I had finished the description Tony got up.

"I won't be a minute," he said, and with that he rushed upstairs.

The man standing in front of me smiled and said, "I like you."

I felt both bemused and embarrassed by his kind compliment.

"Why thank you," I said, wondering what the hell to say next! I hears Tony running downstairs and I looked towards the living room door. As he entered the room I could see he was carrying something.

"Look at this and tell me who it is," he said.

122

It was a photograph of the man who was standing in front of me. I told Tony and asked who he was.

"He's my Dad," confirmed Tony. He looked and sounded both shocked and stunned.

"I'm sorry, love," I said, "I didn't realise it was him," and I tried not to upset Tony by it all.

"No, it's alright," he said. "Go on, please. It's the first time I've ever had contact from him."

Tony's father had died before I met Tony and I had never really asked about him. I had only met his mother a few times and this was the first time I had ever seen a photograph of him, and it was certainly the first time I had met him.

I looked at Tony's father and said to him, "I'm sorry, but I don't remember ever having seen a photograph of you before."

He replied, "Tell Tony about the fish," and he held up a barbel fish.

He added, "Remember to say its name, barbel. He'll know what I mean."

Without further ado I said to Tony,

"He's on about a fish. It looks big to me." My knowledge of fish is limited to say the least! Just then I remembered his Dad saying what it was called so I quickly said, "It's a barbel."

Tony looked amazed. "How did you know that?" he asked with staring eyes.

"Your Dad just told me," I replied.

"That's something you couldn't have known about, Ann," said Tony, and he explained to me that it was the biggest fish his Dad had ever caught and Tony was with him the day he caught it!

"That's amazing," he said, "But I don't understand what you are seeing. It's not that I disbelieve you, but this is extraordinary proof."

I knew what Tony meant for I had told him the spirit was coming to me but I had never been able to give any proof of it before. It wasn't that I had to prove to Tony what was happening to me, but this was a different matter. His very own father was here, in the same room as us, giving his son concrete evidence of life after death. I was thrilled for Tony for I knew how much it meant to him to have communication from his father.

Tony's father wasn't the only visitor that weekend. It was almost as if a whole new world had opened up for me. I could see and hear all of them as clearly as the living, and it was so much easier than just hearing the voices for now I could see who was talking to me. Nearly all the spirit people who communicated were family, including Tony's Uncle Bob, who was a lovely man.

CHAPTER TWELVE

It didn't take very long for me to settle down with the spirit world and the Red Indian was now always present, but in the shadows. Whoever I spoke to from the spirit world I was aware that the Indian was with me too, and I was happy to know he was there. I don't know why, but I felt a bond between us and although I loved the company of the spirit people it was different with the Indian.

Within the two or three months which followed I was able to see and hear the spirit people as perfectly as the living. I still hadn't said a word to Mum and so far only Tony knew what was going on, but I knew I would have to say something sooner or later. There were times when I was saying things without really knowing what I was on about in front of Tony, and I was worried I would do the same with Mum.

So far, when I had gone round to Mum's, nothing had happened but I knew it was more by luck than judgement that nothing slipped out, so that night I decided to tell Mum all about it. When I arrived at Mum's house she was sitting in the living room watching television with my youngest daughter. My eldest daughter was upstairs getting ready to go out.

"Mum, can I have a word with you on your own?" I asked.

"Yes, of course you can," she said as she got up to go into the kitchen. She began to look concerned and asked me if anything was wrong.

"No, there's nothing wrong," I said, "I just want to have a little chat, that's all."

I could tell by the expression on her face that she instantly thought it was a problem regarding the pills, so I put her mind at rest by saying, "I'm fine, really, and before you start worrying it's nothing to do with the pills."

She sighed with relief and smiled, then walked towards the cooker and put the kettle on. As I sat down waiting for her to make the tea I wondered what her reaction would be. I truly wanted her to believe me. She had some idea about spirit for I had always told her about the times I had been to see a medium, but her attitude had always been that when you're dead, you're dead. Very often her comment was, "Do you really believe in all that rubbish?" so I knew what I was up against and it would be nigh impossible to convince her that what had been happening to me was the absolute truth.

Mum made the tea and came over to sit down.

"Well, what's it all about, then?" she asked.

I took a deep breath and proceeded to tell her all about the events of the past months, including the bit about Tony's father and his Uncle Bob and all the other spirit people, but most of all about the Red Indian.

She said nothing for a few minutes but sipped her tea instead.

Eager to get a reaction from her I said, "Aren't you going to say anything, then?"

"Well, you know my opinion on that subject," she replied. "I don't really believe in all that, but on the other hand that doesn't mean I don't believe you."

Thank God for that, I thought.

"Well, at least you accept what I say is true, that's the main thing," I said.

Mum said, "I've never heard you say anything like this before, so I can't see why you should make it all up now."

The one thing about my mother, she would always come straight to the point and speak her mind.

125

"The thing is, Ann, are you happy being able to talk to whoever it is you talk to?" Mum enquired.

I laughed to myself for I knew she wouldn't say 'spirit' and also because she didn't completely understand what it was all about, nor honestly believe in it.

"Yes, Mum, I am," I assured her. "I can't put into words how much I am feeling happier than I have been for a long time."

"Then that's all that counts, love," Mum said. "And have you thought that if you are that happy you might not need the pills any more?"

I sat and stared at her. I hadn't really thought about the pills very much lately. I was still on my four a day, but I must admit that since meeting the spirit world the pills weren't paramount in my life. Mum had certainly come up with the million dollar question, one which hadn't crossed my mind.

"Well let's hope so, Mum, but that would be a miracle in itself," I said.

It was no secret that if Mum had one wish it would be for me to be completely cured of drugs, and in a way I could see a tiny glimmer of hope in her eyes. When I was back home that evening, I was thinking about the Indian. So far he had been in the shadows for some considerable time and I just wished he would show himself to me properly. He hadn't been around all day but I had a feeling he would turn up soon. I had to wait until the following week when I felt his presence much stronger and I hoped my wish would be granted. It happened one evening when I was sitting, reading a book. Tony was upstairs doing some studying when the presence of the Indian seemed very strong indeed. Taking my eyes off the book I looked down and noticed a pair of feet on the floor in front of me. On the feet were a pair of gaily-coloured moccasins and as I stared at them I felt quite excited. Very cautiously I looked straight ahead and, to my astonishment, stood the Red Indian as solid and as normal as any human being on earth. My book dropped out of my hands I was so taken aback. I sat there in awe of this spirit, and as I cast my eyes over him I could see he had such clear, blue eyes which stared back at me. He was silent as he stood there, a good six feet tall and quite majestic in his stance.

Around his head was a band holding his hair off his face and on each side of his face his hair was plaited in brown leather strips. I could see he had a feather hanging loosely down one of his shoulders and another plait down the back of his hair with a feather plaited in between the hair. The feather was white, a brilliant

126

white. It was so bright that I could hardly take my eyes off it.

It was almost as if he and I were two mind locked together, for I knew the feather had some significance, but I wasn't sure exactly what it was. I looked back at the eyes again and somehow I knew they were smiling at me. There were lines around his eyes and I could tell he had somehow earned them in some way or another. He had more lines around his mouth and just then he started to smile. His lips parted and he started to laugh. I expect it was owing to the expression on my face at the time! His beautiful teeth were brilliant white and gleaming. He suddenly stopped laughing but his smile didn't go away. Looking up at him I hoped he wouldn't go and that he would always appear like this.

He was only about twenty-four years old but he looked a bit older. One could tell by looking at his eyes that he had had to grow up quicker than his years would normally expect, but then again he had kept some of his boyish charms. I started to look down past his face and saw he had a thick neck and wide shoulders. He had a very broad chest and as he breathed I could see the muscles rippling. His waist was almost the same size as his hips, but a fraction smaller, and he donned by a loin cloth. His legs were strong-looking and his skin a beautiful bronze colour.

I thought to myself that I had seen many old cowboy and indian films and had I ever wished for a good looking Indian, then here I had one right in front of me. Only this time I knew I wasn't wishing or day-dreaming, he was for real. He started laughing at me again as he stood there with his arms crossed. I noticed he had two arm bands on, one was high up on one arm, the other near to his wrist on the other, and both brightly coloured.

I looked back at his neck to see he had a necklace, which looked like animal teeth hanging from the thread, but what animal they once belonged to I had no idea.

Just then he stopped laughing and unfolded his arms. He lifted one arm up behind him and pulled out an arrow. I hadn't noticed it before, but could now see he had a strap across his chest which held a small leather container on his back where he kept his arrows. Up until now I had only been interested in what he looked like, for I had waited for this moment for months.

He took hold of the arrow and held it out in front of me. I could tell he was trying to say something to me and it then dawned on me why he had only said three words to me in the past. He didn't know all the English language and I didn't really know how much English he did know. It was obvious to me he was trying to tell me something important, don't ask me how I knew, but I could sense he had something to say.

I looked at the arrow he was holding, then looked back at him and said quietly, "What does it mean?"

His other hand moved towards the feather, the one which was hanging down, and he brought it forward, putting the arrow next to it. I looked at the arrow and the feather but I still didn't have a clue what he was trying to tell me. He pointed to the feather with the arrow, but all I could think of was how bright the white of the feather looked, and in a way this seemed to be an important factor. It was the *white* colour of the feather which drew my attention most of all and I knew he was trying to tell me his name.

"*White* what?" I asked him once more and again, he produced both the feather and the arrow. At first I thought of White Feather or White Arrow and when he brought the arrow forward I confirmed it to be White Arrow.

"That's it," I exclaimed, "Your name is White Arrow!"

By the expression on his face I could tell I was right and he smiled at me.

"Hello, White Arrow," I said, smiling back. "It's nice to know your name at last and also to see you so clearly."

He just nodded his head and smiled but said nothing.

I sat there feeling elated, for I was pleased I had worked out his name and so glad I could now actually see him. For a moment, however, I feared he might go away and never come back. I felt so close to him now that I really didn't want him to ever leave and, come to that, I had grown to love the other spirit people too and if they, plus White Arrow, all left me now, I would miss them terribly. If it was meant for them to go then I would rather them go now before I got too attached to them. I had been so terribly hurt in the past and I had promised myself nothing else would hurt me again. As I looked at the Indian I told him this and thought to myself, if only he could speak English. If only someone from the spirit world was around who could explain to him my feelings and anxieties it would make it much easier to communicate with him.

I didn't have the chance to find out if the Indian knew what I was thinking and saying, for Tony came downstairs.

128

"How's the book?" he asked.

I had forgotten all about the book I had been reading by now and started to tell him I had seen the Indian properly just minutes ago and I knew the Indian's name. I didn't tell Tony I didn't want the Indian or the other spirit people to go, for I didn't want to upset him. In a way, Tony had always been under the impression that I had been happy of late, except for having to take the pills of course, and although I knew it was stupid of me not to tell him how I felt about the spirit world and White Arrow, I thought it best not to say anything at this stage.

Tony was eager to hear all about the Indian, what he looked like and if he had told me his name and how, as he guessed, his English may be limited. Tony was aware that the Indian had only spoken three English words to me ever and so I explained fully about the white feather in his hair and the arrow.

"It looks like it will be difficult for you to communicate with him," said Tony.

"Yes, I know," I replied, "But I am hoping he'll learn to speak English as we go along. I'm just pleased I know his name now and in a way it is good that I had understood what he was trying to tell me without him having spoken at all."

From that day on White Arrow was around most of the time, and each time he appeared he was always in a solid, large as life form. No longer was he just a shadow but as a normal human being and, no matter what, I found I now loved him for he had found a way of making me happy. Tony was aware of all this and whenever White Arrow was around Tony knew somehow and I didn't have to tell him. He said that I seemed to change and Tony made a point of it.

One day Tony passed a remark about it to me. I can't explain fully, but I certainly did feel much happier when the spirit people are around me. I told Tony it wasn't only when White Arrow is around but all of them. As I told Tony this I wondered if it upset him in any way and I asked him.

"No, love," he replied. "I just hope they don't take you away from me, that's all."

"Oh, come on, love," I said. I walked towards him and put my arms around him. "They are spirit, people from the next world who were once earthly beings, you are here and very much alive. Nothing can come between us, I promise," I said, trying to console him.

129

"Well, I'm not so sure," he said, and walked away from me.

"What does that mean?" I asked as I followed him out to the kitchen. I couldn't and wouldn't let it rest so I said,

"Come on, you might as well tell me what's bugging you."

"It's him, White Arrow," he replied, and he marched back into the living room.

"Oh, for God's sake, he's only a spirit," I said.

"Yes, I know he is. I'm sorry, but it's just that he seems to take all of your attention lately."

"I'm sorry, love," I said. "This is all new to me as it is to you and I suppose I have ranted on a lot about him and the spirit world, but I didn't mean to, it's just that you are the only one I can really talk to who understands me."

Poor Tony looked so hurt and yet I had no intention of doing so. I wouldn't hurt him for the world and yet I didn't want to give up the spirit world or White Arrow. If it meant Tony getting hurt by all this I would have tried to stop it all and I told Tony so.

"No, I don't want you to do that," he replied. "Just give me time to adjust to it all and I'm sure I'll find it all as intriguing as you do, and I think it's marvellous that you have the ability to communicate with them. But as much as it is new to you, it's also a lot for me to take in."

I could sympathise with Tony and knew we would both have to learn to adjust to what was happening around us. One thing was evident to me now, and that was that our lives would never be the same again.

I found that in my daily life the spirit people would turn up at odd times but always White Arrow would be there, almost as if he was protecting me. I didn't mind and quite enjoyed the company. I also found whenever I was in the company of friends that always someone they once knew who had passed over would pop in to say Hello. I would describe them and whoever they belonged to instantly recognised them. There was never any doubt to my friends that I was actually communicating with the spirit world, but White Arrow had still not said anything at all. That is, until early one evening when we had some friends round. We had all been sitting down, chatting about what had been happening lately, and

I was telling them about White Arrow, when he suddenly turned up at my side. Naturally, I told them he was here and one of my friends asked, "Does he ever say anything?"

I said he doesn't and went on to explain that I understood his English must be rather limited or else he would have done so by ow. I told her that he had only ever said three words to me, and we carried on with our conversation for a while.

Just then, White Arrow made me jump for he said, quite clearly, "Big bird in sky," and he pointed upwards.

I was absolutely taken aback, for he had been silent for so long and now he here was talking about a big bird in the sky!

Tony asked me what the matter was for he saw my attention had been taken away, so I told him that White Arrow had actually said something at long last. I repeated the words White Arrow had said and Tony reckoned he was talking about an aeroplane.

"Of course," I agreed, "It's got to be that."

Tony said White Arrow wouldn't have known the word 'aeroplane' as they wouldn't have had them in his day.

"Maybe I'm going on a journey by 'plane," I said to Tony and our friends.

"Ask him then," said one of my friends.

They were a couple we had known for some time who had always been interested in spiritualism, so it was lovely to be able to share the experience with them. I turned to White Arrow and asked him the question. He pointed to the woman and repeated the words, "Big bird in sky."

"It's for you," I told her. "It's you who will be going on a 'plane journey."

I had a feeling something else was going to be said, don't ask me how, for White Arrow said nothing more, but I asked them all to be quiet for a moment. They all did as I requested and we sat patiently. Just then, a teepee was in front of me. I could see it as clear as day and it was moving backwards and forwards. I sat there, staring at it, when suddenly I seemed to know what it all meant. I looked up at the couple and, without thinking, asked them if they were contemplating moving

131

house. The strange thing is that the movement the teepee was making was very erratic, which made me think they weren't sure about the move being the right decision.

"Well," said my friend, "We are thinking about moving, but we haven't made our minds up what to do for the best yet."

My reply was, "Well, you are going to move, I can assure you," and they both looked at me in amazement. I could tell they weren't quite convinced about what I had told them, but I didn't care. I knew that what I had just seen and told them was going to happen and that one day they would come and tell me they were moving. I also felt it wasn't going to be long before it all happened.

"Is there anything else?" asked Tony.

I sat quietly for a moment, but there was no sound from White Arrow and I couldn't see anything since the teepee was no longer there. I was just about to give up when suddenly I could see a circle with a cross inside it. Once again, I sat bewildered, trying to figure it out. Slowly, the circle started to get darker. It had been a light colour when I first saw it but now it was quite dark. Within seconds of seeing it I knew what it meant. I don't know how, but looking back at the couple I asked them if anyone close to them had been very depressed lately. I felt there had been tears shed by this person and I told them so. They both looked at me surprised and said, "Yes, we're both very worried about a member of our family who is ill. It has caused many tears all round."

For some unknown reason I looked back at the circle and this time it was no longer dark, but the same light colour it was when I first saw it. I turned to my friends and smiled.

"They're going to be alright now," I reassured them.

Just then, White Arrow brought the teepee in again and this time there was another one next to it, but it was a much smaller one. Once more I knew exactly what it meant, but before I could tell them I saw the circle again, this time by the side of the small teepee. The small teepee had illustrated to me that there was small child living in the house, and it was the child who was ill and who they were all worrying about. The circle was still a light colour and I knew instantly that the child would be well, and I passed this information on to them. When they asked me how I knew all that I said I didn't know but they confirmed I was spot on. I was both pleased and puzzled at the same time, pleased because they accepted all that I told them and puzzled because it was amazing how I knew what the objects indicated. White Arrow then vanished and soon afterwards our visitors left.

As I lay in bed that night I thought about the messages and how they had been shown to me, when suddenly it dawned on me. I had known White Arrow couldn't speak much English so he was passing messages on to me in Indian signs. However, what surprised me most was that I knew without asking exactly what they meant and it was the first time White Arrow was actually communicating with me, and I was also pleased it was at a time when I could share it with friends and hopefully it helped them, too.

CHAPTER THIRTEEN

Over the months that followed, most of White Arrow's communication with me was shown in Indian terms, but there were occasions when he tried to speak in English, but it was very broken English. The funny thing is that, whenever he was talking to me in this type of pigeon English, without me realising it, I was doing just the same. I was picking up his way of speaking which was most odd. By now I had told Mum and the girls all about my spirit guide and the spirit people who I had communication with, and thankfully they accepted it fully. In a way I was rather surprised that they should take it all so calmly and accepted it as being an everyday occurrence, and yet I had only been with the spirit world for a relatively short time.

One evening Mum said she had something to say to me and she proceeded to pull me up about the way in which I was talking. I didn't have a clue at first about what she was talking about so I asked her to explain herself.

"I don't know how to put it, Ann," she began, "But you're not talking the way you usually do. Ask Tony to explain it, he can tell you better than I can. It just doesn't sound like you, that's all."

When Tony came to take me home from Mum's house later that evening, I told him what Mum had said to me and said to him, "Would you say there's anything wrong in the way I'm speaking lately?"

"Yes," he replied with no hesitation. "You are often speaking in broken English, well it sounds like broken English anyway. It's not all the time, mind you, but there are times when it comes across strongly."

"What do you mean exactly?" I enquired. I was quite intrigued by it all as I hadn't noticed it myself to that extent.

"Well, I'll give you an example," said Tony. "Instead of saying to me, will you go down the road for some cigarettes, you would now say "go down road", so you seem to be missing out a lot of your words, and I've noticed it happening more when White Arrow's around you. You don't even have to tell me now when he's around because you immediately speak in that way."

"I wish you had told me before," I said.

"Well, I presumed you knew," said Tony.

"No, I had no idea, but in future I'll watch myself," I replied.

It was easier said than done, though, for I wasn't always aware I was doing it. I could only hope it would sort itself out and that White Arrow would pick up the English language quickly so I could stop it.

Mum and the kids liked White Arrow's name and fully accepted him being with me most of the time. It got to the stage that wherever I went he would follow me, but it was very nice having him around and I got used to it. I believe the girls thought it was all a game really at the beginning, for whenever I was at their house they would ask me where he was and what he was doing or saying.

My eldest daughter and I were still not as close as I would have liked, not like I was with my youngest, and I hoped that now that I was feeling much better than I had been for years it would somehow draw us together, but to no avail. The damage was done and I had to accept it as being so. The only thing I could wish for regarding Karen was that in the future things might be different between us in as much as she wouldn't carry the hate she had for me all her life, like I did with my father.

One day, when I was at Mum's house, my eldest daughter was sitting in the living room when she suddenly turned to me and asked me why the spirit world should choose somebody like me to communicate with. I was so surprised and somewhat hurt by her question, but I answered her the best way I could. I told her I honestly

134

didn't know why they chose me and there was no reason for her to ask. I so wanted to give her a definite reply but I just didn't have one.

When I arrived home later that day I asked White Arrow if he could answer my daughter's question. Even though White Arrow's English was not very good, whatever words he used I easily understood. I told White Arrow I was just as confused as she was about my being chosen to speak with the spirit world. Perhaps I was just feeling guilty about my past, which always had a habit of catching up with me, no matter how hard I tried to forget it all. It could be that I was feeling guilty about having something which was so precious to me that I didn't feel as if I deserved it.

Karen's question had sparked off many others in my mind that evening and, when I remembered that look on her face at the time of her asking me it, I knew she didn't feel I was worthy of it. Would this mean other people may well be of the same opinion? As I was wrapped up in my confusion, I heard the words, "I need you, Little One." It was almost as if the words were begging me to listen closer, to listen to whatever White Arrow had to tell me, and not to worry about what other folk thought. It was the first time White Arrow referred to me as Little One and for a moment I was puzzled as to why he called me it.

"You, Little One," explained White Arrow, before I had even thought of asking him.

"What a lovely name to call me," I said, feeling very flattered ad privileged. Then my mind went immediately back to years ago and I distinctly remembered what the nun had said to me the day Mum had come to collect me. What a strange coincidence, I thought, but it soon went out of my mind when White Arrow started to speak to me again.

"You must follow me," he said.

"Where?" I asked, taking it the wrong way, but I very soon found out what he meant.

"You must follow me," he repeated.

"Do you mean follow you as in follow wherever you take me, or what?" I asked, not fully understanding at this point what he meant.

"Speak," he answered, and he pointed to his mouth. I knew then exactly what he meant. Whatever he said, I had to take notice and that's what he meant by following him.

"I do wish you would learn to speak English properly, White Arrow," I said. "It's difficult sometimes knowing what you mean straightaway. So, let me get this right, you want me to take notice of what you say."

"Yes," he replied.

He went on to say, "Daughter did not mean..." but before he could finish his sentence I butted it.

"But she didn't mean to be disrespectful about you, White Arrow," I said.

I didn't really want to hear what he thought about my earlier conversation between Karen and myself. I didn't want to hear what he had to say in case it was something I wouldn't like. I couldn't risk being hurt any more and there had come a time in my life when nobody would hurt me again. I had put up a barrier around me which would let no one in. Perhaps I was kidding myself, but I was going to have a good try, anyway, so the barrier went back up.

"No, Little One," said White Arrow. "No barrier, please," and he spoke in a soft voice.

"I know," I replied, "But I can't be hurt any more," I said, but my barrier was still firmly up just in case.

I wished I knew what the bond was between myself and White Arrow and why he had chosen the name of Little One, but the bond was there and it was special. I had found myself in a strange situation for I looked at Tony, who was sleeping peacefully next to me, and everything seemed crystal clear to me now.

White Arrow was standing by the side of me and as I looked at him I said, "Yes, I love you and maybe I understand why we are so close, but I love him, too," and I looked over at Tony who was still fast asleep. As I looked at my husband Tony, I smiled to myself. It may have been a fact that not everyone thought he was a good man, but to me he was and that was all that mattered, and I loved him dearly. I could see both of them so clearly, which was a weird and wonderful situation to find myself in, to say the least. Here I was, with a husband who was very much alive and well, and also I had a spirit man whom I shared my life with. I repeated that I loved him but as much as I did, my love for Tony was greater.

136

White Arrow accepted this and nodded. As I looked at both of them I wondered if maybe it wasn't such a good idea to tell Tony all this. He was convinced about the spirit world's existence and previous reincarnations, and if I was to tell him I believed I somehow knew White Arrow in a former life, with a bit of luck, he would believe it. Whether he liked it or not remained to be seen. I had a good idea he wouldn't appreciate it so I looked up at White Arrow for his advice. He was shaking his head as if to say "No" and after all it wasn't the right time. There was something about the twinkle in White Arrow's eyes that told me he was full of mischief. I had grown so used to him and his ways by now and made up my mind to tell Tony my conclusions in my own good time.

"White Arrow, if you say anything I'll kill you," I said without thinking.

White Arrow laughed his head off and when I realised what I had said I saw the funny side of it, too. I couldn't kill him, even if I wanted to, for he was already dead!

"You can laugh," I said to him, "But I mean it, I'll tell him when I'm good and ready. Promise me you'll behave yourself!" and with that he vanished. I tried to put it all behind me but somehow I knew White Arrow wouldn't let it drop so I would just have to be on my guard with him. As I looked at Tony I thought, You poor thing, having to put up with a spirit like White Arrow!

It didn't take that long for White Arrow to perfect his English and most of the time he spoke it fluently. I also got to know him a lot better, and the first thing I learnt about him was when he was serious about anything. You just don't argue with him when he's like that but only listen to whatever he has to say. He also has a lovely sense of humour too, and can be quite cheeky when he wants to be. I was enjoying his company and it was so nice having him around.

CHAPTER FOURTEEN

One Sunday afternoon, Tony was sitting reading the paper and I was watching the television relaxing when, suddenly, my mind seemed to go somewhere else. I found myself in a place far, far away from this country and I was no longer in my living room. I was crying...

137

I was crying so much that my mouth felt bone dry, my skin was so hot and burned. The smoke was also burning me and my throat was especially bothersome. There I was, a small baby, and yet I knew and could feel all that was happening around me, and it was so amazing that for one so young to be able to have such a crystal clear picture of the whole scene. I knew I had been there for a time, maybe hours, or perhaps a whole day, and that the wagon was on its side. There were no horses, for as I saw the tracks I could clearly see the broken reins as if the horses had torn them apart as they fled in fear, and yet somehow I knew the Indians had taken them.

Suddenly there was an Indian on a horse in front of me. He was so gentle and as he picked me up the love in his eyes, the strength in his arms, made me stop crying. I felt so safe with him but then, in a flash, I went back in time, to just before the burning smoke had enveloped me.

The wagons were rolling and I knew there were only about ten or twelve wagons around us. I was in the back of our wagon whilst my mother, brother and father were in the front. Father was driving the horses as my brother sat next to him, fast asleep on my mother's lap. It was so hot that my mother had to constantly wipe her face and neck with a scarf as the sweat was pouring from her body. It was still daylight but they were tired from all the travelling they had done all day. By now the dust and heat had got to them and Father looked very tired. I know my brother's name was John and as he lay blissfully sleeping across my mother's lap, her long dark hair pushed back as it hung down her back under the bonnet she was wearing, which was also pushed back. She kept looking behind her to see if I was alright in the back of the wagon and then alternatively wiped father's forehead, taking the perspiration away that was rolling down his face.

Just then a man drew up on a horse at the side of our wagon to speak to my father. Soon we will settle for the night, but we must use as much of the daylight as possible. Father understood as much as he tried, for he knew how important it was to reach our goal and the number of miles we had to cover before the homeland was in sight. They wanted it so badly but with so many more miles yet to go, but they knew they had to rest at night, it being Indian country, and the best time was night-time when it was dark.

Father was becoming more and more concerned about one of the wheels of our wagon as it was not very safe now after all the days of constant travelling, and that night one of the other men helped him repair it. Father had a long dark beard and looked much older than mother, who was about twenty-six but through the tiresome journey she looked older. My brother was about eight years old whilst I was about six months to a year old. My mother was a pretty young woman, and every time my parents looked at each other I could see the deep love they had for each other which showed in their eyes.

Despite the fact that they were both hot and tired they did not exchange any cross words but we were all very happy and looking forward to what was going to be a brand new beginning to the rest of our lives.

Dusk was falling by this time and I think Father must have been in charge, because once again the man on the horse appeared to speak with him to ask if he wanted the wagons to rest for a while or to carry on. Father looked at him and told him that the people are tired and weary and ready for a well-earned rest, so we would go forward until we found a suitable place that would be safe. The man rode off to carry out his instructions.

My brother was waking now. Even at his age he seemed a man as he asked my father if he could help him with the reins. Father looked at him and smiled, then looked at Mother so proudly. He did not have time to look round at me because of his driving the wagon, but asked if I was alright. Mother smiled, "She's fine," and turned to pick me up and put me on her lap. By now my brother was sitting up next to Father and played happily, whilst Father looked full of pride for here was his family, contented in the knowledge that we were on our way to a new land, and he was also so proud to have a son who would carry on his name and proud of his daughter because she looked so much like his wife, the woman he loved so much. By this time I was on my mother's lap. He leant across to stroke my hair and as he did so they smiled lovingly at each other.

Suddenly there was a cry from afar, yet I managed to recognise the voice - it belonged to the man on the horse and he was indicating to us that he had found a place to stop. It was now getting dark and Father was shouting to the wagon behind us that we were going to stop ahead to rest awhile, and in turn the message was passed on to all the other wagons. Gradually, all the wagons formed a circle and slowly came to a halt. Father got down first and then helped mother and, one by one, the rest of us. Mother went to the back of the wagon, taking us with her whilst Father untied the horses to give them a well-earned rest, and something to eat and drink. All the women started to get their pots and pans together to prepare the food for their men and children and themselves. The men, in the meantime, were checking the wagons and horses for safety and started making fires. The children were running about, playing happily.

The air was stifling, it was hot with no breeze, yet the people were comforted

139

with the thought of what tomorrow should bring forth. Very shortly, they were able to relax a lot more after such a long day, so much so that even the men were laughing. The women chatted amongst themselves about the day's events and what tomorrow was to bring. Mother was moaning that her dress had been torn that day; after all, she did not have many to her name, but Father laughed and said that when they reach their new homeland she could make many. Mother laughed for she knew when she made this journey she would, at the end of it, have to lose something, so she did not mind, but in the back of her mind she knew there was just one dress that she would never be able to wear again. It was her wedding dress, and she had never spoken to Father about it for it would have been so trivial in these hard times, but from the day she had me she swore that I would be married in it, for it brought her so much happiness by marrying Father that she had purposely hidden it away for me. They were very holy people and material things were of no importance to them and their people alike, so it was a great secret to Mother (not that she would lie to Father), but it was better that she said nothing to him about it at all.

After the fires were lit, the horses had been tended to and the cooking was all done, everyone began to settle down beside one another by the fire and Mother put me between herself and Father, making sure the blankets were underneath me as the ground was still very hot from the day's brilliant sun. My brother was somewhere about, playing with the other children, my Father keeping a watchful eye on him so he couldn't go too far away. If he did go out of my father's eyes he got called back, knowing the reason was because this was dangerous country.

Father turned to Mother to say he must go and mend the wheel as it would not last another day, and with that he called to his friend and together they went back to the wagon. They were gone for about an hour or so and when Father returned he said to Mother, "It was not as bad as I thought. I hope it will last to the end of the journey."

"I do hope that it will not be too long now," said Mother.

Father stroked her hair and replied, "Wait till we get there and you'll see, you'll be so happy, I know the journey has been hard and trying."

Mother laughed and said to him, "It's alright, I'm not moaning, I just feel sorry for the children. It must be so hard for them."

This time Father spoke very quietly to her, "When we get there and settle down they will soon forget, don't worry," and gazed down at me.

140

It was almost as if he had forgotten all about me, but when he looked at me I could tell by looking in his eyes that he had not. I then turned to face my Mother and held my arms outstretched so she picked me up, and as she cuddled me the love and the warmth she felt for me was all the proof I needed and I felt such deep, sincere love from her.

"I think the children should go to bed now," said my father, "and why don't you go, too, you look so tired."

"Come on, John," my mother shouted to my brother, and many of the other mothers were also calling their children to do the same. John came to her straight away.

"He is a good boy," said my father.

Mother smiled and picked me up and started walking towards the wagon with John holding her hand, and myself with her other arm. She turned to say to Father, "Good night, may God be with you."

It had been agreed that Father would be on watch all night and that Mother would lead the wagons for half the following day so that Father could sleep. She had done it before and had learnt, as women of that time had to, to manage and to help their men in this way so now it was an easy task for her. She had carried out these duties before for months at a time, of taking the role of getting the wagons and horses on the right route whilst Father kept watch during the night.

Mother put me behind the front seat of the wagon. It was now getting cold, so she wrapped me up well. John went to the back of the wagon - he knew where his bed was for he made it himself. Mother looked at him so proudly for he had never asked her how to make his bed and they looked at each other, their eyes telling the bond of love there was between them, and Mother also feeling so proud of having a young son who was trying so hard to be a man. Very soon my brother was asleep and I knew my mother was not worried about him but was now looking at me and caressing me. As she sang to me with her soft voice, I remember her blue eyes and her gentle words. There I was, a blue-eyed, dark-haired baby with a healthy body which was well-fed. A smiling, contented baby with no cares in the world because I was loved. At my tender age nothing mattered to me other than the knowledge that I was being loved and cared for. I did not know or understand that one year ago my parents had been through hard times for my brother and myself, and all because they wished for happiness for their children. As my mother looked at me I remember so vividly her dark hair falling across her face, her skin burnt by the sun and her slim figure. Her eyes were so shiny and bright as if the excitement of thinking of tomorrow was too much to bear. As she bent forward her hair felt so soft between my fingers as I played with it. The words of the lullaby she sang were of the love she had for me and, as my arms stretched out to her, I knew she wanted me to go off to sleep. I felt so contented that her wish came true and within seconds I was fast asleep. The next thing I remember was Mother breast-feeding me. It was still dark yet, the early hours of the following morning, and I could just see the first glimpse of daylight. Mother was singing to me - I say singing, but it was more humming really because there were no words. I felt the silence and as my mother was feeding me I sensed she felt uneasy about something, that there was something not quite right. The silence was almost deafening for there was no sound about us at all - no birds, no insects, just as if the whole world had stopped still. Even at my young age I felt fear and the fear in my mother was growing, but I didn't know the reason why. Just then, my brother seemed to be saying, "Mother", but it did not seem the right word as he had difficulty in getting the word out properly. In my short life I had never seen fear as I was now seeing on my mother's face. The memory I have of that look of hers is so vivid and yet it was probably over in seconds. Somehow it seemed to last forever. The reason for my mother's expression was because between the open flap at the back of our wagon stood an Indian with his bow and arrow ready aimed to fire. My brother had seen him first which was why he tried to call my mother to alarm her, but he was so frightened he could not move fast enough. The Indian had not in fact seen my brother but could only see Mother's back and did not realize she was breast-feeding her baby. The Indian couldn't see me in her arms at all and was unaware of my presence. My brother knew his mother was about to be killed so he moved forward and, although he was frightened of the outcome, it somehow didn't matter to him for he knew what the Indian's intentions were. As he tried to utter the word "Mother" the arrow was released from the bow and within seconds the arrow was deep in my brother's back. He fell, almost to my mother's side, her little son who was a man at just eight years old. Mother screamed in terror and proceeded to lay me to one side whilst she stretched out her arms, grabbing her son to cradle him in her arms, knowing all was lost. The Indian then climbed up into the wagon after seeing he had not killed the one he had intended to, being unaware there had been a young boy there. Mother had a rifle which she always kept close by, as did all the folk in those days. As her dead son lay in her arms she was so angry that this Indian, this total stranger, had killed her boy. She had never had to use a rifle before and had never wanted to and yet now she knew she had to and wanted to. She picked it up and point blank shot him. Mother was shaking, the smell of the gun smoke was strong but she did what she had to do and was so worried about her son. The Indian lay in the wagon and a part of his body was on her son's feet. This revolted her so she pulled her son's body away from the Indian in anger. The arrow had picked the right spot and had killed him outright.

Within seconds she heard gun-firing and screaming. She knew she had lost her son but I was still here safe and well so her next concern was for me. Earlier that morning the men had hitched the wagons to the horses and fed them in order to make an early start before it was completely light. By now the horses were restless by all the noises and gun-fire. Besides her fear for my safety, Mother was so worried about my father. She did not know if he was dead or alive. Just then the wagon went forward, not as if we were on the move but as if the horses were alarmed and frightened. With the jolt, Mother fell over backwards towards the back of the wagon. In fear she grabbed me, but once again fell as the wagon jerked forward, making her fall with me in her arms on top of the dead Indian and her dead son. She screamed hysterically as she saw my brother's eyes were open. The Indian's face was away from us and once again the wagon was lurching forward. The next thing I remember is everything being on top of us - all the things they had brought from their home so far away - all the belongings they had were now tipped upside down, now that the wagon had rolled on its side. Mother managed to hold on to me, albeit by just one arm, but she was bleeding from her head. We were surrounded in upheaval, our clothes and little bits of furniture all about us in disarray. She must have been struck by something which was flying about and landing on us. The blood was trickling down quite badly from her forehead but her main concern was me. She could hear so much noise outside, horses whinnying, guns firing, her people crying and screaming. Mother stopped for a split second as if gathering her thoughts as the wagon lay on its side and then she decided to crawl out of the wagon, dragging me with her. I remained quiet throughout, maybe the reason was fear. Mother crawled away towards the back of the wagon with one arm hanging on to me whilst the other arm was used to push away the things that had fallen everywhere. Her tears were falling down her face but now panic had set in. She was looking and trying to find Father for, amid the screaming and chaos, she hoped in her heart Father would still be alive. At the same time she had to hide me so I would be safe from harm. Little did she know that whilst she was looking and searching for Father she was being watched. I saw her turn her face here and there, looking for somewhere safe to leave me. She opened the flap at the back of the wagon but turned away in fear. I knew she had seen something, something that made her feel all was lost once again. She crawled back out to me and went towards the front of the wagon, dragging me with her by my arm. I was crying now because her pull was hurting me. This did not concern my mother, a small pain did not matter - she just had to find a safe place for me. Suddenly, smoke was coming from nowhere and started getting in our eyes. The smoke was becoming worse and after a few seconds Mother looked back to see it was coming from the back of our wagon, which was on fire.

The smoke was really strong and thick by now and as the wagon was on its side it was difficult for Mother to find a way out. Her fear was for other Indians out there but she knew if we stayed in the wagon we would both be burnt to death, so she grabbed me in her arms so tightly and pushed herself out, praying no one would see her. She rolled over and fell very close to the wagon. She was bleeding even more now as she lay with me next to the wheel of the wagon. She could hear horses but kept thinking of the wagon-wheel for she knew if she could hide me by it if she covered me with all the things that had fallen out of the wagon. She was frightened, however, because another fear which had crossed her mind was the fact that the fire at the back of the wagon must have been due to an arrow which had been aimed at the wagon. It should have set the wagon alight but because of the amount of smoke she knew the fire had gone out, was no longer burning, hence the smouldering dense smoke.

Her dress was long, down to her ankles, as she dragged herself towards the wheel and she tore off her skirt to wrap around me, then, putting me amongst her now ruined belongings behind the wheel. The last thing I remember about her was her fear but, above all, her love for me. She just looked at me, her hair very long, her face so dirty and as she came up close to me she kissed me and said, "I love you, but I must look for your father. I know you do not understand at your tender age why I am leaving you, but I must." She said all this as we were hidden behind the wheel. Of course, at my age, I did not understand, but I knew my mother expected to come back to me. Once again, so much was remembered from one so young.

After Mother had hidden me as much as she could in such a short time she looked towards the wheel and the open space. Her skirt was now missing, just her petticoat was visible, but this didn't matter to her. Suddenly she spotted a small gun; where it came from she did not know and she didn't really care, but she knew it could save her life. It was some yards away from her, maybe two or three feet. Could she take the chance and she could not stay where she was, not knowing what had happened to Father, but at the same time she knew two or three feet would decide with all the horses, Indians, and gun-firing around her. Would she make it? She looked back to see I was right behind her and she laid her hand on me. Somehow I knew she would take the gamble and as she crawled away from me I watched her very closely. It was so clear, like everything else in the past few days had been. Where her strength came from I do not know, except maybe from the fear which had given it to her. She crawled away from me but suddenly she stopped as if she had died. A horse with an Indian went by. I knew she was acting in the hope of fooling the Indian into believing she was dead. She slowly edged

144

forward a little, but within seconds an Indian was jumping down from his horse on top of Mother. He was pulling her hair and she was fighting and screaming, but there was no hope. He had a weapon in one hand and as he pulled her hair so far back her face was looking upwards. The scream was shattering and it was the last time I saw my mother's face. The Indian got up and was walking away - in his hand was long, dark hair and there was blood on his hands.

The vision went - the smoke came back. I was once again with the Indian.

***** *****

APACHE VILLAGE

The village was big and by now I was seven years old. We were camped by a river where there were lots of trees. The other side of the camp was much more open land where the huts, as we called them, were built from leaves and branches. We were playing near the river and now and again played about in the water and thoroughly enjoying ourselves. The weather was very hot and we knew that was the best way of keeping ourselves cool.

Suddenly I hurt my knee, I am not sure how it came about, but I do remember running back home, crying to my mother. My mother was sitting there, laughing at me, but at the same time had her arms outstretched to comfort me. She was a big woman and the dress she wore was folded up to the top of her legs, thus flapping between her legs. By now the other children had come out of the water to see if I was alright. Mother calmed me down and soon I was back playing with the other children. I had a sister who was younger than me and a brother who was older, and the three of us were playing ball so happily and peacefully with all the other children in the village. What struck me as being strange was the fact that there were only old men with the women and children - I could see no young men - including my Father. I say 'strange' for after all in my vision, looking on the outside, it would be, but here I was an Apache girl, so nothing was out of the ordinary.

It appeared that all the young men had gone hunting, which left the old men to look after the women and children. My grandfather was near Mother as our huts were built close together. Some of the children were sitting at his feet as he told them wonderful stories of his adventures and they became very engrossed in his tale.

I looked at Mother and she called out to me, enquiring as to whether my knee was better now or not. I waved and carried on playing happily.

All of a sudden I felt as if there was something wrong, I wasn't sure what, but I could sense it and from where I was playing I turned to look at Mother in the place where I had last seen her sitting down. She was now standing, shouting at us to come and, as there was such an urgent note in her voice, we knew we had to obey immediately. All the other children had also been called in and there was such an air of urgency and fear that some of the children began to cry, purely because of the desperation in their mothers' voices which told them something was wrong. The next thing I remember was that everybody was running about in all directions. I ran straight to my mother's arms, not knowing what was going on, and as she was still crying out to my brother and sister to hurry I could see them coming. Beyond them I could see dust, lots of dust. Dust filled the air as many horsemen were riding towards us. I had seen this sort of thing with the men of our village when they rode out on their hunting trips, but in my heart I knew that it was not my people this time coming home. These were all White Men and there were many of them. Being so young, I had never met a White Man before, although I was White as a baby, but now I was Apache through and through - I felt Apache, I acted Apache - I knew danger was coming. My brother and sister had not reached my mother as quickly as I had and in her fear Mother cried, "Run!" I knew that I had to and that my mother's word was to be trusted, so I followed her command.

The horsemen were coming in from the open land so I ran into the area of trees and the river, for I knew there were big rocks there ideal for one to hide. Without hesitation, off I ran with all my might and as I ran I kept looking back to find that everyone else was still running, that is, women and children first. The old men, and that included my own grandfather, were to stay to fight the White Man. How can an old man possibly win against a young man, be he white or indian, except in fair battle? These men had guns, our old men relied on their bows and arrows for protection. Before I reached cover amongst the trees and rocks I saw one of the old men of the village fall. I could hear lots of gun-fire, and what my people had always taught me and told me of the White Man was true. As I hid, I saw the White Man so clearly coming into the village. The terror they brought with them and the hate they had for the Indians, my people showed it all in their eyes. So hungry to kill, so hungry to hurt. Women, children and old men alike had all been taught of the hate, yet only knew of love from their own people, and here they were now, in front of me, being shot down. White Men were jumping from their horses to run after our women while others were tearing the huts down. The men were dragging some women off to rape them and some of the women gave chase,

146

but were very soon caught and raped on the spot while other Indians were being killed.

Suddenly, there were two children - not my brother or sister - but children of the camp, running through the trees. I shouted at them for I realised I was not in a safe place but knew where there was a suitable place to hide. I knew I had to follow the river and where I had to go, but before I could show them they shouted back at me, "Look out! There are two White Men riding towards us!" There was a large rock with a huge split in it so we headed for cover. I managed to get to the rock first. I pushed myself hard in between the crack in the rock and my friends came beside me. All was silent. All we could hear after a couple of minutes were branches breaking, but we knew the White Men could not bring their horses into the trees. All we could do was to wait where we were, without making a sound, as we could hear them walking through the trees. My body was almost completely through the slit in the rock and I was trying to help one of my friends to come with me but the slit was not big enough. I could feel our bodies shaking and trembling but no sound was made. Even in times of danger we had been taught never to be afraid but to guard our lives - that was the White Spirit's way.

I was trying my best to follow the White Spirit's way, but in my heart I was petrified. Now there were more sounds, more branches broken and they were coming nearer. By now I was very well hidden from the outside but I could see through the slit of the rock. My young friends were trying to do the same, but to no avail for, suddenly, there was the White Man standing there. He grabbed my second friend with one hand and with the other he pointed a gun to his stomach and shot him. The other White Man pulled the girl out of the rock, and as he did so he and the other White Man were laughing, pushing the girl in between them. One of the men walked off, dragging the terrified girl behind him while his friend just stood there, shouting something which I couldn't understand. He did not see me so I made certain I kept as quiet as possible. In a short period of time I heard screaming - it seemed to be so near to me, yet was in fact so far away it was so screeching. The man still stood there near to where I was hiding and then there was no sound at all - a deafening silence. The other White Man appeared and as he stood next to his friend he wiped a knife on his trousers. The first man spoke, victoriously and proudly, "That's finished. Let's go!" This time I could understand his words perfectly and I heard them leave. For a long time I waited there, not daring to leave the rock, the dead boy lying there in a pool of blood being an example as to what could easily happen to me if I wasn't careful enough. Noises were still coming from the village, but were getting less and less now. Night was falling. I could not look at my poor friend any longer and knew I had to leave the rock and follow the river, but I waited till there was no sound at all. It seemed

147

forever, and I waited till dawn until I was absolutely sure there was no-one around who may be able to harm me, or another living person as one could sense that. Even as I came out of the rock I had to see and look back as I walked.

My feet felt wet and as I looked down for a moment I thought I was seeing red sand. It was in fact red blood which came from where my dear friend had lain and died. I followed the trees back to our camp and, being taught the Apache way, I knew no one could see me. Had I walked out of the trees a White Man's way all that would have been in front of me would have been death, White Man's death. Every child, woman and man lay dead as I walked through, and as I searched for my mother a sense of hatred and a sense of loss was with me. Here I was, a child of seven who had been adopted and brought up by the Indians, taught to be brave and grown up before her time and yet, in the middle of all this, how could I be?

Eventually I managed to find Mother. She was in the hut and my grandfather was outside, face down. I could tell it was Grandfather by his clothing and I was too frightened to go in at first but once again my upbringing came to the forefront. I had no fear at this stage and had scoured the camp, looking at many women, many of whom were in such positions as to endorse they had been brutally raped. I knew then what I was to expect of my mother, instead of which I was to see a different scene altogether. Once I had entered the hut I witnessed my sister lying spread-eagled on the floor, completely naked. Mother was sitting in the corner with her head bent down. Having had no hope that she had survived I rushed to her, but as I touched her she fell forward. She was dead, too, as they all were.

I walked away and once again the Indian part of me came flooding back. I had to leave the ones I loved in case the White Man came back. I had no tears for I could show no emotion, feel nothing. I was numb, for I had been so happy and now it had all gone. I walked back to the trees and the river which I knew so well and played (only now it was not play, but survival).

***** ***** *****

THE SIOUX VILLAGE

Daylight was coming so I had to move quickly. Where to, I did not know, but I chose to follow the river. It was many days and nights of running and sleeping. I had been taught how to survive in the wilderness and I lived on many fruits and berries of the wild. The river gave me water, the land gave me food so I knew I

148

was safe from the White Man, for he did not know how to survive in the wilds. However, I knew that there where other dangers I had to watch out for. Although we were taught about the White Man, we were also taught about hostile Indians, Indians who were not of our tribe.

The knee I had injured at the river before the invasion was now hurting and began to swell as I walked and I realised that soon it would give up on me. That night I found some herbs from the ground and once again found a rock to hide and shelter me. I put the herbs on my knee and I knew I was running a fever due to the heat of my body. Whether it was because of my knee or something else - I did not care - I felt I had to lie down, hoping all would be well the following morning. I felt sure the herbs I had found would help. Sleep came upon me quickly.

Upon waking I found, to my amazement, I was not alone. Strangely enough everything was quiet, and considering I had suffered a fever all night and my knee was still painful. I was not as alert as I was brought up to be. As I walked out into the opening in the rock an Indian grabbed me. This was a different kind of Indian from any other I had seen. High up in the rocks were more of them on horses. My immediate concern was the Indian who stood next to me, so I bit him and tried to run off, but he grabbed me again. After what I had been through I was in no mood to give in easily again so I bit him again. However, this time he retaliated by hitting me with his hand, which made me see stars. As a rule, the Indian does not hit children, but this one had no choice. As I fell to the ground I looked up at him to see that he was looking up at the Indians who remained in the high rocks. I followed his eyes and it appeared that he focused them on one indian, the Chief. One knows the difference between the Chief and the others. He lifted his arm high above his head, which was a signal that the Indian was to bring me and follow them all. My life had been spared - they had accepted me.

The Indian picked me up and put me on his horse. We followed the path up to where the group of Indians were waiting and as we reached them I looked at the Chief with such fear within me. He looked so powerful and his eyes just stared at me as he sat on his horse. One could tell he was about six feet tall, lithe and strong and yet graceful, very well proportioned and with skin singularly clear and delicate. He wore no paint, his head was bare and his long hair was gathered in a clump at the back of his neck. His chest and arms were naked and a buffalo robe was hanging from his waist with a belt holding it in place. He was wearing different coloured moccasins on his feet. Looking back at his eyes, which were so proud and forceful, he did not smile - except with his eyes. He had shown me a sign that all was well. I was to be accepted into his tribe which I knew was Sioux.

They moved on once again, we seemed to be travelling for days. I cannot say for sure how many but we would rest at night and then travel again by day. I knew the Sioux were not on their own land for some reason, and that they had been far away, so now they were going home. At night I would sleep on my own, but not far from their watchful eyes. Despite the fact they had accepted me, they still did not trust me.

The Chief would sit at night some yards from the other Indians, praying. Sometimes he talked to himself, which is something I had also noticed about the Apache men, and so I knew he was talking to White Spirit. The other Indians had great respect for this Indian and I knew he must be a big Chief. One night there was great talk of what to call me. I had to have a name, it seemed, but not the Apache name. After some discussion, one of the Indians came across to me to tell me that it was decided upon that my Sioux name was to be Little One. That night I also found out that the big chief was called Sitting Bull, leader of the Sioux.

Soon I was feeling excitement amongst them and I knew their home was not far off, and this pleased them after so much travelling. We were coming into new country now, different from what I had seen before, but then I had not travelled so far. Before, the land was vast with mountains but now there were not as many trees as before, just open space. Suddenly, in front of me in the distance, I could see a village. It looked to be a big village to me with hundreds of huts. I was soon to find out that they were called teepees and they were different from what I had seen before. Looking away from the village I could see buffalo, many of them, and near the village was a river.

As we rode into the village there was much excitement, especially seeing the Chief (as I called him). We rode through the village and I found many of its inhabitants looking at me, pointing and talking about me. The Chief continued and then stopped suddenly, then turned to speak to the Indian who was holding me. He pointed to a teepee and the Indian and I followed the Chief whilst the other Indians went their own way.

We dismounted the horse outside the teepee and I was told to follow the Chief who went in first. I followed closely behind him and I could see an old squaw sitting there. The Chief spoke to her and, judging by their actions and gestures, it was concerning me. The old squaw had great respect for this man but I could tell straight away that she was not at all pleased with what he was saying. All of a sudden he turned without even looking at me, and left.

The teepee was large and very different from our huts, with paintings on the walls, rugs on the floor and the blankets were neatly rolled up around the inside of the teepee. The old squaw sat there, muttering to herself disdainfully for a good few minutes. I just stood there quietly, for I was in a new land with new people so some fear was within me. I knew I had to do as I was told so I stood still for a long time until she was ready to speak to me. Even before she rose from her seated position on the rug I could see the hate in her eyes for me. I was a stranger from another kind of Indian tribe, but what made it worse was the fact that I was white. Having been brought up by the Apaches from a baby, I knew of no other life, but this made absolutely no difference to her so I was treated the same as another White Man. I knew I was different now, not only by the colour of my skin, and yet I knew she would never harm me because the Chief had put me in her charge. He had left me in her care whether she cared or not so I knew she would obey him.

My hair was long and dark and as the squaw touched it she turned to pick something up, turned back and proceeded to cut it! There was no mention of telling me to sit down or anything and, as I watched the hair fall, my mind went back to my Apache brother whose hair was shorter than mine. I thought to myself, ''Now I will look like an Apache boy.'' She left the teepee with me still standing there. I could hear lots of noises outside and voices but could not understand what was going on. The old squaw came back in and grabbed me and led me outside the teepee with her. It was still hot as we had ridden in early that afternoon and, together with anxiety and the heat, the sweat was making my clothes wet through. The Indian with whom I had shared a horse was now sitting on the floor outside the teepee. I felt perhaps he had been put there to guard me but was not sure why. The squaw started walking towards the river which was very nearby, dragging me behind her. She was still muttering to herself, and she carried a blanket on the other arm. As soon as we got to the water's edge she walked in, dragging me with her. She threw the blanket back onto the riverbank and with both hands pushed me under the water! Not knowing if I was with friendly Indians or not, my first thought was that I was about to be killed by drowning, but within seconds she let go and I simply stood there, the water waist-high. She stood there tearing the little clothing I had been wearing into shreds and proceeded to wash me, first my hair, then my body. It seemed to go on and on forever. Without a word still she turned away, dragging me with her towards the bank. She threw the blanket at me in almost a fit of temper and, before I had a chance to put it around me, off she went once again, with me in tow. When we arrived back at the teepee she put me inside, didn't utter one word to me and just left. I sat down, putting the blanket tightly around me. I was still trembling a bit with fear but felt much better after the river bath. I touched my hair which still felt strange, but I knew I had to accept it.

From that day on I was to stay with this old squaw and I accepted that, too. The years with her were not so bad and the old squaw gradually learned to accept me, not like a true Sioux, but the colour of my skin now made no difference to her and day by day, year by year, her love was growing for me.

I did not see the Chief very often after that, and he certainly never came to visit me, but my respect for him and with the love I felt for him, I looked up to him, too. I also knew I was now accepted as a Sioux girl and no longer was I a stranger.

Our camp moved many times over the years, sometimes coming back to places where we had been before. Many seasons came and went. I was growing up now and my hair had grown back to the normal long and dark familiar style. I grew to accept the old squaw as a mother figure and she taught me everything a young girl should know. I was coming to the age of fifteen and growing up fast. I was fairly tall, slim and wore my dress down to my ankles. I had many beads around my neck. I was beginning to show off to the young men of the village, but the old squaw was quick to notice this and would tell me off. Sometimes I did not understand this as there were other girls of the tribe looking and marrying their men at my age, but she would only smile and say, "There's plenty of time."

During this stage of my becoming aware of the opposite sex I would often sneak a look at the young men, but there was one who seemed different from the rest. I had got to know many of the children in the village so I was totally accepted by them, and the young men would not be ashamed to look and smile at me. This different young man always caught my eye because of his eyes. I had seen eyes like his before and I remember the Chief's eyes were the same as this young man's. I put two and two together and realised he was the Chief's son. I had not seen him many times because, like all the other young men of the village, he would go away for days on end hunting, but on the few occasions I did see him he seemed aloof and very different from the other boys.

I would talk to the old squaw about him for in my heart I knew I liked him very much. The old squaw would say nothing but would always listen to me avidly and smile. What I found so strange was that she would never stop me talking about him and yet she did not like me to talk about anyone else. I did not mind this, for at my age I was only too glad to be able to talk about any boy, let alone one I was attracted to.

As that year went by the boy became more and more on my mind. I would hope to see him and waited eagerly till all the young men got back from their hunting trip, but when I did manage to see him I would run away and hide, hoping he did not see my flushed face. Each time I saw him I felt excitement, and I gradually began to fall in love with him. He was so like his father, a strong, fine young man.

Many evenings I would talk to the old squaw about him, but again she would say nothing except, "Have patience, Little One." However, one night she told me there was to be a wedding.

"Whose?" I asked.

"Yours, Little One? You are no longer a child, but a fine young woman. You will have to leave the teepee to join your husband."

I was upset a little to learn this, as by now I loved the old squaw lady dearly. I asked her whom it was I was to marry, but all she said was, "You will be told soon." In my mind I went to all the young men of the village to think of which one it may be. I did not sleep very well that night, knowing I would not be happy, for I loved the Chief's son very much. However, as it was the Indian way, I knew I had to accept whoever he was.

The following day there was a lot of activity in the camp. The old squaw had kept me inside the teepee all day and had rolled up all my belongings in a blanket. I was wearing a long, red dress and wore my hair swept back, which was black and shiny. I had more beads on this day than I had usually worn and, as I looked at myself, I remembered the wedding dress that belonged to a young woman many moons ago. She had been scalped. It was the one and only time I had remembered the woman and her dress, and as quickly as the vision came it went, but made me feel sad for a moment. I realised I was now an Indian woman and that it had happened so long ago and it was soon to be forgotten. It is strange, but although I knew of the woman and her wedding dress, I had forgotten she had been my natural mother and her wedding dress was to have been the one I should be bearing on my wedding day, had she not been killed so violently. What became of that dress I'll never know, but now it was gone forever.

Because of all the excitement of being dressed up for my wedding on this day, in such beautiful clothes and accessories, it somehow didn't matter or seem so important to know who I was to marry. We were once again camped near a river where there were teepees on both sides of it. It was a small river which one could easily walk across.

It was now late afternoon and the old squaw was fussing around me like a mother

153

hen. I could sense the pride and excitement in her, but also knew she was a bit sad for she had looked after me for so long. Suddenly I could hear horses outside the teepee and the old squaw stopped arranging my dress and left the teepee. I felt sick with such a mixture of emotions - excitement, fear but also sadness - for I was to soon leave my home and the old squaw to start a new life with my husband, who was still unknown to me.

The flap of the teepee was then flung open and in walked the Chief. No-one had told me that he would be involved with my wedding among the Sioux tribe as there was no marriage as such. All I had been told was that I was to marry that afternoon, and would simply have to move into my husband's teepee with his family, taking all my belongings with me. That was the marriage I had accepted, along with the usual feasting and exchanging of presents after the ceremony.

The Chief beckoned me to follow him outside, where there was an Indian on a horse waiting for me. He was holding another two horses' reins and the Chief helped me to climb up onto one of the horses. He got on his horse and took the lead, with the other Indian and I following him. I looked back over my shoulder at the old squaw, her face full of smiles because she knew it would not be very long before I was to find out which of the young men I was about to wed.

We approached the river, passing many teepees on the way, and across the river I would see there were a few more of them scattered around, one of which belonged to the Chief. When we reached the river we all dismounted our horses and the Chief pointed to one of the teepees across the river, telling me to go to it. With my belongings in my arms, I waded across the river and walked towards the said teepee. Once more the sickness in my stomach came back as I did not know who was waiting there for me.

It was a surprise to me to have to head for the Chief's teepee, but I carried on telling myself over and over in my mind that it was my duty to make my future husband happy and not to worry about what made me happy. The hem of my dress was wet and I wondered why I could not have ridden my horse through the river, but I did not ponder too much on that thought as one did not argue with the Chief.

I was almost there when, suddenly, the flap of the teepee swung open and in front of me stood the Chief's son. He explained to me that I had been promised to him by his father and that he wished me to be his wife. I understood now why the Chief himself had come to fetch me. The Chief's son held out his hand and, as I stood there looking at him, my mind flashed back to the many evenings I had

154

spent with the old squaw when I had spoken to her of him and how over the past twelve months I had fallen in love with him. There had never been any sign of his feelings being the same towards me but here I was, now standing next to him, about to become his wife. He was taller than me which was news to me, for up until this time I had not been that close to him to know everything about him. His hair was long and tied back with a white feather hanging down at the back. He was wearing white buckskin trousers with a waistcoat to match and he had beads around his neck and armbands on his arms. His complexion was clear and no paint on his face or body like most Sioux men. His body strong, and at the age of seventeen, was very much a man. He was handsome and his eyes, crystal blue, looked at me as if he could see through me. He took my hand and I followed him into the teepee where we were to start our life together as man and wife. I was deliriously happy and realised now that the old squaw had known all along that this was the man I had been promised to, the man that I loved so much.

Our life together was wonderful and I saw the Chief many times now that I was married to his son. My husband's name was White Feather and he was so like his father in lots of ways and very close to him, even though the Chief had other sons. White Feather seemed to be his favourite son though, and we lived for a while with his family. After a short while we moved into our very own teepee. In the first year of our marriage I became with child. White Feather was over the moon about the prospect of becoming a father. He was a very kind and gentle man but sometimes he had to go away, often for days and sometimes weeks at a time, to go on hunting trips but he was always glad to be back. The child was due in the autumn and, as the days grew nearer, White Feather would stay closer to me, not going on his trips. I knew he really wanted a son although not once had he mentioned this to me. I was hoping it would be a boy for his sake. The baby was now due and White Feather, like any other father awaiting the safe arrival of his first child, was panicking and watching me all the time. The baby started coming in the middle of the night and White Feather called his mother for assistance. There was much going on around me but White Feather would not leave my side. Early in the morning our child was born, a beautiful little girl. She was passed to White Feather and as I looked up to him I saw his eyes were full of pride as he held his first child. It did not matter to him that she was a girl and he was fully contented and fulfilled.

The following two years I was to have two more daughters and by now White Feather was becoming a Medicine Man. His father had been a great Medicine Man in his time and like all other Medicine Men he also had great vision of seeing spirit and predicting forthcoming events. The Sioux tribe was very spiritual and its people fully understood the power of spirit.

In the back of mind I was beginning to worry about the fact that I had not been able to bear a son for White Feather. He had been present at the births of each of his three daughters and now eagerly awaited a fine boy. Although he loved his daughters I knew there was a sadness in his eyes. On many occasions White Feather went away to the mountains to pray to the Great White Spirit, not necessarily to pray for a son, but to speak to and see visions.

Very shortly after our third child, I was expecting another baby and White Feather had once again gone away to sit among the mountains, and when he returned this time there was a renewed brightness in his eyes. He put his arms around me and swung me in the air. The White Spirit had spoken to White Feather to tell him that this time I was carrying a son. He was so happy that day as he played with his daughters, in the knowledge that a son would now be following in his footsteps as he had followed his father's. I sat on the river bed holding my youngest child in my arms while White Feather played with the children in the water. I watched him with such love and so glad to see him happy and pleased the White Spirit had given him so much joy. I was grateful to be able to share my life with such a good man and father to my children. He looked back at me and smiled with so much love that it was indeed a day to remember.

Days before I gave birth to my fourth child White Feather became ill and needed constant nursing and attention. This went on for several days and even after our baby was born. He was now too ill to know he had a son at last. His illness followed his being injured by an arrow during a bloody battle with a rival tribe from another village. An arrow had been aimed at him and had embedded itself in his body. Despite the agonising pain it caused him, White Feather carried on fighting, eventually killing the Chief of the other tribe, which was a great feat amongst the Indians. White Feather's father managed to get the arrow-head out of his son's body and made up a mixture of special healing herbs which he changed daily. Although he was very worried about White Feather, the Chief spoke to me of the immense bravery his son had shown. I was so proud but extremely worried about White Feather. Thankfully, he began to improve and slowly was able to sit up and get better again. I showed his newly-born son to him and he was so proud. He thanked the White Spirit for this baby and, looking at me, he said, "From now on I will be known as White Arrow in honour of my victory." Gazing down on his little son he said, "He will have my name, but instead of being known as White Feather he shall be called Small Feather."

With White Arrow completely better now, life carried on as normal. We had our arguments on occasions, like most couples, but on the whole were very happy. One evening, however, we had an argument over something or other and it was on the eve on his preparing to go on another war party. Maybe I was worried and concerned about it after what had happened not so long ago. The following morning we were still not very happy with each other, and I had made up my mind not to help him with his preparations. I usually helped White Arrow with his warpaint, but this particular morning I decided to teach him a lesson and ignored him. When he went I felt sorry about our disagreement and thought to myself, When he comes back, I'll make it up to him.

Days later there was movement in the camp. Whereas it was always so noisy with children and the people going about their everyday chores, suddenly it was deathly quiet. I could see the horses coming with the Chief at the head of them. In his hand he was holding a strap of another horse and, as he led this other horse into our village, I saw an Indian lying draped over it. I instinctively knew it was White Arrow and as the Chief brought him closer to me the Vision faded away, very slowly till I could see no more.

CHAPTER FIFTEEN

Now I was back to the present day and I am sitting in my living room, blinking my eyes and realising I am back again as Ann Walker. It dawned on me why I had been so confused with the names of White Arrow and White Feather, and why there was such a closeness between White Arrow and myself, for we had been man and wife in a previous life.

As I looked across at Tony, who was still asleep, I thought it best not to tell him just at the moment about it unless I had to. It certainly seemed an odd situation to find myself in as now I had two husbands to contend with. I tried my best to put it out of my mind but there was no doubt I felt an affinity with White Arrow, and having been shown my reincarnation confirming this fact was remarkable.

During this period of time Tony's father was a regular visitor to us, and often appeared whilst we were in the car when going out, either on our way to work or pleasure. I liked him very much and would often pass messages on to Tony from him. He appeared to like me, too, and we got on quite well. I had seen Tony's

157

mother once since I became aware of spirit, but that was all. She had popped in one day and said only a few words before vanishing again. Since then it had been Tony's father who was the one to pop in more frequently, and on one particular day, when we were driving to our usual favourite beauty spot called Little Britain, Tony's father was sitting in the back of the car. It was Little Britain where I had first been aware of spirit so it was very special to me.

Suddenly, Tony's father said to me, "This is where I caught the barbel," and he pointed to the exact spot.

"Really?" I replied.

I didn't know one end of a fish from the other but I was polite. I had never seen a barbel and I would have liked to have known what one looked like. I told Tony his father was with us and I said, "Your Dad says it was over there where he caught that barbel fish," and I pointed to the part of the river where he had shown me. Now then, we were parked alongside the river but behind us was also a large lake where the public could freely walk round it. I took it that his father meant he had caught the fish just where we were, when suddenly I saw beside our car a measuring pole sticking up out of the water.

Tony's father then said, "There's a pole just like that one where I caught the fish," and I repeated this information to Tony.

"No, you're wrong," said Tony. "It wasn't here, love, you are mistaken."

I looked back at his Dad who was still sitting on the back seat.

"OK," said his father, "Ask him if we caught the fish here or not."

I asked Tony who replied, "Yes, in these parts, but not where we are now."

God, I thought. I wish I hadn't bothered telling him now, but at the same time I had to find out more, for I wasn't going to be beaten by something so stupid as this! I wasn't in the mood to argue over one fish but at the same time I didn't want to let his Dad down. If he said he caught the fish here, then I wasn't going to let Tony prove him wrong. I knew the measuring pole was important, but exactly how it came into all this, I wasn't rightly sure.

I asked Tony to show me exactly where his Dad had caught the fish.

"Alright," he said, and got out of the car. I got out, too and started to follow. I looked back at the car and said, "I hope you're right," and looked to see if his father was still there. I still hadn't got used to the spirit world completely, remembering they don't need doors to get in and out of cars etc. when all of a sudden his Dad said, "Don't worry, Ann. I am right," and to my astonishment, he was walking right beside me! I still wasn't always prepared for when spirit turn up like that and I stopped in my tracks.

"What's the matter?" asked Tony.

"Nothing," I replied. "It's just that your Dad is here right next to me," and I carried on following Tony.

After a short distance, Tony stopped and turned to look at me.

"It's just round the corner," he said, and walked on with me behind him.

For a moment I thought I'd let him carry on, for if I was right, then I was right, if not, well. I just knelt down by the river, looking at the swans. It was such a lovely day and it felt good to get away from work for a while. I began to throw stones into the water when I suddenly heard Tony call out, "Ann!" His voice had a ring of excitement about it.

"Come here, quickly," he said. "I've got something to show you."

I walked round the corner to where his voice was coming from. It was fairly shady where I had to go as the sun was left behind me, but I could see the water clearly. At the side of me stood the measuring pole which my father-in-law had shown me and told me about. Tony was aghast!

"All the times my father and I used to go fishing here there has never, ever been a measuring pole to my knowledge. Certainly never in this part of the river, anyway, for I know this section like the back of my hand and I swear I have never set eyes on that before!" Tony exclaimed.

He looked flabbergasted and wondered how on earth I knew all about the pole. I shrugged my shoulders and said, "Well, your father did say where he had caught the fish and that there was a measuring pole."

I didn't want to sound cocky, but I was really pleased that I had managed to prove his Dad right, or I should say his Dad proved himself right. At the same time I

159

was surprised that Tony was still being a bit sceptical, or was he? After all, although I knew they were always right, it was still early days for Tony to totally accept and after all, he couldn't see what I could see, nor hear what I could hear, so some things were bound to puzzle and surprise him. When I got back in the car I must admit to feeling a little bit smug and pleased with myself. Tony's father had gone by this time, and when Tony asked me if his Dad was still with us and I told him he had gone, he sounded a bit disappointed.

"Don't worry," I said, "He'll turn up again soon."

In the months that followed, there were many incidents like this which occurred, which absolutely convinced Tony and he never doubted me again. White Arrow never left my side at any time. Whenever anyone else in spirit came into contact with me White Arrow would step back to let them closer, but would never leave me completely. I was at all times fully aware of his presence and Tony was beginning to accept White Arrow to be more like a human being and would ask him many questions through me, of course, about himself and the spirit world in general.

One day, Tony was asking White Arrow something, when suddenly White Arrow replied, "Ask my wife!"

Now, let me take this opportunity to explain. Before I can give myself time to think whenever White Arrow speaks, I just repeat it and think about it afterwards. I could have bitten my tongue in this instance, for as soon as I said it Tony went very quiet and then asked me what White Arrow meant. My mind went back to the reincarnation and I knew somehow White Arrow would not keep his mouth shut, and he had really upset the apple cart this time. Now seemed the appropriate time to tell Tony about my reincarnation, so I explained the whole story to him. Let me tell you about Tony. He has always been a very possessive sort of man and, judging by the look on his face, I could tell that it didn't matter that White Arrow was a spirit or not, the very idea that some other man should call me his wife was most unsavoury and certainly not the right thing to say. As far as he was concerned it was like a red rag to a bull and he didn't like it one iota. Tony had accepted White Arrow to a certain degree, but the same went for White Arrow in accepting Tony as being my present-day husband. It was a very strange triangle to be found in, but up until now I have managed to keep everyone friendly, somehow or another. After that crack from White Arrow I wondered how long the friendship would last between the two men. I didn't want any trouble and things had gone so well, but I could see Tony was not entirely happy about the situation. I turned to White Arrow to have a go at him, but typically of him he had van-

160

ished. It was an old trick of his whenever he was in this mood.

Mentally, I said to White Arrow, "I'll catch up with you later," and I knew he could hear me. I also knew there would be no reply from him.

I looked at Tony and could tell he was still very upset, and in a way I felt sorry for him. After all, it was difficult for him to understand it all in one go, and Tony is a human being and loves me. As he had never seen or heard White Arrow it was an impossible task, for he didn't know who he was competing with.

"Come on, love," I said to him. "That happened well over a hundred years ago and my feelings for you are different from what I feel for him."

I paused for a moment for I realised how daft this all was. Here we were, arguing over someone who was dead!

"Yes, maybe I'm being stupid," said Tony, "But you have to admit that he is calling you *his* wife, when you are *mine*."

This was the first time Tony had not called the Indian White Arrow so I knew he wasn't happy at all.

"Let's forget it, Tony, for goodness sake," I said. "It's not as if White Arrow is living and can run off with me!"

Tony laughed and I could tell he was back to his old self again.

"By the way, where is White Arrow now?" he asked.

"I don't know," I replied, but in my mind I thought, "Just you wait till I catch up with you!"

That night he didn't appear until very late. Tony was reading, and when I told him White Arrow was back he said, "Don't you think you'd better have a word with him?"

I beckoned my finger at White Arrow and said, "I want you. Where have you been all day? I've been waiting for you. I must have a word with you about what you said this afternoon."

"Why?" asked White Arrow, grinning from ear to ear and acting the innocent.

161

"I don't think it's at all funny." I said, keeping a straight face. "You know perfectly well why. It's about you calling me your wife."

White Arrow sat down on the floor and said, "I know, but you are my wife. It's a habit I have of saying."

"Well, I've never heard you say it before," I said, "But in any case could you please try not to say it again because it causes too much friction between Tony and me."

If I can remember correctly, White Arrow replied that he was just being awkward. I had seen White Arrow like this before, but I was in no mood for it now after having seen Tony so upset, and I wasn't prepared to have him distressed any more. I thought to myself, This can't possibly all be happening. Could it really be that two men are arguing over whose wife I was?

"Come on, White Arrow," I said. "You've got to try and understand Tony and his feelings, for it's all very strange to him. Although I understand, it will take Tony time and remember, I've got to live with the pair of you. Do you understand what I am saying? Poor Tony can't see who I am talking to or hear what they are saying to me, and it must be so difficult for him, without you piping in with comments like that one."

He nodded and he wasn't being awkward now.

He said, "I'm sorry, I promise I'll try not to say it again," but as he got up to go his parting words were, "But, you are my wife!!"

I had to smile to myself. The best thing now was to try to forget what he had said, for as long as he didn't upset Tony too much I was happy. No more was said and White Arrow kept his word, well almost; sometimes it would slip out, but only on a very few occasions.

Life was getting good now and I was gradually becoming a different person. Everything around me looked different as I was noticing the flowers and trees, the animals and birds now, whereas, before it didn't bother or interest me. I had left work, too, as my place of work had shut down. That meant I now had more time for the spirit world, but also for what was around me in the living. Mum was much happier too, as she could see a vast improvement in me, and she and the girls had accepted White Arrow completely. Likewise, White Arrow liked them and enjoyed the times when we went round to visit them. After a while it became

162

second nature to me to work with White Arrow and the spirit world. I had forgotten all about the pills, except that I was still taking the four a day, but at least I hadn't gone backwards. The family had not mentioned it but I knew they were glad that I had come as far as I had without taking a retrograde step. Mum and Tony were so pleased with me because in the past I had always suffered from severe depression and so often I was crying. Now, I was much happier, contented, and looked so well, better than I had done for years.

Although White Arrow was around me all the time, apart from the other spirit people popping in to say "Hello" I had animals come to see me, too. This proved to me that our pets live on in the next world, which is such a comforting thought.

One night I went to bed early. There was to be a film on television that I particularly wanted to watch. There had been a good write-up about it in the papers so I left Tony downstairs doing his paperwork and I went upstairs to bed to watch television in comfort. As I got into bed and made myself quite comfy, the film started. I was pleased that I had timed it right and had left the bedroom door open, so if Tony had shouted from downstairs I could hear him. As I leant back on my pillows and pulled the bedclothes around me the film commenced. I became so engrossed in the film when suddenly the sound of the voices in the film seemed to be fading away. I started to get up from my comfortable position to adjust the set when I noticed the lovely smell of perfume in the room. I knew it wasn't mine for I hadn't got any perfume like that. The next thing I knew, I seemed to be drawn to the corner of the bedroom. The television was in the centre of the room where it had always been and I had the bedside lamp on so the room wasn't very well lit, but the television was throwing out some light. Just then, it appeared as if the whole corner of the bedroom was blue, and I was glued to it in amazement as a figure started to build up in front of me. It all happened in a matter of seconds and then, before me, stood a Geisha Girl. She was no more than nineteen years old and as she stood there I was taken in by her looks. She was beautiful beyond words. She stood about five feet three inches and had a slim figure. Her hair was thick and dark and it was piled high on her head and delicately adorned with ribbons and what looked like ornamental sticks which were holding it up in place. The coloured ribbons were attached to the sticks and were hanging down. The darkness of her hair showed up the colours of the ribbons beautifully and the sticks were red and yellow. In contrast, her face looked almost white, but I could see it was her make-up that made it appear so white. Her eyes were a deep shade of brown and her face was small with a gentle smile. Her dress looked very heavy and was made out of a deep mauve fabric with a flowery print all over it. It draped loosely down to her feet and she held her hands in front of her as if in prayer. Suddenly, she bowed to me and I could tell she was greeting me. She

163

began to move closer to me and as she did so her perfume got stronger, the same perfume I had smelt in the room beforehand. I couldn't hear or see the television any more. Instead, my eyes watched every movement she made and I was totally entranced and besotted with her. I couldn't move as I watched her and after a couple of steps she stopped and stood still. I didn't know what she wanted and I didn't care, to be quite honest. I had seen Geisha Girls on the television before, but this was different. Here was one right in front of me and, to me, a very real person. I was completely hypnotised and mesmerised by her when suddenly I was returned to reality by the sound of her soft, feminine voice.

"Hello," she said so quietly, I could just about hear her.

"Hello," I replied.

I leant back on my pillows, and noticed that along with her outstanding beauty, she had well-manicured nails which were very long indeed.

Gosh, you are lovely, I thought to myself, forgetting again that spirit can read our thoughts.

"Thank you," came back her reply. "Do you mind if I tell you my story?"

I found this to be a little strange, for usually the spirit world never bothered to ask me permission, but just went ahead with whatever it was they had to say.

I said, "Of course I don't mind. Please go ahead." I was still overawed by her outstanding beauty, for she was truly a glorious sight. As she proceeded to tell me about her life on earth she had tears in her eyes. She told me all about a great love she had for a young European boy, but her father strongly disapproved of it and stopped her from seeing him. However, because her love for the boy was so great she disobeyed her father. Unfortunately, her father found out and, with a firm warning, told her never to be disobedient again.

The following week the European boy and the Geisha Girl ran away together, but it wasn't long before her father and some of her family caught up with them. This resulted in a terrible argument and fighting broke out, during which the young boy was killed by a knife wound. The poor girl was heartbroken and this explained why she had tears in her eyes as she spoke to me. She was then sent away to another part of the country to relations, but she couldn't forget the European boy whom she loved so dearly. She gradually became so depressed that she decided to take her own life so that she could join him in the next world.

164

At this point I stopped her to ask how she died. I was very intrigued, but she wouldn't tell me. I didn't wish to pursue the matter further, but I asked her if she did manage to join her loved one. She said she did, but it was many years later before they could be together again. I was happy for her and told her so.

She said very quietly, "Thank you for listening to me," and with that she slowly faded away until I could see her no longer.

All this time the television was still on. The Geisha Girl had only been with me for a little while and when I looked back, with a view to following the story of the film, I found I had no interest in it, for my mind was still on the Geisha girl, and I was glad I had missed the film after all, for I was so delighted that I had the privilege to meet her. When I settled myself down to sleep later that night I hoped that I would meet her again some day, but even if I didn't I will always remember her outstanding beauty and shall always treasure that memory.

I always went round to visit Mum and the girls every day and when I had my job Tony had always taken me after work. Now that I wasn't at work it was different. One morning, Mum telephoned to say she had the day off and would I like to pop round. I told her I'd be round as soon as I could and got dressed to go out. I checked I had my front door key. I glanced up at the clock to find it had just gone past ten, so I had plenty of time before Tony would be home for his lunch. That gave me a couple of hours to spend with Mum and I was looking forward to it. I looked out of the window to see what the weather was like. It was sunny outside so I decided to put on a jacket instead of a coat and slammed the front door behind me before I walked up the garden path.

All of a sudden, I saw my dog Sally down at my feet. I stopped in my tracks because for a second I could hardly believe my eyes. I looked again, just to make sure I wasn't seeing things, and there she was. My mind went back to my early years and the times we had shared together. By this stage I had learned that it was only me who could see the spirit world and that I couldn't speak out loud to a spirit when I saw one, otherwise people in the living would surely think I was talking to myself. Therefore, quietly in my mind, I said, "Hello, Sally," and with that her tail started wagging. I felt so choked when she did that, for I would have dearly loved to cuddle her, but I knew it was impossible. As I walked out of the gate, I wondered if she would follow me or just simply disappear but, to my delight, she followed me, because when I first saw her I had no idea how long she would be around.

Sally followed me all the way to Mum's house, but as soon as I reached the door she disappeared. I felt sad for a moment, and hoped it wouldn't be the last time would see her. I didn't mention Sally to Mum, for although she believed in me she had never really wanted to know exactly what it was I could see, so I never pushed myself on to her. After all, she was entitled to her own beliefs and I knew she was just happy to see me so well.

When it was time for me to leave Mum's house, I started to look for Sally straight away, but she wasn't there, so I carried on walking home just the same. On my way home I had to call in at the paper-shop for a paper and some cigarettes. As came out there was Sally sitting on the pavement, waiting for me. I had to check myself once again, as I had often done, for I still wasn't used to telling the difference between the living and the dead.

As I walked off she followed me but when I arrived back home she vanished. This carried on for a few weeks, but after that I didn't see her for some time, and she doesn't stay long nowadays when she pops in, but I'm always glad to see her and truly grateful that she hasn't forgotten me.

Life in general was going along fine with White Arrow by my side and every day I learned something new. For the first time in my life I started to appreciate life and was on top of the world. One day I spent most of the day with Mum. I loved her and am proud to admit it, for she was a good woman and I don't think mother and a daughter could ever be as close as us. We were enjoying life now in a way we never thought possible, and I was as well as could be expected. Both Mum and Tony were proud that I had come this far and that for months now had stayed that way, so now they were both convinced that I was almost cured of the drugs. Therefore, nobody had bothered about the four pills a day I was taking, that is, until that afternoon. I hadn't been in long and made myself a cup of tea. switched on the television to watch when suddenly White Arrow appeared.

"Hi," I said, and once again turned my attention to the television programme was watching. White Arrow often appeared whenever I was sitting watching television, and I gathered that through this media it had been an easy way of h picking up the English language, and I was amused by the fact that he was able learn in this manner. I never commented on it, but let him get on with it and would carry on watching whatever programme was on with him. On this particular day I carried out the same procedure, but to my surprise I heard White Arrow say, "Turn it off."

I looked at him questioningly, but leant forward to turn it off, nevertheless "What's the problem?" I asked him as I lit a cigarette. I leant back on the armchair. It was so unlike White Arrow to order me, so I knew it would have to be something serious he wanted to discuss with me and I was puzzled as I couldn't think what could be so serious a subject. I sat patiently, however, and waited for him to talk to me. By now, White Arrow's English was almost perfect so it was easy to converse with him, which made it much easier for me and, for that matter, I'm sure it did for White Arrow, too.

"Ann," White Arrow said.

Just for a split second my mind wandered off and his calling my name brought me back.

"Yes?" I replied.

"What about the pills?" he asked.

Since I had met White Arrow not once had he ever brought up the subject of my drug-taking and I was completely taken aback. The only thing I could say was, "Well, what about them?"

"Isn't it about time you stopped taking them, for they don't belong in the future," said White Arrow.

I sat still, feeling slightly stunned for a moment and thought about them. I was well now, and hadn't really considered that four pills a day would cause me any harm, but I knew he was right. The truth was, I didn't really want to let go of them. They *were* my past and they had always protected me from being hurt. By now I had stopped hurting my family, but I clung on to the fact that maybe taking only four pills a day wasn't hurting anyone, the least of all me, but I knew I was kidding myself.

Once again White Arrow repeated that they didn't belong in the future.

"I know," I replied. I thought to myself that to many people four pills a day would be nothing to cry about, but they were not normal pills and for twenty-three years I had been addicted to them, and it was my way of life. There is no doubt that they had been my salvation, if you like, and although I was much happier now than I had been for years, the very thought of giving them up completely had never entered my head. I had got this far and I honestly didn't want to stop taking them and the very thought terrified me. I wished White Arrow hadn't brought up the subject, for since I had met him I had been so happy and contented and I

167

didn't want anything to spoil that.

As I looked up at him I knew I should have expected him to want me to stop taking them and, although my family hadn't talked about it to me for ages, I knew deep down that soon they may very well ask me to do the same thing. My mind went back to Dad and when it had all started and just then I was terribly frightened. I just couldn't let anyone or anything hurt me again as I was aware I was still very vulnerable to anything that could cause me pain and anguish; the memory of Dad came flooding back and it was awful.

Forgetting White Arrow could read my mind, he said, "Do you trust me, Little One?" He was speaking softly now.

"You know I do," I replied, "But what if..."

Before I could finish the sentence, White Arrow interrupted and said, "If what, Ann? You can do it. Trust me."

I knew he wouldn't let me down, but I just couldn't help being scared. However, my trust in him was paramount and I so wanted everything to turn out well.

White Arrow said, "Every day won't be like heaven and I won't lie to you, but many good things are in store for you and you will not need or desire the pills any more. The time has come for you to come off them, so that you will be ready for these things that will happen for you in the future."

I looked up at White Arrow and my mind went back to when I had first turned to the church for help from God. Not once since that moment of time had I given it a second thought, and all that happened during the church visit. During the wonderful period in my life that I had White Arrow by my side and the spirit world, I had forgotten about it and never considered that in fact God had listened to my cry and had sent me and given me the greatest gift of all. For the first time I said, "Thank you," and what White Arrow was asking of me seemed such a small request compared with what God had given me in return.

"O.K." I said. "I can't promise, but I'll try my best."

White Arrow smiled and I knew at least I had his strength to back me up. I so wanted to prove to my family I could get well but I had let them down so often. I prayed that this time I would succeed.

168

Since coming to Hillingdon to live, I had signed on with a doctor but had never bothered asking his help to get me off the drugs. The doctor had been quite willing to allow me to stay on that daily dosage, but White Arrow suggested that I should find a new doctor who would help me come off them completely, who would have the patience and conviction to help me come off them instead of giving me the easy option of taking them for the rest of my days. I don't doubt that White Arrow had something to do with the fact that I was able to find the right doctor, for he turned out to be only a young man, but so helpful and under-standing. At the beginning he asked to see me every other day, and slowly but surely started cutting down the pills by just a quarter of a pill a week. During that time White Arrow was always there, and if I felt depressed he would joke about to cheer me up or make suggestions as to what I should do to lighten my load. Sometimes he would just talk to me in the most encouraging way, which was marvellous support for me.

When Tony came home from work every evening, he very often took me out and sometimes we went on to see friends after we had visited Mum and the kids. Sometimes we went for long drives, and I found that with the full support of both Tony and White Arrow, I was winning. The only problem I encountered at this stage was that I was not sleeping at all well and it was nothing for me to still be wide awake at four in the morning.

It was during these restless times when White Arrow would take me back to the past life I had spent with him in North America. After a while it always had the desired effect and I gradually drifted off to sleep.

As White Arrow is my guide who comes from the spirit world, he has taught me that everyone on this earth has their own guide, as he is mine.

Sometimes these guides are referred to as door-keepers and they are linked with you and stay with you from the time you are born till the day you die. There are also some spirit people who are known as helpers. Sometimes they stay with us a long time and maybe just for a short period, it all depends on our needs at the time, but they are just as important in their own right as are our guides. As a rule, guides and helpers are not members of our spirit families but more highly-evolved beings. One night, as I was getting ready for bed, a nun appeared. She wasn't very tall and was a little on the plump side. I would say she was about fifty or sixty years old, and the wonderful feeling of peace which I felt in her presence was remarkable. She said in a very quiet, soft voice, "I've come to help you, my child."

169

"Thank you." I replied, not really understanding what kind of help she was referring to. Up until now I had only known White Arrow to be the learned one who always gave me any help I needed. However, I was very pleased to see her and I adored the serenity she brought with her. I asked her to tell me her name and she said it was Sister Maria.

After having read my mind, she said, "I've come to give help to you at night for your sleep."

Before I could reply she said, "Trust White Arrow. He has called on me for my assistance to help him with this problem of yours."

That made me feel much happier, for I was worried at first that she meant White Arrow was going away and it was the first time such a thought had entered my head, and I didn't like the prospect of not having him around one bit. What if he did go one day? What would I do? How would I feel and how could I go on without him? All these fears and questions were going through my head at a quick pace. My mind was now not on Sister Maria any more and all of a sudden White Arrow appeared and sat on my bed. Sister Maria remained standing at the side of my bed just listening. Just then I became very overcome with emotion and tears began to come to my eyes. I tried so hard not to cry but found it intolerable. "Don't ever leave me, will you White Arrow?"

"Little One," he replied, "While you are on this earth I will be by your side every waking day. You have trusted me so far and I tell you now I am your guide forever, so take the tears and fears away now. From now on and until you are sleeping properly again, Sister Maria will be with you one night and I the next. She is here to help you, so trust her as you do me." Before he left he turned and said to me, "Remember, Little One, I'm at your side, always."

I was happy now he had said that and I turned to speak to Sister Maria.

"I'm so sorry," I said. "I didn't mean to sound disrespectful."

"I understand completely, think nothing of it," she replied.

When it was time for me to turn the light out I wondered how long I would lie there, waiting for sleep to come. Suddenly, Sister Maria took me out of my body and far away to a convent. I found myself with all the nuns and we were all praying together. After our prayers we all walked towards our bedrooms and as walked into one of the rooms I thought to myself how bare they looked. All it had as a cross on the wall and a single bed, and by the side of the bed was a small table. On the table was a side light and a Bible. The sensation of peace and tranquillity in that little room was very strong and I got into bed, picked up the Bible and held it to my chest. I didn't actually read it but lay my head back on the pillow and before I knew it I drifted off to sleep.

The following morning, on waking, I remembered it all and thanked Sister Maria. With both White Arrow and Sister Maria together over the coming months they managed to get me off to sleep normally and I no longer needed their little trips away to settle me.

During this period of getting well, an event happened which showed the other side of White Arrow inasmuch as, if he wanted something done, he would do it without thinking. Let me explain - although most nights I was now sleeping better there were the odd occasions when I wasn't, and this particular weekend, no matter what White Arrow or Sister Maria did to try to help me, it didn't seem to work. Ninety per cent of the time their help was beyond belief, but obviously there were nights when it didn't always work - and this was one of them! I was almost off the pills, but not quite, and the Monday which followed this bad weekend I didn't feel at all well.

I said to Tony, "We'll have an early night tonight as I haven't been sleeping too well the past two nights."

Tony said, "O.K. You go up and I'll bring you up a hot drink in a minute."

"Thanks, love," I replied and went upstairs and as I was walking up the stairs White Arrow appeared and said to me, "Will you go and get some paper and a pen?"

I thought, What on earth should he want me to do that for and I wasn't really in the mood, but I thought, Anything for a peaceful night's sleep.

As I popped back downstairs again, Tony said, "What's the matter?"

"White Arrow wants me write something down."

"What sort of thing?" asked Tony.

"I don't know and haven't the faintest idea till I go back upstairs. With White Arrow you never know what he wants, it could be anything."

Tony laughed and said, "You'd better go up and see."

"I'll be up in a while," he shouted as I turned the corner at the top of the staircase.

As I climbed into my bed White Arrow was sitting on Tony's bed waiting for me. I said to him, "O.K., I've got the paper and pen. What's it all about?" I really hadn't a clue what he had in mind so I was quite intrigued.

Just then, a Cherokee Indian appeared and stood next to White Arrow. They exchanged words but I couldn't hear them. After a couple of minutes I got a bit impatient and said, "Come on, White Arrow, I'm tired," but he completely ignored me and carried on talking to the Cherokee. This continued for about five minutes and then White Arrow stopped the conversation, looked at me, and started to tell me what to do. He told me to draw a picture which he would describe in detail, which would be an Indian symbol. When I finished it I looked at White Arrow, waiting for him to carry on with further instructions and all he said was, "That's it!" and with that both he and the Cherokee vanished. About half an hour later White Arrow returned but was on his own this time. By now, Tony had come up to bed, and I was sitting up having the drink he had made for me.

"What was all that about?" I asked White Arrow.

His only answer was, "It's important," and with that he vanished again.

I had given up trying to solve this baffling guessing game and all I wanted to do was try and get some sleep. Although Sister Maria was with me I could not concentrate on going away to the convent with her this time, so I knew I was going to have another bad night. Sure enough, the following day I felt rough. I had gone for three consecutive nights with hardly any sleep and it had really got to me.

I said to Tony, "If I don't sleep tonight I'll have to see the doctor for some advice."

Tony was a bit surprised as he knew my sleeping had been bad, but he didn't like the thought of the possibility of him putting me back on more pills. I was, after all, almost off them completely now and it would be such a pity to have to go backwards.

172

"It's O.K., Tony, I don't want more pills, I just need a bit of help. After all, I must sleep."

Tony stopped worrying then. White Arrow was around most of that day then early in the evening he vanished again. I had an early night and had only been in bed ten minutes when back he came with the same Cherokee. I had a suspicion that I would be in for a repeat performance somehow so I had already left the paper and pen upstairs ready. This time White Arrow didn't have to talk with the Cherokee and I presume it was because they had spoken before they came to me. I had already told Tony about the previous night, so I turned to him as we sat up in bed and said to him, "They're here again, Tony." Tony said nothing, he only smiled and carried on watching television. White Arrow once again told me to draw a picture of an Indian symbol as he described it, as he had done the night before. A different one this time which meant nothing at all to me and I didn't ask either. They both vanished again and by now I knew the symbols were very important to White Arrow by the way he was acting. Never before had he needed anyone to help him with a message such as this. I went to sleep and put the symbols in the drawer for safe keeping. Again, I had a bad night, so the following morning I made an appointment to see my doctor. Tony took me by car and on the way there White Arrow sat in the back. This was nothing unusual for him but he didn't seem very happy for some reason or another, going by the expression on his face. I didn't take much notice as I wasn't that happy myself, having lost so much sleep. What I did find strange, though, was that White Arrow followed me right into the doctor's surgery. Never before had he ever done such a thing and because he looked so annoyed as we sat waiting to see the doctor, I wondered if it was because he didn't like the idea of my consulting him, and possibly being pre-scribed some drugs to help me sleep.

"Look here, you've got to understand, White Arrow," I said. "I can't go on without sleep for this long. I know and appreciate your and Sister Maria's help. It has been invaluable and has worked up until a few nights ago, but I feel now I'm at the end of my tether and can't cope any longer. Please understand."

He said nothing. I thought to myself, Please yourself!

At last it was my turn to see the doctor and as I entered the doctor's room White Arrow followed me. The doctor was very helpful and, taking my case history into consideration, he prescribed some sleeping pills which were not addictive. I left the surgery thinking, Well at least I'll get a few nights' rest and then it would sort itself out. As I got back in our car White Arrow was sitting on the back seat, mumbling away to himself in his native tongue. This was the first time I had ever heard him speak in his own language and I could tell he was very angry. As I could not understand what he was saying, however, I did not know why. I said to him, "If you're going to persist in speaking to me in your own language and not mine, we're going to get nowhere, are we?" He shut up for a second and I went on, "Well? are we?"

White Arrow said, "Doctors are a waste of time, the symbols are far more important."

First of all I was enraged by his remark and said, "Hold it, White Arrow! Surely my sleep comes first."

"No!" he retorted. "The symbols are more important," and he carried on mumbling to himself once more. I had never seen him like this before and I didn't seem to be doing a very good job of snapping him out of it. Suddenly, from nowhere, an Indian Chief appeared and sat right next to White Arrow. My memories all came flooding back of my reincarnation and I instantly recognised him to be White Arrow's father. I was so pleased to see him for I could remember being fond of this highly-respected man. He spoke to White Arrow in their native tongue and after a short while the Chief looked up at me and smiled. I hadn't forgotten those unmistakable eyes which were so like his son's, then, as quickly as he appeared, he vanished.

I looked at White Arrow, who had calmed down quite a bit by now. He said, "I'm sorry, Little One, but the symbols are so important for you and we only have a short time in which you have to receive them all." From that statement I gathered the Cherokee was to leave soon, but also realised that more were to come. How many more I wasn't sure, but that wasn't the end of it yet.

Everything went back to normal for the rest of that day and I wondered if I would ever see White Arrow's father again. I asked White Arrow what his father had said to him when they were sitting next to each other in our car, and he just intimated that it wasn't very pleasant for him! I knew he had been told off but I wasn't satisfied with that answer and curious to know exactly what he had said.

"Come on, White Arrow, you can tell me."

"Well, besides upsetting you, Little One, my Father told me I was forgetting that I was spirit and not of the living."

I understood what he meant for many times White Arrow seemed to forget he was

174

spirit! Despite all this, however, I felt sorry for White Arrow and told him so. "I prefer you just the way you are."

"Thanks, Little One," said White Arrow, "But I have to take notice and obey him."

By this time I had got to know White Arrow only too well, so I knew he would soon forget the ticking off he had received from his father and be his old self in no time, so I was not unduly worried.

That night, and the following two nights, I received a symbol so by Friday I had five altogether. Apart from knowing they were very important, I didn't know any of their meanings. I kept them safely away in a drawer and nothing more was heard of the Cherokee.

In the days that followed I was becoming more curious about the meaning and significance of the symbols so I said to Tony, "Do me a favour and take me to some libraries to pick up some books on Red Indians."

"Why?" asked Tony, not knowing what I was up to.

"Well, I think I'll try to find out if any of the symbols are in any of the books and if they are they might give some explanation as to their meaning."

Tony is fairly easy going and agreed. What we had not envisaged was how many Red Indian books there are available. It took me three whole months to read all I could about the Indians but didn't come across anything resembling the symbols I was looking for.

One day an idea came into my head and I suggested that Tony and I go to the British Museum. By this stage I think poor Tony had had enough of Indians to last him a life-time so I reassured him by saying, "I promise you that if I find no luck at the British Museum with what I'm trying to find, I'll give up."

He laughed and said, "I've heard that one before!" But when we got there we did manage to find a book on Indian symbols, to my sheer delight (and no doubt Tony's relief!) The author's name was Jefferson and in the book we found very similar drawings to those which I had, in fact, they were almost identical. Unfortunately, that's where our luck ran out, for there was no explanation whatsoever with them. I cannot say I wasn't feeling disappointed but I was glad we had found them anyway as it proved they must be important to be printed in a book.

On the way home I asked White Arrow, "Why don't you tell me what they mean?"

"One day, Little One, you will know the meaning of the symbols, but not now."

I must admit that none of the reading was a waste of time for I had learnt such a lot about the Red Indian. Along with remembering my reincarnation, all the information the books gave me was invaluable and gave me a very clear picture and insight to the Indian people. I still had some Indian books at home and decided to finish reading them before taking them back to the library. I spent most of the following Sunday outstretched on the floor reading the last of the books, so engrossed in what I was reading, when I heard Tony get up to go to the kitchen.

"Do you want anything, love?" I called out.

"No, it's alright," replied Tony.

I carried on reading and when Tony came back into the sitting room he sat on the settee. I looked up at him and was just about to say, "Are you O.K., love?" when I spotted White Arrow. There he was, standing over Tony with a perplexed look upon his face. In his hands Tony was holding a bowl, but what was in it I couldn't quite see. Then White Arrow bent down on his knees, peering into the bowl that Tony was eating from. I was so amused by this that I had to put the book down and sit up to see what White Arrow was up to. Tony looked at me as he must have sensed I was looking at him and unwittingly asked, "What's the matter?"

I said, "White Arrow seems intrigued with whatever it is you're eating."

"It's only a grapefruit," said Tony, in all innocence.

I asked White Arrow what was wrong, to which he replied, "It's alright, Tony's explained what it is he's eating. I've never seen one before."

I thought to myself, Well there's no reason why White Arrow should have seen one before and this was a prime example of the many things which White Arrow would come across enough to puzzle him, but Tony and I would be able to explain things to him which he did not understand before. I carried on reading the book, knowing White Arrow was now happy and contented with the explanation about the grapefruit. I had just eight pages left to finish the book when I found I had to close it for some reason or another and couldn't finish it at all. I had finished all the reading I had to do about Indians and their symbols once and for

176

all.

I was delighted that my family, that is Tony, Mum and the kids, were used to White Arrow now and there was never any question about him being there. He was loved by them as much as I was and nothing could please me more to know White Arrow was beginning to teach me a lot about myself and life that was going on around me. He was very pleased with my progress with the pills and it was obvious to him that I now trusted him completely. My barrier was slowly coming down and it wouldn't be long before I would need no more pills at all. I was right down to virtually no pills at all when one day my doctor said to me, "You'll be completely off them in a couple of weeks, Ann," and you can't imagine how good it was to hear those words. It was coming up to September and I had known White Arrow now for seventeen months. When I went back to see the doctor in September, sure enough, he said, "No more of your pills, Ann, they have been taken off the market."

I knew that White Arrow had known this would happen and why he had helped me so much. From that day on I never looked back. I was now cured completely and there was no turning back. After the doctor had told me this I walked out of his surgery, wondering to myself if I would be able to cope. Suddenly, White Arrow was there by my side and said, "Little One, you'll never look back so go home and tell your family that for the first time there will be no more pills ever again."

I knew Tony and Mum would believe I was cured and also the kids, but that was for the present, wouldn't they be frightened that one day something would make me go back on them? With this, White Arrow said to me, "Between you and me, Little One, we will overcome whatever comes our way."

I found it easy to convince Tony everything would be alright but Mum, love her, trusted White Arrow but I knew she would wait for more time to pass before she was one hundred per cent sure. I knew I had a couple of years ahead of me to prove to the kids that I would stay off the pills.

In the following months I was so happy not having to rely on any more pills. I still had regular check-ups and consultations with my doctor, but overall I was a happier person. The one person I had to prove myself to was my dear mother, for I owed her more than anyone else on this earth. Tony always knew this, even before I had met White Arrow, and had always understood the bond between Mum and me. White Arrow also knew how close Mum and I were and he was as pleased as I was when I saw the trusting look on Mum's face each time I saw her.

She had so much faith in me and I wouldn't, couldn't let her down. We all love our mums and they are all special in their own right, but, because of the hard times Mum and I had shared, we were closer and for me to be able to leave all the drugs behind me was the best present I could possibly give her.

One night, when I went round to see her and the kids, we were all sitting in the kitchen - our favourite chatting place. Now and again I needed someone to give me a pat on the back, a word of encouragement. I asked her, "Mum, are you pleased with me?"

"Ann, I loved you as you were and I will always love you. The only difference now is that I'm proud of you, too. Even without White Arrow being with you I know how difficult it has been for you to get used to no drugs and how bad the pain has been for you to withstand, but I know you better than anyone else, including White Arrow. I always knew that one day something would come along for all us to benefit, something which would take you off the drugs, and for that reason I thank White Arrow from the bottom of my heart. I know how much strength you receive from him and that one day you would prove to me that you would be able to live without them completely."

I was very moved by her kind words and, as we put our arms around each other, I sobbed, "Oh, I love you, Mum," and she repeated the words, "I'm proud of you, Ann. Your girls will be too, you'll see."

We sat down again and composed ourselves. "What about the girls, Mum? Do you think they'll trust me?" I had a nagging doubt at the back of my mind about my eldest daughter regarding this for, although she and I were on speaking terms, we were not as close as I was to my youngest daughter. Almost as if she was reading my mind, Mum said, "Give her time, love."

I said, "I don't think I'll ever be able to make up those lost years to both of them. It doesn't seem possible that the eldest is now nineteen and the young one is sixteen, does it?"

Mum went a bit quiet and then said in a quiet voice, "Do you love them more than anything in this world?"

"I said, "Of course I do."

"Then you will fight to prove it to them in the years to come."

178

I couldn't help thinking, Yes, but how many years would it take, for as much as I loved the life I was now living, my whole past was filled with guilt and pain which was in turn showered upon my children. Those emotions were still there and for the very first time I realised that what my father had done to me I had done to my own children without knowing it. Maybe I had not hit them or they had not seen their mother beaten up daily and the pain that went with it all, but in another way I had caused them another type of pain. By hiding behind pills, they didn't know what their real mother was really like, and even to this day I am eaten up with the guilt I feel.

I told Mum what I had just come to terms with and she leant forward to hold my hand and said, "No matter what you were, Ann, you were a good daughter and you tried your best to be a mother, but what I'm glad about is you realise it now and it isn't too late to prove it to them."

"I hope so, Mum, really I do," I said.

When Tony and I went home later that night I went over the conversation Mum and I had had in my mind. I was very worried about my eldest daughter's opinion of me and thought the damage was already done and irreparable. Just before I went to sleep I prayed it could be rectified. My youngest girl hadn't gone through as much as the eldest, but even that was sheer hell for her, so she and I were a lot closer, which made it easier to cope with somehow. With this knowledge at least I had something to hold on to and I knew this would please Mum, too. My youngest girl was full of love for me and that made me feel good. If only my other daughter could feel the same for me as I loved her just as dearly.

Out of all my doubts and fears I still had White Arrow. He reminded me that he would always be there to overcome any obstacles that arose with him at my side, and that comforted me so much.

CHAPTER SIXTEEN

One Sunday evening Tony and I decided to go to church. The medium got up to give the reading from a passage in a book. It was about a man who had a dream one night. He was walking along the beach with the Lord. Across the sky flashed the scenes from his life and for each scene he noticed two sets of footprints in the sand - one belonging to him, the other to the Lord. When the last scene of his life flashed before him he looked back at the footprints in the sand and noticed that many times along the pathway of his life there was only one set of footprints. He also noticed that this always happened at the lowest and saddest times of his life. This really bothered the man and so he questioned the Lord about it and said, "Lord, you said that once I decided to follow you, you would walk with me all the way, but I have noticed that during the most troublesome times in my life there is only one set of footprints. I don't understand why, when I needed you most, you'd leave me."

The Lord replied, "My precious, precious child. I love you and will never leave you. During your times of trial and suffering, when you saw only one set of footprints, it was then that I carried you."

After the medium had finished the reading I felt quite choked. I had never heard anything so lovely and I was really moved. As I sat there quietly, going over it again in my mind, White Arrow said to me, "Little One, do you remember the night Sister Maria came and you were frightened I would leave you?"

"Yes," I replied, "I shall never forget it."

"Well," said White Arrow. "The words the woman has read from her book are true. Everyone who is put on this earth has, from God, what you have got. That is, a guide to protect and look after you, as I am your guide. We are always with you to overcome whatever is to come."

A question entered my head, one which I hadn't thought to ask before. I asked White Arrow where he had been all my life. Why now, after thirty-seven years of hell? I was so eager to receive the answers to my questions that I wasn't listening to the medium's voice any more. I wanted to know, needed to know, and had suddenly become obsessed with it all. I had momentarily forgotten the lovely reading and, above all, what White Arrow had done for me in the past eighteen months or so. I was recapping the conversation I had had with Mum about my having to prove to the kids I was now cured and how I would try my hardest to get their love and respect back. I was starting to feel angry. Where had White Arrow been all those years and why had he not helped me then? Maybe if he had done so then I wouldn't have to prove myself to the kids now. Maybe Tony and Mum wouldn't have had to go through hell and back if he'd been with me then. I was getting myself in a right old state with maybe this and maybe that...

The service was coming to a close by now and people were starting to chatter

180

amongst themselves. Some of them were talking to us, but my mind was still on what the lady medium had been talking about and I wasn't concentrating on what they were saying to me. It was no good, I would have to continue my questioning with White Arrow later. I was dying to get home and sit down with White Arrow to finish our conversation there. There were so many answers and explanations I needed from him.

When we got home I went straight to bed, telling Tony that I was going to have a few words with White Arrow. Tony asked if they were important questions I was going to put to him and I said firmly, "Yes, very." As I said it, I took a good look at my husband. Not once had I really asked him if all this had bothered him. Our world had turned round this way and that for the past year and a half and I thought it was about time I had considered him more than I had been doing so, so I sat down with Tony before I went upstairs to talk with White Arrow. True enough, Tony had always seemed happy with what was going on, never questioning me, nor asking me how I felt having White Arrow in my life. I had always involved Tony in everything that had been said to me by the spirit world, and White Arrow in particular, but now, for the first time, I was asking, Was it enough? Tony had been with me from the age of sixteen and now he was seeing a different me. I wondered if he was happy with the changed me, did he like me like this? Was he happy with White Arrow and the spirit people? I just wasn't sure and felt a bit guilty and selfish for not having asked him before now how he felt about it all.

"What's the matter?" asked Tony. "I thought you were going to bed."

"I'm thinking," I said.

"What about?" he asked.

"You, Tony, you." I said. "I'd like you to sit down with me for a moment. I'd like to talk to you about something."

"Give me two minutes and I'll be with you," said Tony, and he got up to go into the kitchen to make himself a cup of tea. After he had put the kettle on he said, "What's on your mind? You've been quiet ever since we left church."

"Actually, I was thinking of the reading the lady had given this evening in church and wanted to talk to White Arrow about it."

"Why aren't you, then?" replied Tony.

181

I said, "Well, something else more important was on my mind, and it concerns you."

"Come on then, what's it about?"

"I've never really asked you how you feel about all of this, about my new life with the spirit world and especially White Arrow," I said.

"Well," replied Tony, "I must admit when you first met White Arrow I wasn't at all sure about it, but now you are so well these days, and knowing White Arrow as well as I do now, I really don't mind. After all, you are still mine - nothing at all will ever change that. White Arrow is regarded as one of the family and I like him. That's all there is to it, so don't worry."

He said what I wanted him to say and as long as Tony was O.K., I was satisfied too.

I gave Tony a kiss and got up to go upstairs. He touched my hand and said, "You have no need to worry at all, Ann. I love them as much as you do. I'd soon tell you if I was unhappy and I'm not, so go and have your talk with White Arrow."

Sometimes it seemed so funny to me to have two men around and this was one of those times. Here I was, sharing my time with both of them, but neither of them were jealous of the other. I hoped in my heart it would always be like that. Especially on Tony's part, considering he has never seen White Arrow. I was learning more about the spirit world and one thing was that when we die, although we go to heaven, it doesn't mean that we come back to see our loved ones with wings on our backs! We are the same people as we were on earth. If we were any different we would not be recognised by our families and acquaintances. White Arrow proved to me that he was just like that - he certainly had no wings, even if he was a high guide. He had his moods on earth and they were no different now he was living in heaven, I can assure you!

By the time I got to bed, sure enough, White Arrow was in one of his bad moods. There he was, lying on Tony's bed with both arms and legs crossed.

"Finished now?" he asked sarcastically.

I could read White Arrow like a book so I ignored that remark. He wasn't being funny about Tony at all and showed his true colours. Let's put it this way, patience is not one of his best qualities.

"Come on, White Arrow, I'm not in the mood for this. If you like, I'll ask the questions tomorrow when you are in a better frame of mind." Although I said it, I was really hoping he wouldn't go. Once again I had slipped up by forgetting he could read my mind. He smiled and sat up.

"O.K." he said, "Out with it."

The memory of the reading came flooding back so I said, "Why didn't you show yourself all those years ago when I needed you most of all? Why after thirty-seven years and not before?"

"Little One, from the day you were born I have been with you. I only wish I could have shown myself to you on many occasions. I wanted to, but there is law and order up there (he pointed upwards) and I was not allowed to make you aware of my presence until now. You must know by now that very soon you will have to help other people through me. If you hadn't realised it before, then I'm telling you now. You wouldn't be of any use to them if you had not experienced the pain and suffering they will have had. It is easy to give a message or give a kind word, but it is better still for you to have experienced the same problems so that you know exactly how they hurt and what they are feeling, for you have been through it yourself."

I said, "O.K., I agree that perhaps there was a reason for my suffering, but why my family? That's the bit that hurts me most of all."

"I know," replied White Arrow, "But it is all part of the plan to test everyone who is put on this earth. They each had a pathway to follow. Did you know you choose your own life?"

I laughed at this and said, "What?! You're joking. Only a fool would pick mine!"

"You did, you know," said White Arrow.

What he said was a bit hard to swallow, so I sat there for a few moments thinking back over my life and wondered if he could be right in what he said. Would I have looked and seen that I was going to be a medium myself in the knowledge White Arrow was going to be there, right alongside me? Would I have skipped the early years? What I did know to be true was that I was pleased I had Mum, Tony and the kids and wouldn't have changed that part of my life. I would have definitely chosen all of them for they were my life, even if I hadn't been able to show my love to them all the time, they all meant the world to me.

"Yes, maybe you're right," I said to White Arrow. I knew he was speaking the truth and it made me feel a little bit humble to think my family had also chosen me, even if they were unaware of it.

"Before you go, White Arrow, there's one more thing I'd like to know. Will I be able to make it up to the family for all those years of unhappiness?"

"Yes, Little One, but it will not always be easy. You will have to give more time for the children to forgive and forget."

I understood this as Mum and Tony understood me. The children were still young and it would take them time to forgive and forget, but now I had a renewed strength to wait - the strength of White Arrow.

I heard Tony coming up the stairs and as White Arrow got up from Tony's bed he said, "See you tomorrow, Little One," then he vanished.

When Tony came into the bedroom he said, "Did you ask your questions and, more to the point, did you get the answers you wanted?"

I explained what I had asked and why and White Arrow's answers to them.

"It makes sense," said Tony.

I said, "But there are so many other things I have to find out about."

"I'm sure in good time White Arrow will tell you all you need to know," said Tony, reassuringly, and with that we both got into bed and went to sleep.

* * * * *

At last I was now completely cured of all drugs and was enjoying life to the full. White Arrow was now part of the family and life continued that way. White Arrow had been with me for two years now and I had enjoyed every minute of it. One Sunday, White Arrow came in and sat down. Suddenly, he said, "Little One, the time is coming up for us to help other people." I had a feeling that this would come one day somehow and, as much as I loved White Arrow, I knew I could not keep him to myself and my immediate family. He was a part of me but I knew his real purpose for being here was to help people through me. I had very mixed

184

feelings, because I didn't really want to share him any more than I would like to share Tony, then again I felt a bit selfish for, after all White Arrow had done so much for me - why shouldn't I let others share some of my happiness, it was only fair.

I apologised to White Arrow for my feelings of selfishness and he smiled and I admitted I would be terribly nervous seeing people. "It's not that I don't trust you, you know I do, and I know you'll take care of everything, but I can't help being apprehensive about the whole idea," I said.

"I understand, Little One, but so many people on this earth need our help from the spirit world and that is the main purpose of my being here. As much as I love you and your family, always remember I am here, but not only for you and your loved ones but also I must help the people in your world."

I said, "You're forgetting one thing though, White Arrow. Only the family and close friends know I'm a medium and that I work with you."

"Leave that to me," Little One," White Arrow said, without concern.

Tony was sitting in the armchair so I turned to him and said, "Do you know what White Arrow has just told me, Tony? He wants me to start seeing people, that is, strangers, people I haven't met before."

Tony looked so surprised, for it wasn't that he didn't trust White Arrow's ability to tell the truth, but he hadn't really expected it to happen so quickly.

He said to me, "Will you cope, do you think?"

"I don't know," I replied, "But I have to try for White Arrow's sake. He needs to see the people on this earth, he says that's his whole purpose of being here. I'm so nervous at the very thought of it."

"Don't worry, Ann," said Tony. "White Arrow has always looked after you and he always seems to know what he's doing."

Tony has always had the greatest respect for White Arrow and trusts him totally. It was a great feeling to think Tony had faith in me, too, and I loved him for that.

The following day when White Arrow appeared I was in the middle of deep concentration, questions buzzing around in my head, so I asked White Arrow how

185

it was he intended getting people here to see me. Once again he sat down and said, "I will explain, Little One. Everyone on earth has a family in the spirit world and they know when the people on earth have troubled times. They are able to help as much as they can without the knowledge of their loved ones on earth. If, at times, they feel their guidance isn't enough it is then that they direct the people on earth to a medium. This is also very often carried out without them realising that their spirit family is responsible for this procedure. It is at this point that you come in, for you will be used as an instrument for guides like myself so we can speak through you in order to help these people. There are many forms of help we can provide but what is most important is the fact that we are able to assist them in the first place. There are primarily two main reasons why people will wish to come to see you, either they may have lost loved ones and are perhaps left with a feeling of great grief, and need to have proof of life eternal, or else they have a problem and need advice with it.

"When the sitter arrives and their loved ones from the spirit world come to join them through their love, they are assured that their deeply departed loved ones never leave them. Of course they have work to do on the other side, but if help is needed at any time they are there at once and do not need to be asked twice. It is most important that the people in your world know that their loved ones are still living, albeit in the next world, and will do all they can to help. When these spirit people were living on your earth their families and friends would go to them for help and yet, after they come to my world, it appears the need for their advice ends. It is such a shame when this happens, for why ignore a loved one because you cannot see them?

"So our prime reason of working this way is to prove the existence of my world and that we may give proof of survival. Whatever it is the people are searching for, myself and other guides are here in order to try our best to put them on the right path. It is irrelevant whether their problem be simple or major, whatever it is, they have come to you for advice and comforting words. That does not mean to say that we hold their hands and tell them everything, for there would be no point in that, as you all have to learn about life yourselves, but we do have the capability of knowing the future and so will tell them what is essential for them to know for their sakes and go forward knowing some help has been given, and that what has been said to them is fact and in truth and love. Their families from the spirit world will have been to speak with them through you with evidence of their survival, sometimes speaking of past events. After this, the people of your world will go away, knowing it all to be true, maybe even the truth has been spoken of the future. I say maybe because, until the future has happened, even though their families from the spirit world can give back-up on evidence, the people on earth

186

expect more, and it is only when what they have been told happens that they are 100% certain and can be expected to believe it as being the truth. We do not mind how long it takes as long as our work helps and convinces the people that there really is a spirit world, and then our job is worthwhile. I believe there is so much help needed on your earth and for centuries, since the earth began, we have been here waiting for people to be aware of our existence and to be recognised. This is now happening and it pleases us very much.

"There are so many people on earth like you, Little One, who have contact with us and understand that I must use you as an instrument for me to be able to carry out my work."

I understood all this and it made me feel proud to think I could be of some use to the spirit world and very honoured they had chosen me. I had one question I wanted answered so I asked White Arrow, "Why me, White Arrow? Surely it would have been better to choose someone who had lived a better life and had not done the many wrong things I have done.

"Why, Little One, should I not want you? If you had not had the path you have followed in life you would not have been any good in the work I must do, for at least you will understand the people and will not judge them because you have shared their experiences. Surely, that is why you have been chosen." White Arrow said no more on the subject and left.

I was still a bit nervous, thinking I would have to see strangers in my own home, but as White Arrow had not told me exactly when this was to happen I put it out of my mind and life carried on as normal. My family life was a lot happier, thanks to White Arrow.

One night I went to see Mum and the girls and as we sat in the kitchen I said, 'Guess what, Mum, White Arrow wants me to work with him to help other people."

Mum looked at me and said, "Don't you think you should, after all he has done for you?"

'Oh, I will," I said, "It's just that I'm a bit nervous about it."

'You'll be O.K., love," she said and I could see the look of pride in her eyes. At long last her wish had come true, her daughter was now cured and looking forward to the future, and also she was well enough and trusted enough to work with the spirit world. I loved her so much and thanked White Arrow for giving back to her real daughter, and prayed that in the years to come I could repay some of the happiness she deserved. She had devoted her life to me and my children and had not had much out of life for herself except our love, and I wanted her to have so much more. I flashed back to what White Arrow had told me about choosing our lives and as I looked at her I was sure I had chosen her as my mother. Mum was a bit on the plumpish side and wasn't very tall, being only 5ft. 1in. Her hair was slightly tinted and the light that shone through the kitchen window highlighted the red in her hair. She always wore an apron and had been a very attractive woman in her younger years. She was sixty now and the years had taken their toll. She always put everyone before herself when it came to making sure everyone had what they wanted and then, and only then, would she consider herself. Everybody liked Mum for she was the type of person who would say Hello to everyone and smile, even when there were times she didn't feel like it. On the other hand you could only push Mum so far because, for all her tolerance, there were times when she would lose her temper, but she soon calmed down again and would forget all about it straight away. I thought to myself as I sat admiring her, You just don't know how much I love you.

There was a knock at the door, it was Tony. "I'd better go, Mum," I said, giving her a kiss on the cheek. "I'll see you tomorrow night."

"O.K., love," said Mum, and as I went I popped into the living room to the kids. They were watching television so I called out that I was off home and that I would see them the following evening.

"O.K." they both said, without taking their eyes off the television set - typical of kids, I thought, but I loved them and didn't mind.

Nothing more was said about my working with people for a couple of months, so I carried on learning all I could with White Arrow and the spirit people until one day, right out of the blue, a strange thing happened. We were going along in the car when suddenly a little boy sat on my lap. Instinctively, I knew he was my son and didn't even have to ask White Arrow for confirmation. Although I hadn't completely forgotten the abortion I had in 1978, due to the many events that had occurred over the past two years or more which had completely changed my life, I had put it at the back of my mind and this was the very first time I had any contact with my child. Until now, I hadn't known whether it was a boy or a girl I had been carrying, and now, here was my son. I was unaware that babies and children grow up in the spirit world and up until now the subject had never arisen. My boy was now sitting on my lap with his arms around my neck and, without

188

thinking, I went to give him a kiss but just in time I stopped myself and remembered that, although the spirit world can cuddle us, we cannot reciprocate because their bodies are not solid. I felt very emotional and choked for a moment and before speaking to Tony about his son I turned to White Arrow. I said, "Does he hate me for getting rid of him?"

White Arrow's reply came softly, "Little One, look at your son. Does he not show how much he loves you? Even at his tender age he is much wiser than you for he now knows it was his fate. He chose to be with you for that short time and he chose you to be his mother.

"Will this be the only time I will be able to see him and be as close to him, White Arrow?" I was impelled to ask.

"No," he replied, "You will see your son many times during the course of your lifetime for he will stay with you till the day you die, but he will continue to grow up in spirit and learn. We have many schools here and there are many things for the children to learn, but in between he will visit you occasionally. Remember, God takes nothing away from us."

My little son was now playing and I turned to Tony. This time, I spoke softly and carefully to Tony. "Tony, your son is here."

"Sorry, love, I didn't hear what you said," said Tony.

This time I spoke louder. "Your son is sitting on my lap. You know, the baby we had aborted. It was a boy and he's sitting here," I patted my lap to indicate where our son was sitting.

Tony said nothing but found a place to park the car. When we had stopped he turned to face me and, not doubting me, he said, "Is he really here?"

I nodded.

Tony added, "I'm happy he's around, Ann, but it really hurts me that we had to agree to the abortion." Tony was very remorseful so I tried to cheer him by saying, "Tony, that's all in the past, my love. What counts is he's here with us." I went on to explain what White Arrow had said about babies growing up in the spirit world and that seemed to satisfy Tony.

All of a sudden our son went, so I told Tony and said not to worry for we would see him again. The ride home was quiet, as both of us were deep in our own thoughts, but nevertheless pleased with our son's appearance.

One evening, as we sat watching television, the telephone rang. Tony got up to answer it and said it was for me. It was one of my friends on the line who asked if I would do her a favour. She said she had a friend who had many problems and she suggested that I might see her to try to help solve her anguished state of mind. Without thinking, I said yes, and arranged a day for her to come round. My friend thanked me and rang off. Tony asked what my friend wanted so I told him I had agreed to see her friend in order to help her through with White Arrow's guidance. Just then, the penny dropped, and I said, "God, Tony. I've just realised I'm seeing someone I don't know."

"Don't panic," said Tony, and asked me when I had told her I'd see her. I said that it wasn't till the weekend but I said, "I'll kill White Arrow! He could have warned me in advance that this was going to happen!"

Tony remarked with a smile, that that would be very difficult to do. I looked at him, puzzled. This made Tony laugh and see the funny side of it even more and when I realised what I had just said I could see what he meant. However, I still didn't find the situation funny for I didn't think I was ready to see strangers yet.

"Yes, Ann," said Tony. "But have you considered White Arrow might think you're ready?"

I nodded and said that I hoped so. It seemed daft to worry about it now, it wasn't so much regarding White Arrow, because I was aware of his capabilities - no, it was me. I had worked with people all my life in ordinary jobs but this was something entirely different.

I still had a couple of days to go before my first sitter was due to come and that night I lay awake, thinking it over in my mind. Every time I wanted to have a go at White Arrow he conveniently vanished! The following morning he appeared again and straight away I said to him, "You could have warned me."

"What was the point?" White Arrow replied. "If I had told you weeks ago you would have still been in the same state you are in now, only for longer, so it was better I said nothing."

I thought about it for a moment then said, "Yes, you're right. You did tell me I had to work for you."

190

He smiled and said, "Don't be nervous, Little One, leave it all to me."

"I will!" I replied, trying to act sure of myself, but still thinking I would have to see her in a few days' time.

When the day came I was a bag of nerves. Would she like me, would she be happy with what White Arrow tells her? So many questions and anxieties were going through my mind that by the time she arrived I was totally exhausted from worrying about it. Tony answered the door and showed her in. I was upstairs at the time and Tony came up to tell me she was downstairs. He asked me if I wanted a cup of tea. I said, "Yes, please, love, and would you also make one for the lady?"

As I walked down the stairs I kept saying over and over to myself, "Don't let White Arrow down. Try to relax," but by the time I had got to the door of the room where the lady was, my insides were turning over. I managed to bid her "Hello" and sat down. Before I realised it I was explaining to her how I worked, but I should have said it was coming directly from White Arrow for it seemed as if I had been seeing people all my life. The words just flowed and I was becoming more relaxed as we went along. The woman accepted ninety per cent of what White Arrow was telling her and when we had finished I asked her if she was satisfied with the sitting.

She said, "Yes, very. You've taken a weight off my shoulders. I didn't know which way to turn and now everything is clear to me."

As I got up I said, "Please, do let me know how you get on, I'd be very interested to know."

With that I showed her to the door and as I walked into the front room my face was beaming.

"I know it went well by the look on your face," said Tony.

I said how marvellous White Arrow had been and I couldn't understand why I had been so worried. Tony looked at me and said, "I'm proud of you, Ann." When I asked him why, he went on, "Well, because you could have refused to see the lady, but you didn't and you trusted White Arrow."

From that day on I never doubted nor worried about working with White Arrow, and gradually I began seeing more people and really loving my work. Not only was I making new friends in the living, but also new friends in the spirit world. I felt that White Arrow and I were becoming even closer, if that was at all possible, as we were close anyway and life was taking on a fresh meaning to me. I felt lucky to be alive and cured, my family were happier, plus I had White Arrow, and above all I was now helping other people. Many times I had thanked White Arrow for what he had done for me and I knew in my heart there would be many more thank-yous I would owe to him. Most of all I was proud to think Mum and Tony were proud of me.

Although people were coming and going at our house, life continued much the same as usual with White Arrow. Probably because White Arrow had learned to speak English from watching the television, he was now showing more and more interest in it and at times became quite intrigued by it. He would often pop in and sit with us if there was a programme he particularly wanted to watch. I had got used to all this by now and White Arrow would just plonk himself down any-where on the floor, as long as he had a good view of the set. He still wasn't used to using furniture and, although we were sitting on chairs, he still persisted in sitting on the floor. That is, unless he was in the bedroom which was the only place he would sit on something or else lay down. I had been watching the film for about half an hour when I looked to see if White Arrow was still there. Yes, there he was, sitting in the same place, when all of a sudden I felt the presence of more spirit people in the room. I looked behind me towards the settee, and sure enough, I was right. Sitting completely absorbed in the film sat two people. At first, I thought I was seeing things and I looked over to White Arrow and said mentally, "Who are your friends?"

I asked this question without knowing what else to say as this was the first time this sort of thing had happened. Just then, I thought to myself, Bloomin' cheek They'll be wanting tea and biscuits next!

Once again, I had forgotten White Arrow can read my mind and I heard him say in a deadpan face, "No sugar!"

"Hah! Very funny, White Arrow," I replied, trying not to laugh.

As I took stock of the situation I could see the funny side of it for it all seemed so bizarre. I was gradually getting used to this sort of thing as so many strange occurrences were happening to me.

I looked over at White Arrow and wondered about my future. At least with him with me I was certain I would never get bored! Just then, he turned and looked a me. Trying not to laugh, I said,

"Are you really sure I chose my own life, and that I chose you to come back as my Guide?"

He didn't say a word but just gave me one of those looks and turned his head back to the television set. I felt smug because for the first time he couldn't think of a witty enough answer to give me.

White Arrow told me what the future had in store for me, and one of the things he mentioned was that I would have a car. I had never owned a car of my own before because Tony had always had one, so I was really excited at the prospect of owning my very own.

Time went by and after the following six months I was still waiting for this car to come my way and I was getting a little impatient. I virtually sat waiting for it to arrive on my doorstep, then one morning, as I sat in the living room, I suddenly realised there was no point in my having a car when I couldn't drive and didn't even own a licence. White Arrow nodded his head in acknowledgement.

He said, "That's right, what's the point in giving you a car when you cannot drive? I can't give you the certificate to say you have passed your driving test, that is impossible, so you must go for it yourself. Whatever we give you from the spirit world you must give fifty per cent yourself, otherwise there is no point in it if everything came that easy. You have to meet us half-way and show you can earn it, for you would do nothing to help yourself and wouldn't appreciate anything if it was given to you on a plate."

I fully understood him so that following week I booked my driving lessons. All went well, so when my driving test was coming up I asked White Arrow if I would pass or not.

He said, "Yes," but no more than that, so I was really pleased.

I thought no more about it until the day before, when I was walking round to see Mum and the girls. Suddenly White Arrow told me I would fail. I was so angry with him and said, "Thanks a lot! Why wait until now to tell me?"

He replied, "Tomorrow you will be too sure of yourself and that is why you will fail. I said Yes, you would pass initially, but I didn't necessarily mean it would be tomorrow's test and now you know the reason why."

193

"Rubbish!" I retorted. Although I was nervous about the driving test, the follow
ing day I felt very confident and capable of passing it, so I made up my mind to
ignore what he had said.

When I arrived at Mum's house I had already forgotten what White Arrow had
told me, mainly because I simply did not believe him, and thought he was teasing
me. Mum asked me how I was feeling about the test so I told her that White
Arrow said I would fail, but I was sure I would pass.

Mum laughed and said, "Well, Ann, I sincerely hope you're right, but don't be
too disappointed if you don't. Remember, you always say White Arrow is always
right, so keep an open mind and see what happens."

I thanked Mum for her kind words, for I knew White Arrow meant well and
didn't want to see me upset if I did fail, and that in her heart, Mum hoped I would
pass first time.

The following morning I woke bright and early. I cannot truthfully say I had no
butterflies in my stomach, but I was raring to go. My driving instructor picked me
up and everything went well.

I can remember saying to myself, You're wrong, White Arrow. This time I'll
prove it, and this time *I* am right, and not you!

Throughout the one hour lesson before the test, White Arrow sat in the back of
the car. I tried to ignore him, not that it bothered me him being there, for he
boosted my confidence, but I felt I had to make it on my own.

When we arrived at the driving test centre, he vanished. I was a bag of nerves by
then, so it didn't really concern me where he was exactly, all I cared about was to
get it over and done with.

I felt so uptight I didn't even care if I passed or not. When the examiner walked
me to the car I was shaking like a jelly, but after a few minutes I calmed myself
down and was more in control of my nerves and I whispered under my breath, to
White Arrow to hear wherever he had gone to, that I was going to pass easily.
Everything went fine until I had to reverse round a corner. When the examiner
told me to make this manoeuvre I got a bit too confident, thinking I would

undertake it without any problem. How completely wrong I was! I went up the curb for what seemed a mile around this corner! I knew then that I had failed and that White Arrow was correct in his prediction. I will not write down the exact words that came into my head at that precise moment, but the poor examiner was getting panicky and must have thought to himself, Whenever is she going to stop?? I went to pieces and, for some unknown reason, let go of the wheel, put my foot down hard on the brake so that by the time the car had grounded to a halt with a jerk, the car was facing out on to the road with the back wheels completely up the curb and on the pavement. How embarrassing!

"Er, shall we carry on?" said the examiner sarcastically, as he re-arranged his now hot and sticky collar. I drove off and could tell by the look on his face that I had failed miserably. I was so eager to get back to the centre, if only to have a go at White Arrow. When we pulled up the examiner, who now looked as if he had aged ten years, never said a word, except, "Mrs. Walker, you have failed." It came as no surprise to me.

I had calmed down somewhat by the time I reached home, after all, White Arrow had told me so, but I still wanted to have a word with him. He was sitting on the floor when I went indoors and I said, "Don't bother to tell me I told you so! In future, don't tell me whether I will pass or not."

"O.K." said White Arrow, but I knew him differently and that he would.

To put it mildly, I was not in the best of moods. White Arrow told me to put in for another test straight away and that I would pass it this time. "You have now learnt your lesson to not be too sure of yourself."

I considered this criticism for a moment and unfortunately had to agree with him. Yes, I had been too confident this morning and it was completely my own fault. I had taken the reverse round the corner far too quickly, thinking I could handle it. I looked at White Arrow and said, "Your trouble is, you know too much!"

"That's my job," he replied nonchalantly.

I said, "I give up with you sometimes," to which he replied that he knew best! I decided to give in rather than have another argument as I knew I could never win with White Arrow. When Tony came in at dinner-time he only had to look at my face to tell I had failed my test. He was very sympathetic and told me not to worry. I said I wasn't bothered as White Arrow had told me I'll pass next time. I tried not to sound sarcastic and felt sorry for misbelieving White Arrow. After all,

195

he did tell me I would fail which I did - miserably - but I told Tony I would send off straight away for another test. Tony said if White Arrow told me I'd pass next time, then it would happen.

Mum was on the telephone about ten minutes later to see if I had passed. When I told her I hadn't she said, "Never mind, White Arrow said a car is coming so you will pass next time."

I am so pleased everyone has confidence in White Arrow but, having said that, they all seemed to be on his defence in that he had told me it would happen instead of giving me some credit. Within a fortnight I received my next date for another driving test. No way was I going to ask White Arrow his opinion but the night before the big day, as I sat in bed reading the Highway Code, White Arrow appeared. He reiterated that I would pass so I said to him, "Oh, good, at last I've some good news from you!" He curled up laughing and I said it wasn't funny. He said it was just the expression on my face that made him laugh. Very funny, I thought, thinking it was alright for him. He had never had to take a driving test during his lifetime on earth. He could see I was feeling a bit sensitive about it all and he controlled his laughter. This made me feel much better so I put the Highway Code down, thinking, Well, if I don't know it now, I never will, and made up my mind I wasn't going to worry about the test like I did last time.

The next morning I passed my driving test with flying colours. It was the first time I had actually achieved something by myself apart from coming off the pills. I was highly delighted and pleased with myself and everyone, including White Arrow, congratulated me. I was so excited and on cloud nine that I completely forgot that now I had a full driving licence I could get my very own car.

White Arrow has always said that you can count the number of very close friends we have on one hand and at the time I had three such friends. They were Jean and a couple named Bill and Isobel. All three of them had always taken me for good or bad and if ever I needed help they were first there. I told Jean I had passed my test and two days later she telephoned me to ask me if I wanted a car. I was a bit surprised and said I would love one but I couldn't afford one at the moment. Jean went on to say she knew someone who had a car for sale who would be only too willing for me to pay monthly. It was only £500 and I reckoned I could afford to pay by instalments. I told Jean I would love it and she told me to see her on Sunday to go and have a look at the car. She guaranteed I'd like it. That night I went to bed so excited and as I lay there I asked White Arrow if this was the right car for me that he's promised I'd have. To my amazement he replied, "No, Ann, you can't have this one."

For a moment I thought, Now, I'm not hearing this, and looked up at White Arrow in disbelief. He continued, "Sincerely, this is not the car for you, it is not the one I promised."

"Well, White Arrow," I said haughtily, "I don't care what you think. I'm having this car. All my life I've wanted one and now's my chance," and with that I turned over and went to sleep, having made up my mind I would have it whether he said yes or no.

I could hardly wait for Sunday to arrive. I went along with Jean to look at the car and, without hesitation, agreed to buy it. I drove it home, having made insurance arrangements the previous day as I was so sure about getting it. I showed it to Mum and Tony and the children. I felt so proud of myself to be able, for once in my life, to be capable of doing anything like this on my own. I thought to myself, There you are, White Arrow, I've got the car, but in fact he was very quiet about it and I thought it very strange as he had always put his point of view across about everything I did. As I was so involved with my new acquisition I took no notice but I wish I had done, and had listened to his words of wisdom. By the end of the month I had not earned enough to pay the monthly instalment and so I had to sell it. The car cost me £500 and I reluctantly sold it for £200. The ironic thing here is that a few months after I sold it I could afford to pay for it, but White Arrow had always been determined I wasn't to have this car from the very beginning. I decided to take notice of him and had learnt yet another lesson, the hard way. It wasn't that White Arrow was trying to run my life for me but was trying to tell me that at that particular time I could not possibly afford it. In a short time I bought another car and this time I was able to pay for it without any problem.

White Arrow told me of the many events that were to occur in my lifetime, some of which were more important than others. They were not everyday events because that is not spirits' way, but what he told me had pleased me. Sometimes the good things he told me would happen seemed impossible but I trusted his word and never questioned him and accepted it to be fact. Something was about to happen, however, which he omitted to tell me about, something I would never have expected to ever happen to me, and perhaps this is why White Arrow didn't mention it, for fear that I would not believe him. Or was it that I didn't want to believe it, for it was something that was to hurt me forever. One Saturday morning, my daughter and I set off down the road to so some shopping. As we passed the Post Office I stopped and said to Joyce that I was going to put £1 into a Post Office Savings Account. I had no intention of doing so beforehand but felt impelled to do so at this time. When White Arrow had told me my future some time ago, he told me I would one day go to the United States of America. When he told

197

me this I thought, Yes, and pigs can fly, for at that time there was no way I could ever possibly even consider taking a holiday in America. As we came out of the Post Office I told Joyce that the following year I was going to take them all to America. She looked at me as if I was crazy but said that she hoped so as she would love to go. I said we would definitely go, unaware of how the hell I would be able to raise enough money, but I made my promise. I had opened the Account in the hope that it wouldn't all be a daydream of mine for I so wanted Mum to have a holiday of a lifetime as well as the children. I knew Tony wouldn't fly as he hates the idea, and I also knew he would hate me to go on holiday without him so I said nothing to him about it.

I saved so hard during the months that followed and each night I prayed I would make it. It was as if there was something or someone pushing me to work so hard for this holiday. Whenever I asked White Arrow if I would be able to get them all to America he would just smile and nod his head.

"Little One," he said, "You'll make it, for it is in your destiny."

"But would I make it now?" I asked. He didn't answer me, but just smiled.

The money was growing and by hard work I knew I could do it. During this period my aunt had come round to see my Mum. Mum would revel in showing Aunt Doris my savings book and would probably say to her over a cup of tea "Look, Doris, what Ann has saved. We are going to America."

Considering all the rest of my family never thought it possible I would one day be free from drugs and fully expected me not to survive that long, Doris asked Mum when she thought we might go. I had been saving hard for four months by now and Mum told Doris we would be going this year. She so looked forward to going and had trusted me to carry it out. I knew my mother so well and that she wanted to prove to everyone that as long last we could do the things other families did especially as we had nothing materially before. I loved her for her faith she had me after all these years, and that made me more determined to get her there.

My eldest daughter's twenty-first birthday was coming up in the July and she begged me to throw a big party for her. We had only managed very small birthday parties up until now but, as Mum had a quiet word with me to see if we could afford a big celebration for her, even if it meant foregoing the holiday, I had to agree. After all, she was more important than a holiday but I was sure we could manage the two occasions. I looked at Mum to see how lucky my kids were to have such a wonderful woman for their grandmother. Here was a woman who had never been abroad, with the possibility of a holiday of a lifetime, yet she was willing to give it all up for her granddaughter. This made me appreciate her and love her all the more and made me more determined to take her away to America. I was also determined my daughter would have a party she would never forget, so with a limited amount of money it was possible to go ahead with the party plans. I hired a large hall at the Civic Centre a couple of weeks after Mum had spoken to me about it.

CHAPTER SEVENTEEN

I carried on saving for the holiday for it was now March, and I had gone to church one Sunday with Tony, and as the service started I sat there quietly with my eyes shut. Suddenly I saw a vision, I could see my mother was dead and the fear that was in my heart was almost too much to bear. I wanted to rush out of the church there and then to make sure she was alright, but I knew I couldn't in front of all these people.

As I sat there, praying for the service to finish quickly so that I could rush home to see Mum, another vision appeared. This time it was my Uncle Bill who was dying. I know it sounds dreadful but I felt relief and thought, It's alright, it's not Mum after all. I had made a mistake, it was Uncle Bill. As soon as the service had finished I still felt eager to rush round to Mum's to check on her. I knocked on the door and Mum called out, "Who is it?" Mum never did answer the door without knowing who it was first. As she opened the door to me I felt such relief.

"Hello, Mum, are you alright?" I asked.

"Of course I am," she replied, wondering why I had an anxious tone in my voice. I kissed her on the cheek, being so glad the vision I had witnessed was not true, and put it all behind me. I didn't even tell Tony as I thought it was so silly and that it was all my imagination playing tricks on me. Also, White Arrow had not told me Mum was going to die yet.

It was almost July and I had managed to book our holiday. Tony said he didn't mind not going. I had asked him, of course, but he wouldn't come with me. My eldest daughter also declined my offer to spend our very first holiday abroad together because she said if I didn't mind she'd rather go somewhere else with her

199

friend. I can't pretend I wasn't disappointed because I had really hoped all the family would come with me and now it was just myself, Mum and my youngest daughter. I wanted both the girls to come with us for Mum's sake, but she didn't seem too disappointed but looked forward to the holiday anyway, she was only too pleased to be able to go herself.

It was two weeks before the party when I had a dream that my cousin and grandmother were both in spirit and they were at my eldest daughter's party. They were sitting at a table reading a Will which I could not understand, but took it that my eldest daughter was about to depart from this world. It was a horrible dream and in it I was crying and yet the party carried on, and it was my wish that it did.

The following morning I was so upset when I awoke that I had to have a word with White Arrow about my terrible dream. I asked him if anything was wrong with reference to my bad dream but he said nothing, so I presumed there was nothing to worry about or surely he would have warned me.

The party went really well with lots of laughter and fun. All the family came along with my eldest girl's friends. She was so thrilled and thoroughly enjoyed herself, which pleased me no end because I remembered only too vividly the suffering she had endured in the past and hoped she could now forget the wrong-doings I had done to her and to her sister.

We were due to fly out a fortnight after the party, one year almost to the day that I had put the first pound into the Post Office. I think White Arrow had performed a miracle because I had never achieved so much in my lifetime as I had in the past twelve months. Mum had never flown before and was getting really excited about the prospect of going overseas. My youngest daughter had a boyfriend by this time but was also looking forward to the holiday as she had never been abroad either. I had decided to include my friend Jean to come along with us, remember her? Jean was one of those friends you can count on one hand? We were to fly out on the Monday and at the airport I kissed Tony goodbye and promised to ring him when we arrived at the hotel. My eldest daughter had flown out the previous day so she was alright.

Going back to when White Arrow had told me what my future held in store for me, at the time some of the things seemed out of the question but whilst we were on holiday in America I was to experience a few of them. Typical of my luck, when we arrived at the first hotel we were booked into it turned out not to be up to standard but, luckily, Jean managed to change hotels and the next one we went to was great. We spent a whole week there before moving on to Disney World.

The first hotel we stayed at for our first week was on the beach and the very first day I fell asleep. Having lain in the sun too long I got badly sunburnt. I felt very ill that night but didn't want to spoil anyone's fun, so the following day I agreed to go to the beach again, provided I could use a canopy which would keep me in the shade. My daughter and my friend went for a walk whilst I stayed talking to Mum. They returned half an hour later and had arranged to go on a boat trip and came back to ask us if we would be interested in going, too. I was beginning to feel a lot better despite the fact that the heat was killing me as it was in the 90's. I asked Mum if she wanted to go but she said she'd prefer to stay in her hotel room and watch television where it would be cooler.

We all walked Mum back to the hotel and got changed for the boat trip which was going to an island called Shell Island. I was quite looking forward to it really so off we went to make our way to the boat. We all climbed on board with me wearing Mum's hat and Jean's shawl around my shoulders and I sat back enjoying the trip. I thought back to White Arrow once telling me I would one day go on a catamaran so I looked up and to my surprise realised the boat was indeed a catamaran. I suppose with my suffering sunstroke I hadn't taken much notice of the type of boat we had boarded. Well done White Arrow! I said in my mind, and then it dawned on me that I hadn't seen him since we had arrived and asked, "Where are you?" I got no reply so just carried on enjoying myself.

As the boat nearly reached the Island I made up my mind I would be the very first to jump off the boat. The man in charge hadn't said otherwise so, with my hat on my head, and the shawl still around my shoulders, we touched the shore - and I jumped. The next thing I knew I was going down, down and down. The hat went one day, the shawl the other, and there seemed to be no bottom to the water. I was sinking deeper and I said to myself, "Here we go again, Ann. It could only happen to you!" It was a good job I am a good swimmer for as soon as I decided I had gone down far enough I swam back up.

Gasping for breath, I managed to reach the boat and as I looked back at the boat everyone else was still on it and as I crawled onto the sands they were all laughing at me. Fine, I thought, yesterday I got sunstroke and today I go on a catamaran which White Arrow had told me about and yet forgets to tell me I would nearly drown. As I lay there I thought, Don't give up, Ann, you've another twelve days to go yet. It's got to get better!

And it did - well almost. A few things happened which were not that serious, but by the time we flew home there were some people who would not be keen to fly with me again, which I don't blame them for. You see, the flight normally takes

201

eight to ten hours but, yes, you've guessed it, our return journey had to be different. We left our hotel at 9.30 a.m. on Monday morning but didn't arrive at Heathrow Airport until 1.00 p.m. Tuesday. There was a long delay at Kennedy Airport for hours and then, having to go to Ireland for another five hours, it didn't help matters at all.

When we eventually reached home I wondered if spirit didn't really want me to have this holiday after all, but despite all our mishaps we had a fantastic time. It had been a wonderful, new experience for us all and all looked so well on our return. We were very anxious and eager to see Tony and Karen, only to find they were happy and had enjoyed themselves in our absence. We came back at the end of August which, so far, had been a good year for us all. White Arrow had made a few appearances on holiday but had only stayed a very short time so I had not seen that much of him and missed him as much as Tony. As much as I enjoyed my holiday, I was glad to be home for I had missed my work. Our holiday meant so much to all of us and I was only too grateful to have been able to take Mum and Joyce with me. I had never had so much fun in my whole life, and I know the same applied to them, too, as well as my friend Jean.

It is amazing how very quickly life returns to the old familiar routine and pattern, and things went back to normal very soon. We were in September by now and it turned out not to be a very good month for us. My youngest daughter had broken up with her boyfriend, my eldest had to go into hospital for a minor operation, and Mum was not well. I wondered at first if the heat had been too great for her when we were on holiday, or perhaps the travelling had upset her system, but with all three of them having problems I didn't know whether I was coming or going.

Towards the end of September, the girls had managed to sort themselves out but Mum was still not well. She went to the doctor as she was having pain in her shoulder, near her chest. The doctor sent her to have an X-Ray. I had been continuing my work with White Arrow as before, but had noticed he wasn't his usual self but very quiet in between clients. It didn't worry me that much as I was more concerned about Mum and not once did I consider asking White Arrow what the matter was with Mum. On reflection, this was odd, as I had always turned to him for advice and guidance.

Mum was due for a hospital visit on the Thursday morning and that morning my mind went back to before the holiday. I had forgotten so many things which had been told to me by the spirit world, only when it seemed important did I remember - and I was remembering now. Tony was home that morning and as I sat down reflecting on the things I had been shown and told, I felt just as if I was dying of

ancer. This frightened me as it was quite a horrible sensation so I had to tell
ʼony about it. I said to him, "Tony, I think I'm going to die of cancer, you
now."

ʼGood God," said Tony, half scared to death. "What on earth makes you say
ιat?"

ʼI don't know. I keep feeling I've got cancer. I was well aware I was frightening
im and tried to lighten the atmosphere by saying, "Don't worry, love, maybe
ʼm picking up someone else's condition and it isn't me after all."

ʼhe memory came back of the bad dream I had had back in July and then it made
ιe re-think. Not Mum, surely not, not my Mum. I was saying it over and over in
ιy head in disbelief. I didn't want to ask White Arrow for fear he would tell me
 was true, and I suppose I didn't want to hear the truth. I tried to convince
ιyself that I was over-reacting, after all, she's only got a pain in her shoulder and
ʼhest. Surely you can't have cancer in the shoulder. I was hoping that after the X-
ay we would know for certain and I would be able to relax a little. No news
ιme from the hospital for about a week but I was worried about Mum as she was
ot looking at all well, and I was very annoyed with the hospital staff for not
ɪtting us know the facts sooner.

ʼhen one morning Mum ʼphoned me to say she had received a letter from the
ospital to say they wanted to see her again for another X-Ray. Mum must have
ɪnsed my concern and reaction because she told me not to worry. Maybe the first
-Ray didn't come out properly and I hoped to God she was right. She said she
ıd an appointment for the following Thursday so I said to try not to think about
 and that I was sure all would be O.K.

 said, "I'll see you later, but please stop worrying, Mum," and she said she
ould do her best.

fter I put the ʼphone down I sat there, thinking about how much she meant to
e. I had to speak to White Arrow about it so I said to him, "White Arrow, I'm
ɔ scared about losing Mum. Please, don't let anything happen to her."

ʼLittle One, I am here. I will give you all the strength you need," he said, but
ɔthing more, and sat next to me. I kept going over in my mind how much that
onderful woman had done for me all those years. She had brought me into the
orld, fed and clothed me, and loved me all that time, not once complaining
ɔout the trouble I had given her. I was filled with fear that morning and turned to

203

look at White Arrow and said, with tears in my eyes, "If anything, White Arrow, I would even go without you rather than anything happen to Mum, for she is my life. I owe her so much and I need time to repay her. Please, give me that chance." For the first time, I saw tears in White Arrow's eyes, which really upset me all the more. He had never before cried in front of me and as he put his arms round me he said gently, "Little One, what is to be, will be, but I promise you your mother will never leave you."

Perhaps I shouldn't have said what I did but at that stage I was clutching at straws, holding onto anything that would allow me to keep my mother.

As the dreaded Thursday appointment drew nearer I could take no more of it, and it wasn't fair on White Arrow to ask him any more on the subject. In the past few days he had been like my shadow, following me everywhere. Mum's appointment at the hospital was in the afternoon, and it had been arranged that Aunty Doris would take Mum and pick me up on the way there. Before they arrived I decided to telephone my medium friend, Derek, to ask him what was wrong with Mum. Within seconds there was an immense power circulating around me, a power full of so much strength and love, way beyond my wildest dreams. It was almost overpowering me and then I heard Derek talking to his guide. He came back to say, "Ann, I'm sorry, but as I understand it, your Mum has cancer."

All I could think of to say was, "Thanks, Derek, for your help," and I put the receiver down. For some reason or another it did not sink in but kept repeating that horrid word over and over. Should I tell my aunt my fears? I never doubted the spirit world so I thought, No, let's wait and see what the hospital says. I looked at White Arrow and the same unbelievable strength was as strong as ever around me. He was still so close to me and I decided that I wouldn't ask just yet. I'd wait for Mum to come home first and see what happens then.

We went to the hospital and they took another X-Ray. To my amazement everything was clear. I was so relieved and delighted with the result and so glad I hadn't told Aunt what Derek had said. When I got back home I couldn't wait for Tony to come in. As soon as he got in the front door he asked how Mum was.

"Fine!" I said, "So what do you think about Derek's telling me Mum has cancer?"

"Ann, I really don't know what to think. Does White Arrow say nothing at all about it?" Tony asked.

I replied, "Well, he seems so unhappy and not his usual self at all which worries me."

Tony said, "Do you think he's not telling you everything?"

"No," I replied, "He told me Mum was going to be with me always, so it can't be that bad."

Tony kissed me and told me to try not to worry. He suggested we go by what the hospital results had proved to be and to accept that the news was good after all, and not to take any notice of what Derek had told me. It was the middle of October by now and Mum was getting no better. The pain in her shoulder was still there and now she was suffering pain in her stomach. Once again the doctor sent her for an X-Ray, this time for her stomach. I was beside myself with worry since the pain in her stomach had started, but still White Arrow was saying nothing about it.

One morning I said to Tony, "Tony, I've had enough. I'm going to see Mum's doctor because she is in so much pain all the time and yet nothing seems to be done about it." Tony agreed with me and made the appointment for me there and then. He made it for that evening but I didn't tell Mum I was going when I spoke to her on the 'phone earlier in the day, not until I had spoken to the doctor.

When I entered Mum's doctor's surgery I found him to be a very pleasant man. I was very taken with his soft and caring voice. I had to remind myself that I was there to talk about Mum and not to dwell on how nice her doctor was. Inside my head I was asking, "Where are you, White Arrow? I need you." Then he appeared. He put his hand on my shoulder, which calmed me a little, and I proceeded in telling the doctor my feelings for Mum, as well, of course, of my utmost concern for her well-being.

"Mrs Walker," the doctor replied, "I would not like you to repeat to anyone what I am about to tell you, but the hospital think your mother has a tumour in her stomach. We cannot be certain how serious it is until we have carried out more tests."

"Thank you," I said, mostly for his honesty and, as there was nothing else to say, I left. As I was walking to the car I thought, Well, they can remove a tumour so there's hope yet, but somehow, deep down, I knew I was kidding myself. It was almost as if I was being prepared without realising it. God knew how I loved that woman and that night when I went to see her there was pain in my heart. Once

205

again, I said to White Arrow, "Don't let anything happen to her." His reply was what he had told me before, "You'll never lose her, Little One."

I understood it, as I had the first time he told me, that she was going to pull through and that everything would be alright. However, I felt I couldn't take all the responsibility of knowing she was ill by myself, so Tony suggested I contact my brother and tell him as he had the right to know. My brother has three daughters, two of which can hear and speak quite clearly, but the other, like her father, was deaf and dumb. When I telephoned him the middle one answered. "Could you tell daddy I want to see him tonight, darling?" She went away to speak to Raymond and when she came back she said, "Daddy is coming over now." I said goodbye and tried to make up my mind as to how I could tell my brother his mother is very ill.

When I had seen Mum earlier that day both my daughters were out, but before Raymond arrived Mum 'phoned me to ask me to go round to see her for a little while because she wasn't feeling at all well.

I said I couldn't possibly make it for about an hour and made up some excuse about having someone coming to see me, but really it was because I had to be home for Raymond when he arrived, and didn't want Mum to know he was coming. Mum said, "O.K. but try not to be too long, will you, love."

As I rang off I started panicking because it was so unlike Mum to call me so late in the day. It was already about 9 o'clock when Ray arrived and I explained to him as quickly as possible what the doctor had told me and that Mum had been on the 'phone complaining of not feeling well. Raymond suggested he'd go round to Mum's first in case she thought something was wrong if we both arrived together. He looked worked but both of us were still of the opinion all would be well. We stayed with Mum till my girls came in.

The following morning I was not coping with the situation at all well. Although White Arrow was still with me for my clients I felt the need to visit my doctor. related my predicament and he was very reluctant to put me back on drugs and therefore he prescribed Valium, five a day.

The Valium took the edge off to start with, but Mum took a turn for the worse later that week and was due for a check-up at the hospital on the following Monday. When the doctor saw her he decided she was too ill to go home but would keep her in hospital in order to take tests straight away.

I went to the hospital half an hour earlier than visiting time was to start, so that I could have a word with the doctor. Tony stayed outside, knowing I wanted to be on my own with the doctor. I walked into the Sister's Office and the doctor was in there talking to her. "Can I have a word with you please, Doctor?" I said, and explained who I was. He was very kind and agreed to speak with me. The sister left so that we could speak privately and the doctor told me about Mum's problem. At first he hesitated so I told him I wanted to know the truth. Mum lay in her hospital bed, unaware I was there and with the doctor. It was 2.30 p.m. on the Tuesday afternoon and surely the results of the tests they had carried out the previous day would be finalised.

I thought to myself, Please hurry and spit it out, we've only thirty minutes to discuss my mother's future before visitors are permitted and if I'm not with Mum at 3 o'clock on the dot she'll worry. Although I told him I wanted the truth, deep in my heart I didn't want to know it.

The doctor then told me Mum had cancer of the liver. It came like a bolt out of the blue, for I knew there was no turning back and that he couldn't have made a mistake, as he had the results of her tests in his hands.

There I was, standing on my own for the very first time in my life, with no mother to support me. My first thought was, "God damn him," and yet it wasn't his fault, poor man. I had asked him for the truth and that's what he told me. My mind was divided - half was on the doctor, the other with my mother whose bed I could see down the middle of the ward. It could have only been a matter of seconds but, even so, a million and one questions entered my head. How do I tell the kids? How do I tell Tony and Raymond? How on earth would I be able to cope without her, the woman I adored?

I realised I hadn't asked him how long Mum had to live. He said she had three months to a year, that was all. Once again I took the optimistic approach, well, a year, if only they could keep her alive for a year, maybe... my heart started to jump, maybe there was a glimmer of hope, that she may be able to live a long time yet, maybe... lots of maybe's came into my mind. I didn't want to believe it, but the worst was yet to come. I knew I had to go home to tell my children their grandmother was terminally ill. She was the one woman who had kept us all together and she was part of us and had done everything for us unassumingly.

The doctor went on to tell me what tests they had carried out on Mum, then I told him what Mum's own G.P. had told me in confidence. Whether it was the Valium or White Arrow's influence, I don't know, but any other time I wouldn't have been able to ask for the truth, let alone hearing and accepting it. The doctor's words had got through to me but somehow it was as if they bounced off me.

By the time I got to Tony I was crying uncontrollably. The tears were flowing down my face and I said, "Oh, Tony, she's dying. What do I do now?"

I kept sobbing when, suddenly, another arm was around me. It was my aunt who had come up to see Mum with my Uncle. I told her what the doctor had said and started to wipe my tears away as visitors were now arriving. I didn't want Mum to see my tears and however I kept them at bay I will never know. As I walked up towards Mum's bed I smiled at her and said, "Doris and Eddie are here, Mum, so I won't stay long but will be up tonight, alright?" To be honest, I couldn't get away quick enough, for that was one of the hardest things I have ever had to do, and even as I left the hospital I knew I would have to face yet another impossible task, that of telling my two daughters.

I cried all the way home and by the time I reached home the pain inside me was intolerable. Why her, God? Anyone else, but not her. All her life she has given her love to us and now she was dying. Now He was going to take her.

"It's just isn't fair, it just isn't fair," I screamed.

"Come on, love," Tony said, "Try and pull yourself together. The kids have got to know and you're the one who'll have to tell them. It'll come better from you."

I told Tony I would have to take a Valium tablet if I was to tell them right now. My intake of pills had doubled but I knew I couldn't cope without them. Tony was getting worried about this, I knew, but he didn't say anything about it. Without them I wouldn't be able to cope at all and I had to do that for Mum's sake and the children, and it was the only way I could do it.

My eldest girl was in that afternoon and so I saw her first, and when we picked up my youngest daughter from work I then told her about their grandmother. Both of them were in tears and very stunned. I knew they hadn't taken it all in, as I hadn't when I was first told, and their first reaction was to rush to the hospital to see her. It was too early for her to receive visitors so we all sat around and waited for an hour and a half to pass before we would be allowed in. It seemed we were sitting there for a lifetime, with hardly a word exchanged between us. There was still my brother to tell, but I thought I'd leave it till I had seen Mum, then get him to come over to see me.

208

Both the girls and I were all wearing heavy make-up to hide our red eyes and when we were permitted to go into the ward the girls sat one either side of her bed. I felt so proud of them because they put on a brave face, laughing and smiling, yet they must have felt wretched inside. Now and again they would pop outside in turn to have a weep and then compose themselves once more before going back to see her.

When it was time for us to leave we kissed Mum in turn, trying not to let her know anything was amiss, almost as if we were playing a cheating game. All the way home we were each silent, wrapped up in our own private thoughts. All our hearts weighed heavy in the knowledge we would soon be losing her. I managed to get in touch with Raymond, which was always difficult with his being deaf and dumb. He couldn't express himself as clearly as we could and as I told him the sad news he just sat there and cried, "I love her." We cuddled each other for a while and realised no words were needed to express our combined emotions.

When Raymond left he said he would meet me at the hospital the following day.

The following week I asked the doctor at the hospital if it was at all possible for us to take Mum home. He agreed because he said there was nothing more they could do for her. We picked her up on the Friday and I am not sure if Mum knew in her heart or not she was going to die, but she dreaded the thought of going home. Perhaps she had put two and two together, thinking the hospital were unable to do any more for her and so had sent her home as the last resort. I had asked the doctors not to tell Mum of their diagnosis and they kept their promise.

We all took shifts to look after Mum. We brought the bed down for her into the back room where there was a back door. My family felt it better for me to continue seeing clients as normal as this would hopefully prevent my mother from thinking there was something very wrong, and so I took the night shift. I used to sleep in the same room as her and then, in the morning, we would do everything that was necessary and then both my daughters took over in the afternoon and evening. My mother never really believed in spirit, as I have mentioned before, but one night, right out of the blue, I remember saying to her, "Can I put my hands on your shoulder, Mum?" She was in terrible pain from the cancer and, although I had always believed one was either directed to be a medium or a healer, and not both, I put my hands on her shoulder and gave her spiritual healing for the very first time. A couple of nights later I asked Mum how the pain was and she said that the only time she had relief from it was when I had laid my hands on her. I will never forget that.

My Mum's sister (my aunt) and my grandfather, who are both in spirit, had been very much around for a couple of days and one evening, because it was such a warm evening, I had the back door open. My mother said to me, "There's a man at the door, Ann. I can see him."

"That's alright, Mum," I said, "I'll show him out into the back garden and then I'll shut the door." It was of course my grandfather and I knew she had seen him. He had come for her to help her pass to spirit. Everything is to do with fate. I would never allow the nurses to be with my mother at night because I wanted to look after her at night time. Having said that, however, the nurses who were on hand since Mum had been back home with us told me that I must have a night off because I was getting so tired, and that if I didn't get my rest I would be no good to anybody.

At first I argued with them, but they were so insistent that I agreed to take the night off. My God, am I glad I did. I slept on the sofa and the night nurse sat up all night with my mother until she woke me up at 5.00 a.m. to tell me my mother was dying. This gave me time to get my family together. As we gathered round the bed, I looked down at the bottom of the bed, and there stood my mother. However, my grief was so great that I just turned away and looked back at her body lying in the bed. My mother had gone.

As we all left the room, both my girls went into the hall holding each other, crying. Raymond sat on the stairs, crying. I cuddled him and he cuddled me. All of us felt such a great loss. Tony stood in the background, ready to comfort me when I needed him. As I embraced my brother, I looked over his shoulder and up the stairs and there, standing at the top, was my mother once again. In my distress I shut my eyes tight - No, I thought, it couldn't be possible. I opened my eyes again but this time she had gone.

There were so many things to be done that day and, although I was distraught, strength was coming from somewhere. My brother and I made the funeral arrangements and we stayed till early evening making sure the girls would be alright, then returned home.

During these difficult and testing weeks, White Arrow had been with me throughout, but because I had so much on my mind with Mum, I had hardly spoken to him, but as I knew him so well, I knew he understood. I felt numb all day, an odd sensation as if it wasn't really me. Tony was marvellous and said, "Would you like a cup of tea, love, or something to eat? I'll tell you what, you go upstairs and rest and I'll bring you up something later."

He knew I wanted to be left on my own and I thanked him for his understanding and never-ending support. I took his advice and went upstairs and as I climbed into bed I reached for my Bible which was on the bedside table.

It took me back to the last Christmas when Mum had asked me what I would like as a present from her, and this was the Bible which she bought me. I have never been a religious person so, to be honest, I was surprised at myself for wanting it, and Mum had said to me, "Well, Ann, if that's what you want, I'll get you one."

As I opened the front of my Bible I saw her words which were written on the inside cover, "To Ann, Love Mum xxx". It all came back to me and I remembered only too clearly how I had asked Mum to write in it for me. I looked for a pen and wrote beneath Mum's words, "Mum passed to spirit. Look after her God. God Bless her. I will miss her very much." I clung to the Bible and was so glad I had asked Mum for it. It had been the first time that day that I had been on my own and suddenly it hit me. I sat back, the tears rolling down my cheeks, thinking how we had done everything together, we had been inseparable, so what was I going to do without her? The pain in me was intolerable and I grieved, when all of a sudden White Arrow appeared. I said to him, "Not now, White Arrow." I didn't mean to hurt him but I wanted to be left on my own with my thoughts of Mum, but White Arrow was insistent and said, "Little One, look up, please."

My head was in my hands. White Arrow went on, "I have brought your mother with me to see you as I am looking after her."

I slowly lifted my head and at first I couldn't see her, only him.

Realising my anticipation, he said, "She's here, Little One," then, when I looked again, she was standing next to him. She looked exactly the same as when I saw her that morning, only this time she didn't go but sat down beside me on the bed. I so wanted to hold her and never let her go, but I had already learnt that I couldn't possibly hold her. She held her hand out and laid it on mine and said, "Don't cry, Ann. I haven't gone away from you, but have come back to you and the girls. Nothing in the world could have stopped me from returning to you and the girls because I love you too much."

By this time White Arrow had gone to leave Mum and I to talk alone.

"Why you, Mum, why you? Surely it would have been better for me to have gone instead of you." I was thinking of the children and the love that they had for Mum. I knew I could never take her place in their eyes or would want to.

211

"Ann," Mum replied, "My time was up but at least you and I are more fortunate than most, for you can still see me and hear me, there are many who can't and it must be more difficult for them to accept."

I understood what Mum was saying but it didn't ease the pain.

"Mum," I said, "I want to join you. I can't carry on and don't want to go on without you. I don't care about my future, just you."

"Now, don't be daft, Ann," Mum said, "Whatever you do in the future be sure I'll always be there with you. Nothing has changed." I looked at her and knew she was right. After all, wasn't she sitting there next to me with her hand on mine? It still wasn't the same as cuddling her and oh, how I wanted to.

"You must go on," Mum continued. "Not only for your sake but for Tony's and the children's. They all need you now and in the future."

I just couldn't accept this, for Mum had been the only person who had kept the family together, and without her around I knew it would fall apart.

"Mum," I said, "I want to come to you. I want to die..." and at this juncture White Arrow appeared. He spoke very quietly, "Little One, I cannot order you not to take your own life but if you do decide to take it you will not be able to join your mother."

I hated him for saying that and it made me very angry so I told him so. "You promised me I would be able to make it up to Mum for all the wrong doings I had done in the past. You promised me she would always be around, you promised." I repeated it over and over and getting myself into a terrible state.

White Arrow said, "Little One, I have kept my promise. She is here."

"It's not the same," I replied, sobbing. I tried to make White Arrow see my point of view and at the same time was so glad Mum was here right next to me. I was so confused.

Just then, we heard Tony coming up the stairs. Mum kissed me and said, "I'll be back, you'll see." I fell asleep that night, having cried myself to sleep, for I knew I was fortunate enough to see and speak to Mum in her spirit form but was far from over the absence of her physical being.

In between making the arrangements for the funeral, White Arrow had me working non-stop. Mum's body was taken to the Chapel of Rest and when I was working with the spirit world and White Arrow they managed to take the pain of grief away, but in between clients I had to come back to face reality. I made up my mind to see Mum in the Chapel of Rest and as I stood there looking at her silent, unreal form, standing next to her coffin stood White Arrow and Mum together. As the tears started to flow once more, I begged Mum to go back into her body to come back to the living, but she did not answer me. I turned to White Arrow and begged him on my knees, "Please, I'll do anything, just bring her back to me."

I seemed to be kneeling forever, sobbing my heart out and when I got up I touched Mum. She looked so normal so I stroked her face and hair, still wishing the impossible. I knew I couldn't stay there much longer as the children wanted to see her to pay their last respects, but at the same time I didn't want to leave her. It was crazy really, for I knew I would be able to see her again the following day.

My intake of Valium had steadily increased to the grand total of seventeen a day. The funeral was only a few days away and I was dreading it. I had to visit my doctor every other day as he was keeping a close eye on me in case I did anything silly. He didn't want me to attend Mum's funeral for he didn't think I'd be able to cope with the situation, but of course I had to go. On one of my visits to him he said to me, "Ann, surely, as you work with the spirit world, death should not be that important to you as you understand about it all."

I was rather taken aback by his statement and considered it foolish of him to suggest such a thing. Did he not realise I am human and have real emotions and feelings? He didn't seem to realise what a great loss I had encountered and was finding it virtually impossible to cope with the knowledge that I could never again hold her in my arms the same way as when she was alive. I said nothing in reply to him - what could I say?

The day of the funeral arrived and, like anyone else who's lost a loved one, I was in a complete daze. I felt as if part of me had died with her. The rest of the family were so good and supportive to the four of us for they knew how much Mum had meant to us all.

That night, when it was all over, I crept into bed, exhausted, and tried to block the day out of my mind. As I drifted off to sleep my last thoughts were that this had been one of the unhappiest days of my life.

My depression began to lift when Mum began to come to me a few days later, and then she was with me most of the time. My anger with White Arrow had almost gone and I felt I owed him an apology.

Mum appeared one evening after the funeral and she sat at the side of me.

"Ann," she said, distinctly, "Promise me you won't take any more Valium. Don't go backwards, love. I don't want to see you ill again."

I promised her and the following morning I went back to see the doctor. He was so pleased that I wanted to come off them and agreed to help me. It was difficult, but I started that day and when I got down to ten a day I started to feel ill. I was having shooting pains in my chest and left arm.

I told Tony and he suggested I tell the doctor about it.

"Oh, I'll go in a couple of days, you never know, it might go away," I said.

"No you won't," said Tony. "I'll make you an appointment for today. It can't be right to have pains in your chest and arms, Ann, you know that."

I knew Tony was right and, as he was involved with homeopathic medicine, I accepted his advice. The doctor examined me and sent me to the hospital for a check-up.

We had an appointment for the following day. An E.C.G. was carried out by a nurse who explained it all to me afterwards.

"Mrs. Walker," she said, "I would like you to see the doctor so can you come back in two hours' time?"

What else could I do but agree? so we set off for home only to have to return a little later.

Tony looked really worried and said he hoped there was nothing seriously wrong. I told him not to worry and that I was sure I was alright.

When we returned to see the doctor at the hospital he told me he wanted me to go into hospital as I had suffered a slight heart attack. I was panic-stricken, not because of the heart attack being diagnosed, but I could remember Mum being in hospital during her last illness and I couldn't face going in myself just now.

214

made out that I was experiencing many problems at home and couldn't possibly come in. Tony gave me one of those looks - but after knowing me all these years he knew it was no use arguing with me once I had made up my mind not to do something.

All he said to me on our way home was, "Are you feeling alright, Ann?" Other than that he was very quiet and subdued. As soon as we got indoors, Tony said, "Ann, please go into hospital and do what they tell you to do. It's for your own good."

I said, "Tony, if I went in just now, it would kill me, I can't go, I'm sorry."

Suddenly White Arrow appeared. I hadn't seen him all day and I was very surprised he hadn't mentioned this little lot to me.

White Arrow had an important message for Tony. He told me he wanted Tony to take me to see a different doctor.

"Fine," I said, "but who, and why?"

He told me the name of a doctor I had known years ago and was surprised White Arrow should mention him as I didn't think he knew him.

"He will give you both the answer to your problem, but tell Tony you are definitely not coming to the spirit world yet, for there is still a lot of work for you to do." I passed on everything White Arrow said, and added that White Arrow had never been wrong before so we had to trust him.

Tony accepted White Arrow's words for he trusted him implicitly. He seemed a bit brighter to hear this news and said it made him feel a bit better, but we'd have to see what the doctor says about it all.

The following day we made an appointment with the doctor whom White Arrow had suggested we consulted. I went privately so that I could have check-ups without going into hospital, and this had been White Arrow's plan all along. He knew how terrified I was of going into hospital and that Tony was frightened of losing me, so this was the best way round it.

After all the necessary checks were carried out it was decided that I was suffering from Angina and that many people live for many years with this complaint, which, relieved both Tony and myself.

It meant I could go back to my promise to Mum and that was all that really mattered. I managed to come off all pills by Christmas and from that time on I never looked back, as I had kept my promise to Mum and was feeling much better in health again. I thanked White Arrow for his assistance for without his help I couldn't have done it.

That Christmas, however, was terrible for all of us. It was the first one without Mum and we found it difficult to enjoy ourselves and just wanted it to hurry up and be done with. We all tried hard at making the most of the festive season but we each had our minds on Mum.

As I was able to see and hear Mum, perhaps it wasn't as bad for me, and I told the others that Mum wanted us to try and enjoy Christmas, but it wasn't the same.

On Christmas Day Tony asked if I wanted to go out for a drive. I felt right down in the dumps, having lost faith in my ability as a medium when it came to giving messages to clients from their loved ones in the spirit world. It was the first time I had ever questioned or doubted my working with spirit. They had always been right up until now so why should I be feeling like this now? White Arrow soon picked up my train of thought and appeared on the back seat of the car. He showed no emotion at all in his face.

"Little One," he said, "Remember this. All you are to me is an instrument. What I tell you, you say. If you are losing your confidence that's your hard luck, but there are people who need the spirit world to help them and that is my work - to help them. I know you have suffered in the past weeks, but you cannot let others suffer because of your pain."

He was very abrupt and to the point, and with that, he vanished.

My first thought was, "And a Merry Christmas to you, too!" but then I realised he was correct. I was being selfish and wallowing in my own self-pity.

He certainly chose the right words, for it did the trick. It pulled me out of the doldrums by being so blunt with me. At long last I now accepted that it was my mother's destiny to die at that time. Although I knew it all along, I wouldn't accept it until that Christmas Day's afternoon drive. I went back to work after the holiday, not giving one hundred per cent any more, but one hundred and fifty per cent. I had been made to see I was not the only one with worries and grief to contend with, and it took White Arrow's cutting me down to size to make me see sense.

216

As promised, White Arrow was also right in saying Mum would never leave me. When he had told me way back when I had been told she only had a short time in which to live, I had taken it the wrong way. I could see things more clearly once again and life was almost back to normal. I say 'normal', because, although I was seeing a lot of Mum, it wasn't the same as when she was alive when I could actually cuddle her, but it made me truly thankful to God that I was privileged to be able to see Mum in spirit form.

Gradually, as time went by, the pain got easier. I was still missing her living presence, but I was so grateful that I could still communicate with her in spirit. My work with White Arrow got busier and I loved helping the people through him. In working with White Arrow I learnt so many things, but most of all I learnt to care for other people. My experiences of the past had made me realise how important it was for me to have gone through it all, for without the hell I had been through how could I possibly understand their anxieties and troubles. No problem seemed too big or too small for White Arrow and the greatest joy of all, up to this present day, is seeing the end result. I am always at my happiest when working with for the spirit world, after all, I do work for a perfect world, and I know that where the spirit are, that is heaven.

There are so many stories to tell about White Arrow and the spirit world, but my whole purpose of writing this book is not to tell you of the wonderful things the spirit can do through me, but the wonderful things that *your* guides and your families can do for you. It is then, after you have left after sitting with a medium, that your Guides and families carry on performing the miracles for you, not us.

As I sit here, writing my last few lines, I look back over the years and can remember what I have learnt through White Arrow's teachings. He told me once that on earth we all have a pathway to live and that at times it would very likely be like sheer hell to us, but before we pass on to spirit, that is, returning to heaven where we lived before coming to earth, that it was no use to us returning to spirit before our allotted time for we would only have to return to earth again to learn it all over again.

I thought about my past and the times I had wanted to leave this earth in the hope of finding happiness in heaven, but then I met White Arrow. I looked at him and said, "No, heaven can come later," and for the first time I was pleased I was here.

White Arrow winked at me and I knew he understood, and I knew that whatever was in store for me I could make it with him by my side.

THE END